Effective Teacher Collaboration for English Language Learners

This volume explores the value of teacher collaboration in meeting the needs of diverse English language learners (ELLs). A range of research-based chapters demonstrate examples of effective collaboration between English language specialists and content area teachers and offer recommendations for collaborative practice.

Foregrounding the ways in which teacher collaboration can better support the needs of ELLs in elementary, middle, and high school classrooms, this volume provides evidence-based insights and suggestions to underpin effective teacher collaboration across the curriculum. Through case study examples, readers can understand common challenges and pitfalls, as well as best practices and how to apply teacher collaboration in real classroom settings. Research studies in subject areas including mathematics, science, and English language arts provide a basis for practical, evidence-based recommendations to engender mutual trust, teacher agency, and the development of shared goals to enhance instruction for ELLs' achievement.

This book provides educators with new insights from empirical studies, and is vital reading for researchers, scholars, teachers, and teacher educators who are aware of the importance of collaboration for student success. Those involved in ESL, bilingual, and dual language programs may be particularly interested in this volume.

Bogum Yoon, Ph.D., is Professor of Literacy Education in the Department of Teaching, Learning, and Educational Leadership at the State University of New York at Binghamton, USA.

Routledge Research in Language Education

The *Routledge Research in Language Education* series provides a platform for established and emerging scholars to present their latest research and discuss key issues in Language Education. This series welcomes books on all areas of language teaching and learning, including but not limited to language education policy and politics, multilingualism, literacy, L1, L2 or foreign language acquisition, curriculum, classroom practice, pedagogy, teaching materials, and language teacher education and development. Books in the series are not limited to the discussion of the teaching and learning of English only.

Books in the series include:

Developing Cross-Cultural Relational Ability in Foreign Language Learning
Asset-Based Pedagogy to Enhance Pragmatic Competence
Gerrard Mugford

Effective Teacher Collaboration for English Language Learners
Cross-Curricular Insights from K-12 Settings
Edited by Bogum Yoon

Multilingual Perspectives from Europe and Beyond on Language Policy and Practice
Edited by Bruna Di Sabato and Bronwen Hughes

Training Teachers of Chinese in Australia
Theoretic foundations and practical applications
Chen Shen

Being and Becoming a TESOL Teacher Educator
Research and Practice
Edited by Rui Yuan and Icy Lee

For more information about the series, please visit www.routledge.com/Routledge-Research-in-Language-Education/book-series/RRLE

Effective Teacher Collaboration for English Language Learners

Cross-Curricular Insights from K-12 Settings

Edited by Bogum Yoon

NEW YORK AND LONDON

First published 2022
by Routledge
605 Third Avenue, New York, NY 10158

and by Routledge
2 Park Square, Milton Park, Abingdon, Oxon, OX14 4RN

Routledge is an imprint of the Taylor & Francis Group, an informa business

Library of Congress Cataloging-in-Publication Data
A catalog record for this title has been requested

ISBN: 978-0-367-52196-7 (hbk)
ISBN: 978-1-032-04982-3 (pbk)
ISBN: 978-1-003-05831-1 (ebk)

DOI: 10.4324/9781003058311

Typeset in Sabon
by SPi Technologies India Pvt Ltd (Straive)

Contents

Figures and Tables

Figures

Tables

About the Editor and Contributing Authors

Editor

Bogum Yoon, Ph.D., is Professor of Literacy Education in the Department of Teaching, Learning, and Educational Leadership at the State University of New York at Binghamton. Her research interests include teacher education, critical global literacies, English language learners (ELLs), and critical multicultural education. Effective teacher collaboration to support the needs of ELLs is one of her specialized research areas. She has conducted numerous qualitative studies in diverse classroom settings on how content area teachers and ESL teachers work together to support ELLs' language and literacy learning. Her email is byoon@binghamton.edu.

Contributors

Laura Eggleston has been working as an English as a New Language Specialist for the past 4 years. Prior to that, she taught Kindergarten for 6 years, first grade for 10 years and served as a Teacher on Special Assignment in Literacy for 2 years. Laura serves as a capital region co-chair for the NYS TESOL Association. Laura is a Mentor and Instructional Leader within the school district where she teaches. Her email is leggleston@mohonasen.org.

Dr. Tiffany L. Gallagher is a Professor in the Faculty of Education at Brock University in the Niagara Region and the Director of the Brock Learning Lab. She is recognized for her research that aims to enhance the professional learning of teachers through coaching and the learning of students with literacy difficulties and learning challenges. Her email is tgallagher@brocku.ca.

Amanda Giles, Ph.D., is an ESL teacher at a middle school in the Southeastern United States. She completed her Ph.D. degree in the Department of Curriculum and Instruction at the University of Alabama. Her research interests include collaboration between ESL and content area teachers, literacy, language policy, and effective assessment practices for ESL students. Her recent work appears in *Language Teaching, Research in Middle Level Education Online* and *TESL Canada Journal*. Her email is amanda.k.giles@gmail.com.

Dr. Andrea Honigsfeld is Associate Dean and Director of the Doctoral Program (Educational Leadership for Diverse Learning Communities) at Molloy College, Rockville Centre, NY. A Fulbright Scholar and sought after national presenter, Andrea is the coauthor or coeditor of over 20 books on education and numerous chapters and research articles related to the needs of diverse learners. Her email is ahonigsfeld@molloy.edu.

Heeok Jeong, Ph.D., is a visiting scholar in the Teacher Education and Curriculum Studies Department at University of Massachusetts Amherst. Her interdisciplinary research focuses on three areas: teacher education and practices toward culturally sustaining translanguaging pedagogy; classroom discourse and multicultural literature that promote multilingualism and multiculturalism; and participatory action research with teachers and students that amplify voices and promote agencies of students from non-dominant communities. Her email is jheeok@umass.edu.

Dr. Carrie McDermott is the Coordinator of Graduate and Post-Graduate TESOL/Bilingual Programs and is Director of Bilingual and TESOL Grants in the School of Education and Human Services at Molloy College, Rockville Centre, NY. Carrie is a national speaker and presenter, author, national grant writer, curriculum writer, instructional coach, and researcher. Her email is cmcdermott@molloy.edu.

Suzanne E. McLeod, Ed.D., is the Coordinator of the Educational Leadership Program at Binghamton University. She retired as the Superintendent of the Union Endicott Central School District. Previously, Suzanne worked as an Assistant Superintendent for Business, Curriculum Director, and Building Administrator at both the elementary and secondary levels. Suzanne authored professional articles on the topics of trust, home schooling, and bullying, the book *A Principal's Guide to No Child Left Behind*, and teaches workshops to aspiring leaders. Her email is smcleod@binghamton.edu.

Daniel Ness, Ph.D., is Professor of Curriculum and Instruction at St. John's University in New York. With a specialization in STEAM education, he has authored numerous articles on the development of mathematical and scientific thinking, which focus on spatial cognition from birth through adolescence. Ness has co-edited *Alternatives to Privatizing Public Education and Curriculum*, which was awarded the

Society of Professors of Education Outstanding Book Award in 2018. His email is nessd@stjohns.edu.

Yvonne Pratt-Johnson, Ed.D., specializes in TESOL and serves as Chair of the Department of Education Specialties at St. John's University. The recipient of the 2013 Sigma Delta Phi Educator of the Year award and several Fulbright-Hays grants, her research interests include literacy development, language acquisition, study abroad, equity in teaching, and strategies for teaching linguistically and culturally diverse students. She holds degrees from Stony Brook University, Georgetown University, and Teachers College, Columbia University. Her email is prattjoy@stjohns.edu.

Christine Uliassi, Ed.D., is a Visiting Assistant Professor in the Childhood and Early Childhood department at the State University of New York at Cortland. Her research interests include critical literacy, culturally responsive instruction, and multilingual education. Prior to her work in teacher preparation, she was both an elementary and ESL educator in Fairfax County Public Schools (Virginia) for 12 years. Her email is Christine.Uliassi@cortland.edu.

Ana Vintan is a professor in the School of English and Liberal Studies at Seneca College. She has a passion for teaching, and research in the areas of professional learning, connections among curriculum, instruction, and assessment. Her email is anav_ro@hotmail.com.

Min Wang, Ph.D., is Assistant Professor of TESOL and Bilingual Education in the Department of Education Specialties at St. John's University. Dr. Wang's research interest includes critical applied linguistics, discourse analysis, positioning, and agency. Her recent book entitled *Multimodalities and Chinese students' L2 literacies: Positioning, agency, and communities* addresses the complicated interactions among multimodality, positioning, and agency in increasingly digitized, multilingual, and multicultural contexts in and through which Chinese international students practiced their L2 literacies. Her email is wangm@stjohns.edu.

Acknowledgments

Bogum Yoon

The publication of this edited book, *Effective Teacher Collaboration for English Language Learners: Cross-Curricular Insights from K-12 Settings*, is the meaningful product of many devoted educational scholars' contributions. The situation during the pandemic may have been challenging, but it did not hinder the educational scholars' commitment to contribute to this volume of the book.

As the editor of this book, I truly appreciate each chapter author who conducted case studies on teacher collaboration for the needs of English language learners (ELLs) and worked with me throughout the writing process for this collection. The vivid picture of the teachers' collaborative practices in each chapter was possible through the contributing authors' dedication to the improvement of teacher education for ELLs.

The contribution by the anonymous reviewers must be acknowledged. They read my initial proposal, along with the sample chapters that I wrote, and provided me with thoughtful feedback. Their insightful and constructive suggestions contributed to further developing my ideas on collaboration between content area teachers and ESL teachers. Additionally, I would like to thank my respectful friend and scholar, Anne Simpson, who allowed her time to listen to my thoughts on this project, to review some of the manuscripts during the chapter selection process, and to provide thoughtful comments on them.

My special thanks extend to Elsbeth Wright, Routledge editor in education research, who worked with me throughout the entire process of this book project as part of *Routledge Research in Education Series*. Her utmost professionalism and deep insights on education research made me feel that I made the right decision to select Routledge as the outlet of my work. It has been such a pleasant experience working with her and her professional team for this important book project.

Finally, I thank Emily Pressler, Ying Li, and Ashley Frantellizzi for their editing work on the manuscripts during the chapter authors' final revision process. All of them are graduate students who are studying in my current institution, State University of New York at Binghamton. I appreciate my school's support for this project by allowing me to work with these promising future scholars.

Preface

This edited book, *Effective Teacher Collaboration for English Language Learners: Cross-Curricular Insights from K-12 Settings*, discusses the current issue of teacher collaboration to meet the needs of diverse English language learners (ELLs), "learners who are in the process of acquiring English as a new language" (Yoon, 2021, p. 23). It provides the foundational knowledge of teacher collaboration, broadly defined as *the practice of groups of teachers working together with shared common goals to support students' learning*. This book includes case studies, suggestions, and future directions for effective teacher collaboration across the curriculum. Suggestions and implications are drawn from actual studies in the classroom, school, and community setting to help the reader to see the interactive dynamics between teachers. Through the presented case study examples, the reader will see how teacher collaboration is applied in a real classroom setting.

This collection of chapters also addresses the needs of educators who seek out new insights from recent empirical studies to support the increasing population of ELLs around the world. Although many researchers, scholars, teacher educators, and teachers are aware of the importance of collaboration for student success, they might not know what evidence the current research studies provide in actual settings. This book is intended to serve this audience by providing research-based insights on how both groups of teachers, ESL/bilingual teachers and content area teachers, can establish collaborative partnerships to promote ELLs' successful learning in language, literacy, and content.

This book, with highlighted case examples, will be particularly helpful for researchers, scholars, teachers, and teacher educators who work with pre- and in-service teachers in education programs. As McClure and Cahnmann-Taylor (2010) pointed out about the current reality of teacher collaboration, "the partners who are expected to collaborate in the future actually never get together during this critical time of exploring and thinking through what it means to collaborate with other teachers" (p. 125). We need a research-based resource for researchers, scholars, and teacher educators who work with both ESL/bilingual teachers and content area teachers to help them prepare for effective teacher collaboration before going out into the teaching field and so that they can gain an understanding of various perspectives. I hope this edited book unites different teacher communities together, providing greater opportunities for dialogue through authentic examples across the curriculum.

Indeed, the premise of this book is to affirm that teacher collaboration is important because it provides opportunities for teachers' professional learning (Cochran-Smith & Lytle, 2009; Darling-Hammond & Richardson, 2009; Hargreaves, 2019). Yet, I remind the reader that this book does not adopt a "romanticized" and "simplistic" perspective that teacher collaboration can be "perfectly" done in any situation. Given that ESL/bilingual teachers and content area teachers work in different contexts with different specialized content areas, it is important to understand the complexities of the school context and the factors that limit or facilitate their collaboration. It is also central to understand that not all teachers will seek out a collaborative partnership. By using the evidence from the case studies that were conducted in diverse settings across the curriculum, this book will help the reader to see the difficult realities of teacher collaboration and how these situations could be handled more effectively.

As a teacher educator and researcher who has been working with pre-service and in-service teachers for almost two decades, I have often observed that many teachers feel it daunting to work with ELLs and other teachers in order to support their students due to their lack of experiences. This book, filled with case study examples on teacher collaboration, offers space for researchers, scholars, teacher educators, and teachers to deepen their understanding of ELLs' needs and of collaborative partnerships. It also provides teacher education programs with the opportunity to gain future directions for effective collaboration.

In terms of the organization of the book, it consists of three parts: Part I (two chapters of foundational knowledge on teacher collaboration), Part II (seven chapters with research studies), and Part III (two concluding chapters of implications and suggestions for future research and practice). For instance, Chapter 1, provides an overview of this book. It discusses the need of teacher collaboration between ESL/bilingual and content area teachers, particularly drawn from my own research experiences in diverse school settings. In the following chapter, Chapter 2, the reader will have opportunities to engage in important theoretical concepts and perspectives with relation to teacher collaboration. These theoretical perspectives are fundamental to better understand the case examples shown in the subsequent Chapters (3–9). Chapter 2 will serve as a condensed version of current research on teacher collaboration between ESL/bilingual teachers and content area teachers. Overall, Part I will offer space for the scholarly audience to consider collaborative partnerships as a tool to help meet the needs of the increasing population of ELLs in this global era.

After the presentation of theoretical perspectives of teacher collaboration in the following chapter, the reader will see these specific collaborative examples in Part II, from Chapters 3–9 in various settings. The diverse authors of these seven chapters will present research studies on teacher collaboration in elementary, middle, and high school settings and across curriculums. Some of the authors in the chapters use the term ELLs (English language learners) interchangeably with other terms such as ESL (English as a second language), ENL (English as a new language), or MLLs (multilingual learners). Instead of suggesting one consistent term for this book, ELLs, I accommodate the authors' different use of the term that fits their topics and contexts.

Specifically, Chapter 3 introduces teachers' collaborative practices in two English language arts (ELA) classrooms in an elementary school setting drawn from year-long qualitative data collection. As a researcher, Uliassi describes the experiences of an ESL teacher, working with two general education teachers: a fourth grade teacher quite experienced with ELLs, and a fifth grade teacher new to teaching ELLs. Drawn from the findings, suggestions for how researchers, educators, and school leaders can advance meaningful partnerships for educational equity for ELLs are provided.

Like Chapters 3, Chapter 4 discusses teacher collaboration in an elementary school setting, but the grade level (e.g., kindergarten, first, and second grade) and the co-teaching content (e.g., both ELA and math) are different. In this chapter, Jung and Eggleston examine collaborative practices between an ESL teacher and three primary school teachers (e.g., K-2). By using collaborative professionalism as a theoretical framework, the authors discuss both possibilities and challenges that the participant teachers encountered during 4 years of collaboration.

After these two studies in elementary school settings, the book includes a chapter that explores teachers' collaborative practices in both elementary and middle school settings (K-8) in Ontario, Canada. In this chapter, Chapter 5, Vintan and Gallagher share their qualitative case study on how ESL teachers collaborated with classroom teachers and a technology coach to utilize educational resources for ELLs' learning needs.

Additionally, this book introduces two studies in middle school settings. For example, Chapter 6 explores teachers' collaborative practices in a social studies classroom. In this chapter, Giles shows how she, as an English as a second language (ESL) teacher and researcher, worked with a social studies teacher in planning for and teaching ELLs in an eighth grade collaboratively taught social studies classroom. Through the qualitative case study method, the author discusses both possibilities and challenges that she and the social studies teacher encountered as they collaborated. After this study in a social studies classroom, the book introduces a case study in a middle school science class. In Chapter 7, Wang and Ness discuss the efficacy of co-teaching for ELLs guided by positioning theory. The authors examine how a seventh grade science teacher and an ESL certified special education teacher collaborated in a seventh grade cohort science classroom.

This book also includes two studies that are guided by culturally inclusive pedagogy in discussing teacher collaboration across curriculums. For instance, Chapter 8 explores teacher collaboration in relation to mathematics. Guided by culturally responsive-sustaining framework, McDermott and Honigsfeld present a case study of one high-school co-teaching team consisting of a mathematics teacher and an ESL teacher. As a final case study chapter in this book, in Chapter 9, Pratt-Johnson discusses her case study on a program in which ESL and content teachers (e.g., ELA, science, and math) collaborated on planning lessons during an excursion that took New York City teachers to West Bengal, India. Both groups of teachers studied the heritage language and culture for a growing number of ELLs in the United States of America.

After presenting all case study examples in Part II, this book concludes with two final chapters in Part III. One chapter discusses what the presented case studies imply to school leaders and addresses the question on how school principals can support teacher collaboration for ELLs. Specifically, in Chapter 10, Mcleod, who has worked as a school and district leader for decades, provides specific suggestions for school principals. Her perspectives are drawn from the findings of the research studies in this book as well as her own professional experiences.

Finally, the chapters presented in Part II, from various school contexts and across content areas, are summarized and synthesized in Chapter 11. In this concluding chapter, as the editor of this book, I provide suggestions for future research as well as suggestions for effective teacher collaboration among content area and ESL/bilingual teachers drawn from the teachers' voices and ELLs' learning experiences. This final chapter will provide opportunities for educational scholars to reflect on the case studies and evidence-based implications for teacher collaboration practices for ELLs' successful learning across the curriculum.

In conclusion, through these chapters, scholarly audiences will see what teacher collaboration looks like in actual settings. I hope that this organization of the book serves the main purpose of this edited book by providing research-based insights on teacher collaboration for ELLs' needs across the curriculum. Educators make a life-long commitment to their students and supporting ELLs for their learning successes is of paramount importance to them. I hope that all educators join me in creating possibilities for effective teacher collaboration for ELLs who are both academic and cultural assets to this world.

Bogum Yoon
State University of New York at Binghamton
January 2021

References

Cochran-Smith, M., & Lytle, S. L. (2009). *Inquiry as stance: Practitioner research for the next generation*. New York, NY: Teachers College Press.

Darling-Hammond, L., & Richardson, N. (2009). Teacher learning: What matters. *Educational Leadership*, 66(5), 46–53.

Hargreaves, A. (2019). Teacher collaboration: Thirty years of research on its nature, forms, limitations and effects. *Teaching and Teachers: Theory and Practice*, 25, 603–621.

McClure, G., & Cahnmann-Taylor, M. (2010). Pushing back against push-in: ESOL teacher resistance and the complexities of coteaching. *TESOL Journal*, 1(1), 101–129.

Yoon, B. (2021). English language learners' language and literacy development: A brief synopsis of theoretical orientations for middle school teachers. *Middle School Journal*, 52(1), 2–29.

Part I

Overview and Theoretical Perspectives

1 Introduction

The Need of Teacher Collaboration for ELLs

Bogum Yoon

There are many terms that refer to students whose primary language is not English and who learn English as a new language, such as "emergent bilingual learners," "English as a second language (ESL) students," or "multilingual learners." In this chapter, the more inclusive and general term, English language learners (ELLs), will be used, which is defined as *learners who are in the process of acquiring English as a new language* (Yoon, 2021, p. 23). ELLs continuously populate classrooms around the world, including classrooms right here in the United States. For instance, according to the recent data by the National Center for Education Statistics (NCES, 2020), ELLs in the United States "constituted an average of 14.7 percent of total public school enrollment in cities, 9.6 percent in suburban areas, 6.8 percent in towns, and 4.1 percent in rural areas" (n.d.).

These data imply that teachers will have ELLs in their own classrooms, regardless of the city, suburban, and rural area in which they work. It also implies that responsibility for teaching ELLs is no longer only delegated to English as second language (ESL) or bilingual teachers. It is every teacher's responsibility since many ELLs receive instruction both in the general and ESL/bilingual classroom settings. ELLs will benefit from both content area teachers with expertise in the specific subject area and ESL/bilingual teachers with expertise in the language and literacy area. Communication, interaction, and dialogue between these two expert groups of teachers are crucial for ELLs' successful learning across the curriculum.

When working with ELLs, teachers will understand that ELLs' needs are unique. ELLs are in a situation that requires them to learn content knowledge while simultaneously acquiring a new language in order to be successful in academic learning. This situation creates the need for both general education and ESL/bilingual teachers to work together by sharing common goals to support ELLs' academic, cultural, and social needs. Given that ELLs' language and literacy skills (i.e., broadly defined reading, writing, speaking, listening, viewing, and critiquing) are fundamental to be successful in all content areas, collaboration between the two groups of teachers has become a necessity, not an option.

DOI: 10.4324/9781003058311-2

Situating Teacher Collaboration in My Experiences

As a teacher educator and researcher who has been working with pre- and in-service teachers throughout my professional career, my inquiry of teacher collaboration between ESL/bilingual teachers and content area teachers has developed through my studies on ELLs (e.g., Yoon, 2004, 2008, 2015, 2020; Yoon & Haag, 2012) and my ongoing observations of the needs of teachers in teacher education programs.

Although teacher collaboration is considered an important practice for student success (DelliCarpini, 2008; Dove & Honigsfeld, 2018; Goddard, Goddard, & Tschannen-Moran, 2007; Hargreaves, 2019; Lassonde & Israel, 2010; Leonard & Leonard, 2003; Ronfeldt, Farmer, McQueen, & Grissom, 2015), it is not clearly known what challenges and issues exist from actual classroom studies. Identifying challenges and issues might be a priority to provide specific suggestions for effective teacher collaboration and to offer possibilities for educators to attempt in their own settings. With these issues in mind, I have conducted classroom studies to see how teachers work together to support ELLs in diverse settings (elementary, middle, and high schools) throughout my academic career.

My identities as a researcher and mother of two sons who were English language learners in the US context also prompted my motive to pursue this topic of teacher collaboration. Given that many teachers in the United States are monolingual and have few experiences working with ELLs, I wondered how mainstream teachers work with ESL/ bilingual teachers to support diverse ELLs' language and literacy learning. Thus, I explored the interactive dynamics among teachers both in the ESL classroom and in content area classes, focusing on English language arts. Since the teachers' collaborative dynamics are shown through the way they work with and for ELLs, I also observed and interviewed ELLs.

In conducting these qualitative case studies, I found that teachers have different views of their roles regarding ELLs' needs. An intriguing finding was that ELLs participated more actively in classroom activities when all teachers – bilingual, ESL, and content teachers – have common goals and a clear understanding of ELLs' cultural, social, and academic needs, compared to the classrooms of the teachers who have little interaction with each other. These experiences helped me find both possibilities and challenges of teacher collaboration.

To compare these findings from my classroom studies, my colleague and I (Yoon & Haag, 2012) have also conducted a survey study, which collected 75 teachers' responses on teacher collaboration for ELLs' learning. Findings suggest that collaboration between general/content area teachers and ESL/bilingual teachers is challenging due to both groups' epistemological perspectives on teachers' roles and the lack of the institutions' initiatives. For instance, some of the "regular" classroom (i.e., general, mainstream, content) teachers viewed themselves as "content" knowledge teachers and viewed ESL teachers in a "supporting" role. They expected the ESL teachers to come to them in order to check on ELLs' needs and to support their content teaching.

On the other hand, the ESL/bilingual teachers tended to view themselves as "language teachers," and acknowledged that the content area teachers did not always have a deep understanding of language acquisition and ELLs' needs. They shared that the content teachers were not always aware of how challenging it was to learn a new language while also learning a new culture and content. These findings suggest that these teachers were not all viewing each other as co-equal partners, and because of this there was tension between them. The teachers' perceptions of their roles (i.e., "content" vs. "language" teachers) may have hindered their attempts to promote collaboration.

Along with these survey study findings, my extensive literature review also helped me find a gap and prompted me to pursue this book project. My review of the literature shows that the topic of teacher collaboration among content area teachers and ESL/bilingual teachers is not new in the educational field, but the realities of teacher collaboration in practice is rather lacking. For instance, there are many insightful ideas on teacher collaboration presented in professional journals and books (e.g., Dove & Honigsfeld, 2018; Honigsfeld & Dove, 2019; Kim, Walker, & Manarino-Leggett, 2012; Pawan & Ortloff, 2011; Walker, & Edstam, 2013).

However, a noticeable finding was that there are few books that discuss the issue of teacher collaboration using empirical studies that can show the context of how these two groups of teachers actually work together to meet ELLs' particular needs across the curriculum. Although there are some exceptions (e.g., York-Barr, Ghere, & Sommerness, 2007), specific examples from empirical studies that show the context and the process of teacher collaboration were severely lacking. In addition, I found that the field of TESOL education and the field of literacy education and other content areas tend to discuss teacher collaboration issues from the perspective of their own expertise area and do not include others' views about the possibilities and challenges of teacher collaboration.

This gap led me to think about how I can integrate these separate discussions together for scholarly audiences and how I can provide research-based insights on teacher collaboration to extend their current understanding of teaching ELLs and their learning processes. The individual research projects in diverse settings in this book will expand current understandings of teacher collaboration for ELLs' successful learning across the curriculum. I hope that this book will create a dialogue among scholars and educators about the opportunities and challenges presented through the authentic case examples.

References

DelliCarpini, M. (2008). Teacher collaboration for ESL/EFL academic success. *Internet TESL Journal, 14*(8). Retrieved from http://iteslj.org/

Dove, M. G., & Honigsfeld, A. (2018). *Co-teaching for English learners: A guide to collaborative planning, instruction, assessment, and reflection.* Thousand Oaks, CA: Corwin.

Goddard, Y. L., Goddard, R. D., & Tschannen-Moran, M. (2007). A theoretical and empirical investigation of teacher collaboration for school improvement and student achievement in public elementary schools. *Teacher College Record, 109*(4), 877–896.

Hargreaves, A. (2019). Teacher collaboration: Thirty years of research on its nature, forms, limitations and effects. *Teachers and Teaching: Theory and Practice, 25*(5), 603–621.

Honigsfeld, A., & Dove, M. G. (2019). *Collaborating for English learners: A foundational guide to integrated practices* (2nd ed.). Thousand Oaks, CA: Corwin.

Kim, J. Y., Walker, C., & Manarino-Leggett, P. (2012). Equipping classroom teachers for English language learners. *TESOL Journal, 3*(4), 722–734.

Lassonde, C. A., & Israel, S. E. (2010). *Teacher collaboration for professional learning: Facilitating study, research, and inquiry communities.* San Francisco, CA: Jossey-Bass.

Leonard, L., & Leonard, P. (2003). The continuing trouble with collaboration: Teachers talk. *Current Issues in Education, 6*(15). Retrieved from http://cie.ed.asu.edu/volume

National Center for Education Statistics (2020). Retrieved from January 9, 2021. https://nces.ed.gov/programs/coe/indicator_cgf.asp

Pawan, F., & Ortloff, J. H. (2011). Sustaining collaboration: English-as-a-second-language, and content-area teachers. *Teaching and Teacher Education, 27*(2), 463–471.

Ronfeldt, M., Farmer, S., McQueen, K., & Grissom, J. (2015). Teacher collaboration in instructional teams and student achievement. *American Educational Research Journal, 52*(3), 475–514.

Walker, C., & Edstam, T. S. (2013). Staff development while you teach: Collaborating to serve English learners. *TESOL Journal, 4*(2), 345–359.

Yoon, B. (2004). Uninvited guests: The impact of English and ESL teachers' beliefs, roles, and pedagogies on the identities of English language learners (Doctoral dissertation, University at Buffalo, 2004). *Dissertation Abstracts International, 65*, 885.

Yoon, B. (2008). Uninvited guests: The influence of teachers' roles and pedagogies on the positioning of English language learners in regular classrooms. *American Educational Research Journal, 45*(2), 495–522.

Yoon, B. (2015). A case study: One novice middle level teacher's beliefs, challenges, and practices for young adolescent English language learners. In K. F. Malu & M. B. Schaefer (Eds.), *Research on teaching and learning with the literacies of young adolescents* (pp. 3–19). Charlotte, NC: Information Age Publishing.

Yoon, B. (2020). *Key elements of teacher collaboration for English language learners' literacy learning: Classroom examples from a case study.* Paper presented at a virtual conference of the Literacy Research Association.

Yoon, B. (2021). English language learners' language and literacy development: A brief synopsis of theoretical orientations for middle school teachers. *Middle School Journal, 52*(1), 23–29.

Yoon, B. & Haag, C. (2012). The epistemological and institutional challenges of teacher collaboration for English language learners' literacy learning. In M. T. Cowart & G. Anderson (Eds.), *English language learners in 21st century classrooms: Challenges and expectations* (pp. 244–257). Denton, TX: Canh Nam Publishers.

York-Barr, J., Ghere, G., & Sommerness, J. (2007). Collaborative teaching to increase ELL student learning: A three-year urban elementary case study. *Journal of Education for Students Placed at Risk, 12*(3), 301–335.

2 Theoretical Perspectives of Teacher Collaboration

Bogum Yoon

Scholars in the educational field define teacher collaboration in various ways. As noted earlier, in this book, I define teacher collaboration as "the practice of groups of teachers working together with shared common goals to support students' learning." It means that at least two teachers will be involved in collaboration. This broad definition is drawn from several scholars' work on collaboration. For instance, Friend and Cook (2007) defined collaboration as "a style for direct interaction between at least two co-equal parties voluntarily engaged in shared decision making as they work toward a common goal" (p. 7). This definition is particularly helpful in its emphasis on collaboration requiring the element of a common goal between two parties. In this book, the two parties refer to ESL/bilingual teachers and classroom/content area teachers. I posit that both groups of teachers' roles are equally important as experts in their own field.

Along with Friend and Cook's definition, Shakenova's (2017) idea on collaboration also contributed to the construction of my own definition of teacher collaboration. She noted that collaboration is "shared values through teachers' learning which influences teaching practice and students' achievements" (p. 35). This definition indicates that there is a link between teachers' collaborative practices and students' learning outcome. It implies that the purpose of teacher collaboration is to support students' accomplishments in learning. Shakenova's definition offers a particularly useful reminder for teachers to understand the purpose when considering collaboration.

The definition of teacher collaboration in this book emphasizes two major elements: "goals" (i.e., shared goals between teachers) and "purpose" (i.e., students' needs and achievements as a main purpose of teacher collaboration). My definition implies that it is important for two parties of teachers as co-equal partners to establish a shared goal to address ELLs' different needs. It also implies that the purpose of collaboration between ESL/bilingual and content area teachers is to meet ELLs' needs and to support their learning across the curriculum.

DOI: 10.4324/9781003058311-3

Research Synthesis on Teacher Collaboration

Current educational reform promotes more collaborative partnerships between teachers for student success across the curriculum. However, teacher collaboration is a complex process that involves benefits and challenges. Research suggests that there are negative elements of teacher collaboration such as the lack of teacher autonomy (Johnson, 2003), but the benefits that teachers obtain through collaboration are undeniable. Given that many ELLs receive instruction from both general education and ESL/bilingual education classrooms, the collaboration between the teachers of these two particular fields becomes more important than that of any other teachers in terms of meeting the diverse needs of ELLs. To this end, the specific benefits and challenges of teacher collaboration must be considered.

Benefits of Teacher Collaboration

Research suggests that collaboration between ESL/bilingual teachers and content area teachers is beneficial because it invites both groups to share their expertise, different opinions, and experiences for the benefit of ELLs' successful learning. As language specialists, ESL/bilingual teachers can share their expertise with content area teachers who can also share their knowledge as content specialists with ESL/bilingual teachers. Given that ELLs acquire content knowledge more successfully through the use of language in an integrated manner, not in a separate manner, the exchange of both groups of teachers' knowledge is important. Through collaborative practice, both groups of teachers can learn how the components of language can be effectively integrated to the content curriculum (see Echevarria, Vogt, & Short, 2008) for details on the language and content integration).

The exchange of ideas and insights that were developed through different teacher education programs and professional experiences is crucially important. Both groups of teachers might have certain beliefs and implicit assumptions about their content areas through these experiences. Through this exchanging and sharing process, both groups of teachers can establish new and shared beliefs about ELLs' needs. Both sides' expertise is equally important and valuable. Yet, it is also central that both groups of teachers recognize that there are areas in which they need to grow professionally.

Although Teaching English to Speakers of Other Languages (TESOL) education programs are increasingly including more content-based curriculum, these programs, which are mostly originated from applied linguistic studies, focus on linguistic perspectives such as grammar. Due to this orientation, ESL/bilingual teachers might miss opportunities to deepen their learning of how to teach ELLs content curriculum. Likewise, content area teacher programs focus on specific subject knowledge and they might not have sufficient opportunities to learn how ELLs acquire a second language through second language acquisition theories and practice. This situation provides the rational as to why both groups of teachers should involve the collaborative process of sharing ideas and reflecting on their instruction for ELLs' development in language, literacy, and content learning.

Another important benefit of collaboration is that it invites both ESL/bilingual teachers and content area teachers to position themselves as active learners who can co-construct the meaning of learning. Knowledge is not fixed (Bruner, 1961; Vygotsky, 1962), and it is created through active collaboration and interaction. Although both groups of teachers have expert knowledge in their own field, they might learn through the collaborative process that their learned knowledge is limited and might not be applied to any student and to any context. Not all ELLs learn in the same way and by the same method. This situation requires a collaborative practice to construct and reconstruct knowledge and meaning to meet ELLs' different needs.

As Vygotsky (1978) pointed out, learning is a social practice achieved through active interaction with individuals and continuous reflection on the experiences. Teachers are professional learners, and they can create a "community of practice" (Lave & Wenger, 1991) through the active process of collaboration. Collaborative partnerships between these two groups of teachers can provide useful opportunities for teachers to challenge their preconceived assumptions about ELLs' learning through in depth discussions. Continual interactive and reflective processes can promote professional growth and new knowledge creation, which will eventually lead to ELLs' successful learning.

Challenges of Teacher Collaboration

Along with the benefits of teacher collaboration, current research also indicates that there are accompanying challenges. The challenges are not in the outcome of teacher collaboration, but in the process of establishing partnerships due to the involvement of diverse internal and external factors. Research suggests that teacher collaboration is not a simple practice since it involves both institutional dynamics (e.g., school structure and school culture) and interpersonal dynamics (e.g., teachers' attitudes, beliefs, and philosophies). The success of teacher collaboration depends on how these complex dynamics are operated and integrated.

The challenging effects of these dynamics are most relevant in the process of collaboration. Although research suggests that the lack of the common planning time was considered as one of the obstacles in the process of establishing partnerships (e.g., Collinson & Cook, 2001; Yoon, 2004; Yoon & Haag, 2012), more serious issues seem to be related to both groups of teachers' views of their own and each other's roles and responsibilities for ELLs. The uncertainty of their own roles and responsibilities for ELLs is evident in the current literature (e.g., Burgess, 2011; Yoon, 2015).

In addition, teachers' perception of unequal status was also viewed as a challenge to implementing a successful collaborative practice. Particularly, ESL/bilingual teachers feel that they do not have the same professional status as the content area teachers (Arkoudis, 2006; Burgess, 2011) and they often assume the role of the classroom paraprofessional (Coltrane, 2002). ESL/bilingual teachers also perceive that content area teachers view them as "supporting" and "paraprofessional" roles, rather than as legitimate and equal partners with whom they work. These perceptions of unequal professional status seem to bring tension to the two groups of teachers, which hinders the process of effective teacher collaboration and influences ELLs' learning accordingly.

These challenges offer space for both ESL/bilingual and content area teachers to examine the issues and ways to resolve them. Teacher collaboration brings numerous benefits, but successful and effective teacher collaboration does not happen without strenuous attempts and commitments from both groups of teachers. What components do the teachers need to consider for successful collaboration? Let us examine this question by focusing on fundamental elements that current research suggests.

Elements for Effective Teacher Collaboration

I discuss research findings by focusing on four major themes for effective teacher collaboration: (1) co-planning time for shared goals, (2) teacher agency for voluntary collaboration, (3) mutual trust, and (4) equal positioning between two parties. I remind the reader that these four components are not exhaustive. Indeed, there are many other elements and factors that influence teacher collaboration positively. Yet, these four themes are the recurring patterns on teacher collaboration that I have found in review of the literature and through my own qualitative case studies over the last two decades. To augment explanations of these themes, I provide examples from my own previous studies, along with other studies that I have found through the extensive literature review.

Co-Planning Time for Shared Goals

Current research consistently suggests that effective teacher collaboration requires a common planning time among teachers to establish shared goals to meet the needs of ELLs. The element of co-planning time is a consistent theme from survey and interview studies (e.g., Davison, 2006; Yoon & Haag, 2012). Although there are not many empirical studies that discuss the two groups of teachers' collaboration in the classroom and the school setting, I found that the co-planning time is still a consistent theme across the educational research (e.g., Arkoudis, 2006; Bauler & Kang, 2020; Burgess, 2011; Duke & Mabbott, 2000; Lassonde & Israel, 2010).

One of the main reasons to have co-planning time is to establish a focused goal to meet ELLs' diverse needs. Numerous scholars in the field of collaboration suggest the co-planning element as the beginning stage of effective teacher collaboration. For instance, DuFour (2003) included planning as one of the four elements of collaboration (i.e., planning, co-teaching, assessment, and reflection). DuFour's idea is similar to Honigsfeld and Dove's (2015) suggestion that the first cycle for effective co-teaching is co-planning, followed by instruction, assessment, and reflection. ESL/bilingual teachers and content area teachers planning together for ELLs' learning is a prerequisite element for effective teacher collaboration.

Any teacher might be engaged in planning before instruction. Yet, the importance of co-planning time between ESL/bilingual teachers and content area teachers is obvious when ELLs are viewed as heterogeneous, who are in different stages of learning development and have different cultural experiences in their home country. For example, some ELLs have formal schooling experiences in their primary country while some might not have them. Some ELLs have high literacy skills in their own native language and some might not have. Some ELLs have thorough knowledge of math and science in their own language, but they might not know how to transfer this knowledge in acquiring content knowledge in English. Some ELLs might be refugees who had to move to several different countries from their war-torn home country. Some ELLs can speak multiple languages, but they might not know how to express their thoughts in a written form. Some ELLs are immigrants who might have highly educated parents who have a social network to support their children. Some immigrant ELLs might not have the similar supporting home environment and system.

As such, ELLs' heterogeneous characteristics, situations, and experiences are endless. Lumping all ELLs into one group without considering this diversity will result in limited instructional practices. These ELLs' different experiences and backgrounds need to be considered when planning lessons (Yoon, 2008). The situations that ELLs face necessitate that both groups of teachers have more consistent and extended co-planning time to discuss how they can meet ELLs' academic, cultural, and social needs to succeed in school. Having formal co-planning time is essential to set up a specific common goal that both groups of teachers need to discuss. Through this co-planning time, both teachers have opportunities to share and deepen their understanding of ELLs' diverse needs and abilities. Through this formal co-planning time, both groups of teachers can share their focused vision for ELLs.

Despite the importance of formal co-planning time for effective teacher collaboration, research suggests that many teachers struggle to find common planning time (Bauler & Kang, 2020; Burgess, 2011). Through my own studies (Yoon, 2004, 2015), I also found that teachers have difficulties finding common planning time. One of the major reasons is that ESL/bilingual teachers often have different schedules from content area teachers. They serve ELLs in their own ESL/bilingual classrooms for ESL "pull-out" programs and they serve ELLs in their mainstream classrooms as well for "push-in" programs on a daily basis. When content area teachers have weekly or monthly curriculum meeting time, these ESL/bilingual teachers might need to work with ELLs in their own classrooms.

If this is the case for most teachers who cannot find common planning time for shared goals, what options do they have, then? An intriguing finding from my own studies is that both ESL/bilingual teachers and content area teachers who could not find formal co-planning time overcame the obstacle through a flexible and informal co-planning time. For instance, in my recent study at a local middle school in 2018, I observed that both an ESL teacher and an English language arts teacher with different schedules attempted to collaborate by using their lunch time, hallway time, and frequent e-mail communications, even on the weekends, to discuss ELLs' needs. Through both physical and virtual communicating processes, they were able to establish a shared goal for ELLs each week. In their interviews with me, both teachers expressed that it would be better to have more official co-planning time for effective collaboration, but it did not greatly influence the way they interacted with each other.

Additionally, in another one of my studies at a local middle school (Yoon, 2007), one content area teacher who taught social studies, reading, and ELA for sixth-grade students effectively worked with an ESL teacher by understanding ELLs' academic, cultural, and social needs. The ESL teacher worked for both elementary and middle schools in the district. Since she served her elementary ELLs in the morning, she was only available in the middle school building in the afternoon. In that context, both the ESL teacher and the content area teacher frequently exchanged e-mails when there were issues that they had to work through together to meet the needs of the ELLs.

More specifically, when the content area teacher was concerned about the academic progress of one of her ELLs, who often did not complete his homework and did not actively participate in the classroom activities, she e-mailed the ESL teacher to learn more about his participatory behavior in the ESL classroom. The content area teacher was curious about whether the issue was related to English ability, his learning disability, or any other issue. She also contacted the student's parents after getting the phone number from the ESL teacher. Both the content area teacher and the ESL teacher had a conference with his mother. Through this conference, the teachers learned that the issue was not related to any of his abilities, but was more related to social factors such as motivation to learn and peer dynamics, which helped the teachers to establish a new goal for the student. Additionally, when there were events after school such as international festival days that the ESL teacher organized for the social needs of ELLs, the content area teacher participated in the events and used the time to learn more about ELLs and their families.

This case illustrates that collaboration takes many different forms that can occur in or out of class and can occur any time when there is a need for ELLs. It indicates an instance of a content area teacher's initiative and an ESL teacher's active response to the content area teacher's needs, and vice versa. It also shows that the two teachers voluntarily seek informal time to discuss ELLs' needs when a formal co-planning time was not allowed in the school setting. This finding supports Hargreaves's (1994) claim that collaboration can happen any time and in any space. It also supports Strahan's (2003) point that "informal get-togethers" (p. 143) is important for collaboration in practice.

In sum, co-planning time for shared goals is important to meet ELLs' needs and it can be achieved through both formal and informal settings. According to school contexts, teachers who are involved with collaboration might seek out both possibilities. To have effective teacher collaboration, there is no doubt that schools need to provide organizational support through teachers' scheduling. However, as shown in the teachers' case above, teachers themselves also need to initiate and take a leadership role by taking responsibilities to support ELLs.

Teacher Agency for Voluntary Collaboration

Another important element found in the research is that teacher collaboration must be voluntary, initiated by teachers themselves, not as a mandated task governed by school administrators (Bronstein, 2013; Danielson, 2011; Hargreaves, 1994; Tobin & Roth, 2005). That is, teacher agency for voluntary collaboration is fundamental for effective teacher collaboration. Hargreaves's (1994) point is particularly significant. He claimed that when collaboration is controlled by administration, teachers often work without desire and, accordingly, genuine and meaningful teacher collaboration does not occur. Collaboration is not effective when teachers are coerced to interact. Hargreaves's perspectives imply that both ESL/bilingual teachers and content area teachers' agency regarding their ability, initiative, and commitment to collaborate for professional growth is essential.

Although collaboration mandated and governed by administration is not effective, it does not mean that school administration can only depend on teachers' desire and commitment without any support. Teachers' initiative, desire, and commitment are interconnected with the school culture and system. They influence and interact with each other in the educational context. To help both groups of teachers sustain their desire and commitment to collaborative partnerships, promoting school culture that values collaboration is key to meet ELLs' needs. Indeed, it is the individual teacher's own decision and choice to make collaboration effective and successful, but such success also requires administrators' support.

The question, then, is what type of support do both groups of teachers need for activating their agency and sustaining their motivation for collaboration? Research suggests that it is vital for schools to provide physical space and time for both groups of teachers to plan and implement collaborative practices. Specifically, schools can consider the proximity by offering classroom space on the same floor so that both groups of teachers can more easily access each other to discuss the needs of ELLs.

For instance, through my own studies in 2015 and 2018, I observed that, compared to the teachers who were on different floors or otherwise not in close proximity, the teachers who were on the same floor and with classrooms closer to each other tended to have more interactive processes. Although other factors such as interpersonal relationships might be involved in the degree of interaction, research suggests that the issue of proximity cannot be ignored for collaborative practices.

In sum, to have more consistent and stable collaboration among teachers, both groups of teachers' desire and commitment to collaboration, along with school support for common space and time, is essential.

Mutual Trust

Another component for effective teacher collaboration suggested by the research is mutual trust (Tschannen-Moran, 2001, 2014). Mutual trust is fundamental for promoting open dialogue between ESL/bilingual teachers and content area teachers. No matter how important both groups of teachers believe that collaboration is for ELLs' learning, collaboration cannot successfully occur when there is little mutual trust, or when dialogue is not promoted among teachers in school settings.

An important research finding is that when mutual trust is discussed, it is often in the context of a personal level, which includes teachers' social dispositions such as their personality and emotion (Fullan & Hargreaves, 1992). This personal level of trust is important to establish a collaborative relationship. For example, both ESL/bilingual teachers and content area teachers might think they are likely to feel more comfortable to collaborate with partner teachers who are more "friendly." This personal dynamic influences the establishment of trust for teacher collaboration.

However, trust at the personal level is insufficient for effective teacher collaboration. As Fullan and Hargreaves (1992) noted, trust in expertise level is also important. That is, mutual trust is not only established through the personal dynamic between the two groups of teachers; it is also established through how they view and value each other's expertise and role. For instance, if ESL/bilingual teachers respect content area teachers' deep knowledge and expertise in language and literacy while content area teachers value ESL/bilingual teachers' innovative strategies on teaching content curriculum, possibilities for promoting and sustaining mutual trust can be enhanced.

Building trust takes time and can be made possible through openness. Both ESL/bilingual teachers and content area teachers need to be ready to offer their views about how they feel about each other's role and expertise in working with ELLs. Comfort and willingness to express their opinions freely is particularly important for collaborative practice between ESL/bilingual and content area teachers since both groups of teachers are from different backgrounds and disciplines. Their view of how ELLs learn might be different due to their different teacher education programs, their different philosophical orientations, and their experiences in personal and professional settings.

This openness comes when both groups of teachers recognize that their learning opportunities in the teacher education programs might be different from each other. TESOL programs focus more on the special linguistic needs of ELLs while content area teacher programs concentrate more on "general education" students who use English as their native language. Although respect is one of the key elements for effective teacher collaboration (Silva & Morgado, 2005), it cannot be achieved without recognizing the different curriculum orientations. Silva and Morgado (2005) asserted that teachers should be willing to accept other teachers' diverse opinions. Authentic collaboration between ESL/bilingual teachers and content area teachers starts from recognition of such differences.

Along with openness and recognition of difference, mutual trust can also be accomplished based on shared responsibility between the two groups of teachers. Given that both teachers' roles become more expanded as they work with an increasingly diverse population of students including ELLs, it is important to clarify and share their roles and responsibilities before, during, and after engaging in collaborative practices. Friend and Cook (2013) noted that collaboration depends on shared responsibility for participation. This principle implies that not only ESL/bilingual teachers, but also content area teachers need to be actively engaged in participating and sharing responsibility for ELLs in the classroom to build trust and to open dialogue.

In sum, both groups of teachers' mutual trust is built upon their expertise, respect, and openness. The element of mutual trust for effective teacher collaboration provides insights that interrelate with other elements such as teachers' agency for voluntary collaborative practices.

View of Equal-Positioning

Both groups of teachers' view of their roles as equal partners is central to have effective teacher collaboration. Yet, research consistently suggests that there is an uneven power dynamic and hierarchical imbalance between ESL/bilingual teachers and content area teachers (Arkoudis, 2006; Burgess, 2011; Creese, 2002; George, 2009; Harper & de Jong, 2009; Liggett, 2010). Friend and Cook (2003) noted that collaboration requires parity among participants. Parity refers to a "situation in which each person's contribution to an interaction is equally valued, and each person has equal power in decision making." (Friend & Cook, 2003, p. 7). Parity is an important principle for any professional teamwork to take place. Effective collaboration will not be possible if individuals' power is exercised over others, and it will not be possible if teachers perceive that there is unequal status within a team of teachers.

For instance, if content area teachers position themselves as being more knowledgeable about what needs to be covered in the curriculum and see ESL/bilingual curricular goals as secondary in status, the ESL/bilingual teachers might perceive an unequal status in decision making. Likewise, if ESL/bilingual teachers position themselves as being more experienced about what needs to be covered for ELLs' learning without considering content area teachers' knowledge, parity is unlikely to develop.

The important element of teachers' view of professional status as equals for effective collaboration is shown through empirical studies in the classroom. The teacher's professional status seems to be related to the curriculum status as well. Arkoudis (2006) noted that the ESL curriculum has not been considered as important as content areas such as math and science in school settings. She asserted that there is a sense of curriculum hierarchy that influences teachers' professional status and positioning. The prevalent curriculum hierarchy seems to influence the way that teachers position themselves and position the partner teachers.

My own classroom studies on teacher collaboration (Yoon, 2004, 2015) reflect the dynamic phenomenon. I found that ESL/bilingual teachers feel marginalized in school settings. They feel their classrooms are placed in the corner and not in desirable places (e.g., no windows) (Yoon, 2004). In addition, ESL/bilingual teachers tend to resist some of content area teachers' view of them as "supporting roles," by positioning themselves as legitimate language specialists (Yoon, 2015). When ESL teachers perceive that their partner teachers do not view them as co-equal partners, I observed that there were fewer interactions between them and content area teachers. There was tension between teachers and their expectations toward each other were incongruent.

More specifically, in my study in an elementary school (Yoon, 2015), the ESL teacher that I observed and interviewed shared her uncomfortable feeling regarding the way that one of the classroom teachers "treats" her and views her as a "supporting" aide, not as a language specialist. The classroom teacher, on the other hand, shared in an interview with me, that she did not feel she received sufficient support from the ESL teacher. Through the observation and the interviews with both teachers, I found that tension was obvious and that it was clearly related to the absence of a shared understanding of their roles. There was little openness and candid conversations between these two parties. The classroom teacher expected the ESL teacher to help ELLs with their homework for the class while the ESL teacher did not agree that her role was to assist ELLs with homework for the general education class. The ESL teacher shared that, as a language specialist, she felt that she had other roles, such as focusing on developing ELLs' vocabulary and language use.

In this context, I rarely saw interactions between the ESL teacher and the classroom teacher over the course of one semester. This study clearly shows an example of both teachers' conflicting expectations and misunderstandings about their roles. It appears that the teachers' positioning of themselves and their positioning of the other partner needs to be considered for effective teacher collaboration.

This finding implies that, for effective teacher collaboration, both ESL/bilingual teachers and general education teachers need to clarify their roles and discuss how they can share responsibilities to support ELLs. Although it is both groups of teachers' role and responsibility to work with ELLs, specific roles can be negotiated by two involved teachers based on the ELLs' needs and their expertise and experiences. The finding also implies that substantive and in-depth discussions are needed to resolve issues and reconcile relationships. If there is little conversation and interaction between these two groups of teachers, ELLs are the ones who suffer in learning.

In sum, I discussed the four major elements for effective teacher collaboration that I found throughout the course of my own studies and the extensive literature review. Although I discussed these elements separately to help the reader understand each element in a more in-depth manner, the reader likely recognizes that they are interrelated. For instance, the two groups of teachers' co-planning time could be voluntarily initiated, negotiated, and expanded through their mutual trust in their personal and expertise level and through positioning each partner as important and as a valuable knowledge contributor.

When personal, professional, and organizational factors work together (Silva & Morgado, 2005), possibilities are more available for effective teacher collaboration. When these elements seamlessly work together, both groups of teachers have more opportunities to establish collaborative professional relationships (Hargreaves, & O'Connor, 2018). The research-supported elements clearly reflect this. Teacher collaboration for ELLs should be pursued as an important professional development. As with other students, ELLs have equal rights to receive the best educational service (Hakuta, 2011). When both ESL/bilingual teachers and content area teachers can be used as important sources for ELLs, the students' learning can be maximized.

In conclusion, these four elements of effective teacher collaboration (i.e., co-planning time for shared goals, teacher agency for voluntary collaboration, mutual trust, and equal positioning between two parties) will be reflected and expanded in the subsequent chapters in Part II (Chapters 3–9) through the interactive dynamics among teachers.

References

Arkoudis, S. (2006). Negotiating the rough ground between ESL and mainstream teachers. *The International Journal of Bilingual Education and Bilingualism*, 9(4), 415–433.

Bauler, C. V., & Kang, E. J. S. (2020). Elementary ESOL and content teachers' resilient co-teaching practices: a long-term analysis. *International Multilingual Research Journal*, 14(4), 338–354.

Bronstein, A. S. (2013). *Teacher collaboration in the age of teaching standards: The study of a small, suburban school district*. Retrieved from http://proxy.binghamton.edu/login?url=https://search-proquest-com.proxy.binghamton.edu/docview/1436986293?accountid=14168.

Bruner, J. S. (1961). The act of discovery. *Harvard Educational Review*, 31(1), 21–32.

Burgess, M. (2011). *Best practices for collaboration between ESL and general education teachers*. Theses, Dissertations, and Other Capstone Projects. Minnesota State University at Mankato.

Collinson, V. & Cook, T. F. (2001). I don't have enough time: Teachers' interpretations of time as a key to learning and school change. *Journal of Educational Administration*, 39(3), 266–281.

Coltrane, B. (2002). Team teaching: Meeting the needs of English language learners through collaboration. *Center for Applied Linguistics Newsletter*, 25(2), 1–5.

Creese, A. (2002). Discursive construction of power in teacher relationships. *TESOL Quarterly*, 36(4), 597–616.

Danielson, C. (2011). *The framework for teaching rubric: 2011 revised edition*. San Francisco, CA: Teachscape.

Davison, C. (2006). Collaboration between ESL and content teachers: How do we know when we are doing it right. *The International Journal of Billingual Education and Bilingualism*, 9(4), 454–475.

DuFour, R. (2003). Leading edge: 'Collaboration lite' puts student achievement on a starvation diet. *Journal of Staff Development*, 24(3), 14–23.

Duke, K. & Mabbott, A. (2000). An alternative model for novice-level elementary ESL education. *MinneTESOL/WITESOL Journal*, 17, 11–30. Retrieved from https://files.eric.ed.gov/fulltext/ED458807.pdf.

Echevarria, J., Vogt, M. E., & Short, D. J. (2008). *Making content comprehensible for English learners: The SIOP model*. Boston, MA: Pearson/Allyn & Bacon.

Friend, M., & Cook, L. (2003). *Interactions: Collaboration skills for school professionals* (4th ed.). Boston, MA: Allyn and Bacon.

Friend, M., & Cook, L. (2007). *Interactions: Collaboration skills for school professionals* (5th ed.). Boston, MA: Allyn & Bacon.

Friend, M., & Cook, L. (2013). *Interactions: Collaboration skills for school professionals* (7th ed.). Boston, MA: Pearson.

Fullan, M., & Hargreaves, A. (1992). *What's worth fighting for in your school? Working together for improvement*. Berkshire, England: Open University Press.

George, C. (2009). Marginalization or collaboration: First year ESL teachers & the middle school context. *Middle Grades Research Journal*, 4(1), 25–52.

Hakuta, K. (2011). Educating minority students and affirming their equal rights: Research and practical perspectives. *Educational Researcher*, 40(4), 163–174.

Hargreaves, A. (1994). *Changing teachers changing times: Teachers' work and culture in the postmodern age.* New York, NY: Teachers College Press.

Hargreaves, A., & O'Connor, M. T. (2018). *Collaborative professionalism: When teaching together means learning for all.* Thousand Oaks, CA: Corwin.

Harper, C. A., & de Jong, E. J. (2009). English language teacher expertise: The elephant in the room. *Language and Education, 23*(2), 137–151.

Honigsfeld, A., & Dove, M. G. (2015). *Collaboration and co-teaching for English learners: A leader's guide.* Thousand Oaks, CA: Corwin.

Johnson, B. (2003): Teacher collaboration:Good for some, not so good for others. *Educational Studies, 29*(4), 337–350.

Lassonde, C. A., & Israel, S. E. (2010). *Teacher collaboration for professional learning: Facilitating study, research, and inquiry communities.* San Francisco, CA: Jossey-Bass.

Lave, J., & Wenger, E. (1991). *Situated learning legitimate peripheral participation.* Cambridge, MA: Cambridge University Press.

Liggett, T. (2010). "A little bit marginalized": The structural marginalization of English language teachers in urban and rural public schools. *Teaching Education, 21*(3), 217

Shakenova, L. (2017). The theoretical framework of teacher collaboration. *Khazar Journal of Humanities and Social Sciences, 20*(2), 34–48.

Silva, J. C., & Morgado, J. (2005). *Facilitators to collaboration between teachers: Effects of gender, teaching experience and subject area.* Paper presented at the Inclusive and Supportive Education Congress International Special Education Conference Inclusion: Celebrating Diversity? Retrieved from http://www.isec2005.org.uk/isec/abstracts/papers_c/castrosilva_j.shtml

Strahan, D. (2003). Promoting a collaborative professional culture in three elementary schools that have beaten the odds. *The Elementary School Journal, 104*(2), 127–146.

Tobin, K., & Roth, W.-M. (2005). Implementing coteaching and cogenerative dialoguing in urban science education. *School Science and Mathematics, 105*(6), 313–322.

Tschannen-Moran, M. (2001). Collaboration and the need for trust. *Journal of Educational Administration, 39*, 308–331.

Tschannen-Moran, M. (2014). *Trust matters: Leadership for successful schools* (2nd ed.). San Francisco, CA: Jossey-Bass.

Vygotsky, L. S. (1962). *Thought and language.* Cambridge, MA: MIT Press.

Vygotsky, L. S. (1978). *Mind in society: The development of higher psychological processes.* Cambridge, MA: Harvard University Press.

Yoon, B. (2004). Uninvited guests: The impact of English and ESL teachers' beliefs, roles, and pedagogies on the identities of English language learners (Doctoral dissertation, University at Buffalo, 2004). *Dissertation Abstracts International, 65*, 885.

Yoon, B. (2007). Offering or limiting opportunities: Teachers' roles and approaches to English language learners' participation in literacy activities. *The Reading Teacher, 61*(3), 216–225.

Yoon, B. (2008). Uninvited guests: The influence of teachers' roles and pedagogies on the positioning of English language learners in regular classrooms. *American Educational Research Journal, 45*(2), 495–522.

Yoon, B. (2015). A case study: One novice middle level teacher's beliefs, challenges, and practices for young adolescent English language learners. In K. F. Malu & M. B. Schaefer (Eds.), *Research on teaching and learning with the literacies of young adolescents* (pp. 3–19). Charlotte, NC: Information Age Publishing.

Yoon, B. & Haag, C. (2012). The epistemological and institutional challenges of teacher collaboration for English language learners' literacy learning. In M. T. Cowart, & G. Anderson (Eds.), *English language learners in 21st century classrooms: Challenges and expectations* (pp. 244–257). Denton, TX: Canh Nam Publishers.

Part II

Case Examples in K-12 Settings and across Curricula

3 Both Teachers' Names are on the Door

ESL and Classroom Teacher Collaboration

Christine Uliassi

It is September and fourth grade teacher, Kathy (pseudonym as all other names) and English as a second language (ESL) teacher, Megan, are guiding students to write biographies about their classmates to share their stories. The students are in the middle of interviewing their partners. Megan and Kathy realize that the English language learners (ELLs) need more support in notetaking during interviews, so they decide to revisit the concept. The teachers decide to replay a Brain POP video on notetaking. There was one important notetaking tip from the video that none of the fourth graders have been utilizing. The classroom teacher, Kathy, starts, "When we watch it again, *keep your eyes peeled*! That is an idiom...an expression. Does anyone know what *keep your eyes peeled* means?" Eh Tah, an ELL, says "It is like when you peel a banana!" "Yes," the ESL teacher, Megan, jumps in, "*peel* in this phrase means open or wide open, so you should be looking carefully and paying close attention for the last tip in the video." During the lesson described, Kathy and Megan are both at the front of the class as students sit in table groups. They are teaching in the fourth grade classroom, and both their names are on the door.

This teaching vignette illustrates the collaboration between a classroom teacher and an ESL teacher as they co-taught lessons after reflecting on their ELLs' learning needs. Their synergy promoted ELLs' understanding. The pair recognized a need to revisit a concept of notetaking, and the teachers, familiar with the complexities of the English language, intuitively explained an idiom that was used in the lesson. This exemplifies how elementary school teachers can work together for ELLs in an inclusive setting.

Effective teacher collaboration for ELLs in elementary settings is more important now than ever. An estimated 10% of public school students are ELLs (National Center for Education Statistics, 2017). The growing number of ELLs in elementary schools and the goal to ensure educational equity for these children has led to more inclusive models for providing instruction. The model of self-contained ESL classrooms, while still used at times, is less common. Agencies like the US Department of Education (US DOE) and the US Department of Justice (US DOJ) as

DOI: 10.4324/9781003058311-5

well as state agencies are recommending – and often mandating – that schools limit the amount of time ELLs are pulled out of mainstream classrooms and urging teachers to provide services that meet the needs of ELLs within inclusive mainstream settings (US DOE & US DOJ, 2015). As this is being expedited at the elementary level, ESL and classroom teachers chart new territory in teacher collaboration, co-teaching, and co-planning. However, collaboration "requires more than simply placing teachers together" (Peercy & Martin-Beltran, 2012, p. 70).

The purpose of this study is to examine how two elementary classroom teachers, *one experienced* and *one new* to teaching ELLs, collaborated with the school's ESL teacher to support students' literacy development. The research question guiding this case study was: What possibilities or challenges do ESL and classroom teachers encounter when they collaborate for ELLs' literacy development? To inform the study, a review of recent research on teacher collaboration for ELLs was conducted.

Research on Collaboration between ESL and Classroom Teachers

The opportunity for collaboration allows ESL and classroom teachers to build their teaching repertoire and schools to bolster their teaching capacity for diverse learners, yet it is not without challenges. Research sheds some light on the complexities that classroom teachers and ESL teachers face when collaborating (Batt, 2008; George, 2009; Peercy & Martin-Beltran, 2012; Vintan & Gallagher, 2019). First, misinterpretations of teaching roles and responsibilities can cause tension (Peercy & Martin-Beltran, 2012; Vintan & Gallagher, 2019). Vintan and Gallagher (2019) found that classroom teachers who are used to being the sole authority in the classroom struggled with an additional teacher in their classroom space. Some even reported initially feeling threatened by having another teacher in the classroom. Once classroom teachers understood that the purpose of ESL teachers was not to be critical of their lessons and practices, collaboration became easier. Conversely, ESL teachers often feel marginalized in their teaching roles (George, 2009; Peercy & Martin-Beltran, 2012; Vintan & Gallagher, 2019). George (2009) used the term "marginalized experts" because ESL teachers were so knowledgeable, but not given opportunities to collaborate and share their knowledge. Like the ELLs, they felt like they were not fully included in the classroom or school community.

In addition to the misperceptions surrounding collaborative roles, lingering misconceptions about ELLs' cultural and linguistic needs can create challenges. For example, Vintan and Gallagher (2019) found classroom teachers' problematic expectations about students such as needing to learn English from ESL teachers before participating in classroom work or not allowing ELLs to use home languages. When surveyed, many ESL teachers indicated that their classroom partners lacked an understanding of culturally and linguistically responsive education. In many collaborative spaces, the ESL teachers feel the weight of having that responsibility (Batt, 2008). Classroom teachers may not realize the language demands of curriculum, and ESL teachers may struggle to be well versed in content and grade specific learning standards (Davison, 2006). Additionally, both ESL and classroom teachers' collaborative relationships can be strained because of teachers' differing visions and lack of common planning time (Peercy & Martin-Beltran, 2012).

It is important to look briefly at how the separation of ESL and classroom teachers' roles may cause tensions in collaboration to arise. Studies fault separation of Teaching English to Speakers of Other Languages (TESOL) and classroom teacher education programs (Dykes, Gilliam, Neel, & Everling, 2012; Evans, Arnot-Hopffer & Jurich, 2005; Nieto, 2009). Evans et al. (2005) argues that this separation creates a "destructive divide and an illusory division of responsibility" (p. 77). Teacher education programs are so different and so isolated when the learning for both classroom teachers and bilingual educators should be very similar, if not identical for the benefit of ELLs in inclusive settings. The University of Texas at Tyler combined students from mainstream teacher education and bilingual education programs who normally take separate courses into a combined block of modified courses so teacher candidates could learn from professors and students in both programs (Dykes et al., 2012).

Since there is a dearth of programs like this, teachers from separate educational backgrounds often need to determine their specific co-teaching responsibilities and learn from each other's expertise on the job. Vintan and Gallagher (2020) found that authentic collaboration takes a long time to develop. Yet, they noted districts can support teachers in this process by offering shared professional development opportunities focusing on teacher collaboration for ELLs. As teachers' roles become more dependent on each other, it is important to further research on the complexities of collaborative partnerships that help or hinder ELLs' learning.

Theoretical Framework

Davison's (2006) framework guided this study on teachers' collaborative efforts for ELLs' literacy learning. The framework, based on extensive research in inclusive settings, describes teaching characteristics, attitudes, and expectations at different levels of collaboration between elementary ESL and classroom teachers. While Davison defines "levels" or "stages," it is not necessary to think of it as a continuum that teachers progress through. The first stage is pseudocompliance or passive resistance. As the name implies, teachers are not buying into collaboration and would rather maintain the status quo of pull-out or self-contained ESL. There is very little time or effort invested into the co-planning or co-teaching. Classroom teachers may have strong relationships with other classroom teachers, not with their ESL counterparts. The next level is compliance. Here, teachers are more responsive, but often frustrated by collaboration and view it in very concrete terms (i.e., generating ESL worksheets, adapting texts). For example, teachers may want more outside training on what each teacher's role should be, but still see the roles as separate. At the accommodation stage, there is more willingness to implement strategies and techniques, but little critical examination of beliefs or pedagogical practices. Practices are limited in growth as teachers do not feel comfortable challenging each other's beliefs on learning styles or language development.

At the highest levels of convergence (level 4) and creative co-construction (level 5), teachers are highly positive about collaboration fostering a productive learning environment. At convergence, many practices and beliefs become shared. For example, teachers may have lengthy dialogue on ELLs' responses to a lesson, eagerly planning a needed follow up. Teachers at this stage respect each other greatly but may still struggle to share views that contradict one another's. At the creative co-construction level, teaching is intuitive, creative, and fluid. At both the highest levels, teachers see positive outcomes of collaboration and have a strong sense of agency. Conversations about students are very specific and use shared terminologies. At the advanced levels, there is more of a focus on the theoretical underpinnings of instructional ideas and decisions compared with the lower levels' focus on lesson delivery.

Study Context for Teacher Collaboration

As a researcher, I collected the data at an elementary school in a small northeastern city serving 350 students. About 20% of the students receive English as a New Language (ENL) services. About 40% of the students receive free or reduced-price meals. This school serves diverse ELLs, including children of international faculty as well as students, refugees, and first-and second-generation language learners. There is a large community of Karen people in the school community. The Karen are an ethnic group from Burma (Myanmar), many of whom fled Burma due to religious and ethnic persecution by the government. The school is known locally for its cultural, socioeconomic, and linguistic diversity.

Participants

Three teachers participated in this study. Megan was the ESL teacher (8 years teaching experience) who collaborated with Kathy (4th grade, 16 years teaching experience) and Alice (5th grade, 6 years teaching experience) to provide inclusive support for ELLs. All three teachers were white and monolingual.

Megan decided to get her graduate degree in TESOL after finding a passion for language and culture while living and working abroad. She had taught both high school and elementary ESL in the district for 8 years at the time of the study. She was very knowledgeable about the backgrounds and experiences of her students and their families. She had been collaborating with Kathy for 3 years. They ate lunch together most days, chatting and planning informally. Of the 22 students in their fourth class, 8 were ELLs, including 1 student who joined very late in the school year. Four students were from Burma and spoke the Karen language. One student was from Ethiopia and spoke Amharic, two students spoke Spanish (Ecuador and Spain), and one student was from Iraq and her first language was Arabic. There were other bilingual students (Chinese- and Spanish-speaking) who were not in the ENL program.

Kathy had extensive experience working with ELLs in the classroom and sponsoring local refugee families. She had a 20-year career in another field before returning to school to get a bachelor's degree in elementary education. She did not feel prepared for the needs of the many ELLs, so she returned to get her master's degree in literacy. To continue her learning, she regularly attends local conferences on teaching culturally and linguistically diverse learners as well as national or international organizations, including NAME (National Association for Multicultural Education) and TESOL (Teaching English to Speakers of Other Languages) conferences. She is knowledgeable about the Karen refugee community, which she supports as a sponsor.

Alice was in her sixth year as a fifth grade teacher and working with upper-grade ELLs for the first time. After obtaining an undergraduate health degree, she worked in teaching-related fields (tutoring, job training) and decided to get her master's degree in childhood education. Until the year of the study, her classroom was often the inclusion classroom for students with special needs. Because of this, she had experience with collaborative teaching.

Even though Alice and Megan had never worked together before, they were friends from years of sharing a hallway. The fifth grade class of 18 students included 3 receiving ENL services and 1 recently exited bilingual student. One student had recently arrived from South Korea and the others were from Burma and spoke the Karen language. Two other students were bilingual (Lithuanian and Hebrew) who were not in the ENL program. Because of student numbers and levels, Megan spent 90 minutes a day in fourth grade while only about 30 minutes in fifth grade.

Data Collection and Sources

I, as the primary researcher, drew upon a year-long qualitative study on teachers' practices for ELLs' literacy development. I collected data during the 2017–2018 school year. I spent approximately 200 hours observing the teaching and learning dynamics in the classrooms. The primary data sources were teacher interviews and classroom observations.

During the teacher interviews (two 1-hour interviews with each teacher), I asked questions to find out more about the teachers' backgrounds, their approaches to literacy, and their methods of supporting ELLs. I used observation data from English Language Arts lessons and collaborative planning meetings. These field notes detailed teachers' instruction and interactions with the ELLs and the teachers' dynamics with one another. The content of these field notes included verbal descriptions of activities, as well as some direct quotes.

Data Analysis

I began my analysis by looking at my notes from lessons, planning sessions, and interview transcripts. I looked each case separately and developing preliminary themes. I used Corbin and Strauss' (2015) coding methods so that categories developed after exploring data. Coding strategies included open coding, in vivo coding (participant's words), axial coding, and selective coding. During open coding, incidents found to be conceptually similar to previously coded incidents were given the same conceptual label.

Next, I looked at where these themes converged in the two cases, especially in relation to the complexities of teacher collaboration. The lens of Davison's (2006) teacher collaboration was engaged to determine if categories related to the study's research question on possibilities and challenges. Selective coding involved returning to the data to seek out any data that relates to the themes. For example, initial codes of "consult," "problem solve," "sharing strategies," and the in vivo code "She is my sounding board" led to the axial concept of "sounding board." This developed into the theme "having a sounding board for discussing challenges." Trustworthiness of the study was provided by using rich descriptions, triangulation, and peer debriefings.

Researcher's Positionality

To ensure sincerity in qualitative literacy research, it is important to share researchers' biases, beliefs, and values, which are shaped by their linguistic and ethnic backgrounds (Yoon & Uliassi, 2019). My identity as a white, English-speaking, middle class, former teacher and current researcher is relevant. I worked in linguistically diverse communities in the Washington D.C. area as a classroom teacher for 10 years before becoming an ESL teacher. I became a certified ESL teacher because of my passion for working with diverse families, but also because I did not feel prepared to meet the literacy needs of ELLs in my classroom. My experiences as an ESL teacher pushing into mainstream classrooms often left me feeling undervalued. When I moved to upstate New York, I left behind this urban, multicultural community. I began teaching methods courses in elementary education with practicums in mainly rural communities without many multilingual families. I felt challenged by the disconnect of methodology courses and practicums, focused so much on monolingual classroom teaching, and my previous experiences in diverse, multilingual environments.

These shifting experiences directed me to do research in equitable practices for ELLs, including ESL and classroom teacher collaboration. Because of my experiences as an ESL teacher and my focus on language, power, and equity, I avoided using the terms "Kathy's classroom" or "Alice's classroom" which marginalizes Megan. I used "fourth grade class" and "fifth grade class."

Findings

This analysis led to four main findings about the collaboration for ELLs in the two partnerships. First, both partnerships leveraged ELLs' experiences in literacy lessons. Second, the teaching partners had a "sounding board" to discuss challenges. Third, the teachers shared the role of providing language support. Lastly, the teachers negotiated the limited time with ELLs. As each finding is expanded, I will provide examples of how Megan's collaboration varied with Kathy, experienced with ELLs, and Alice, new to teaching ELLs. Overall, both partnerships consistently reflected characteristics of the convergence level of Davison's (2006) framework displaying high levels of mutual respect and trust. The partnership with Megan and Kathy, at times, demonstrated aspects of Davison's (2006) creative co-construction (level 5) as critical reflection was evident in their co-planning. At times, the partnership between Megan and Alice showed aspects of Davison's (2006) accommodation stage (level 3) as concrete ESL strategies were seen as central to planning.

Leveraging ELLs' Experiences in Literacy Lessons

Both classroom teachers greatly valued Megan's role and the experiences of the ELLs which enhanced their collaboration. The two partnerships thoughtfully selected texts about refugees, immigrants, and others marginalized characters, and used their experiences as a lens to understand texts and participate in conversations.

In fourth grade, Kathy and Megan shared a similar critical multicultural stance that was reflected in their literacy planning and lessons. They believed literacy should promote non-dominant perspectives and awareness of social justice issues. Kathy and Megan noticed how impassioned several of the ELLs became when talking about issues of equality, so they frequently planned topics related to social justice and inequality in English and Social studies.

Their "Immigrants Make America Great" project was one example of how their collaboration enriched ELLs' learning. Both teachers were affected by the negative messages about immigrants by the current US administration during the time of this study. In response, they created a unit entitled, "Immigrants Make America Great" – a pushback toward the Trump campaign message "Make America Great Again." Each student read a picture book about an immigrant in America, took notes on their background and contributions using a graphic organizer, and then prepared a poster to display outside the classroom. Megan supported ELLs by guiding them to texts related to their interests and helped them fill out the graphic organizer with key information. Kathy instructed the students to use technology tools to create small posters and displayed them under the giant hallway banner "Immigrants Make America Great." The fourth graders selected texts on diverse individuals from Albert Einstein to DJ Kool Herc, a Jamaican immigrant credited with major contributions to hip-hop music, to Sylvia Mendez and her family, activists who helped end school segregation for Mexican children. Kathy reflected, "They really liked that project. We want to do it again next year...a lot of people have been looking at the bulletin board." The partnership in fourth grade led to meaningful critical tasks building off of ELLs' diverse backgrounds.

Leveraging ELLs' immigration experiences in literacy lessons was also shown in the fifth grade partnerships. Here, Megan took the lead in connecting literacy tasks to students' cultural assets. For instance, she helped the classroom teacher, Alice, select and display multicultural texts to welcome ELLs at the beginning of the year. Moreover, Alice asked Megan to help her select guided reading books for the whole class but wanted them to specifically connect to the diverse ELLs' lives. During a planning session, Megan brought reading group book options to Alice. They examined the texts together and determined the best options, based on text complexity, students' cultural backgrounds, as well as literacy standards. They agreed upon the text *Goodbye Vietnam* (Whelan, 1993), a story about a family that has to leave their homeland to escape uncertainty and threats of violence from the government. Alice appreciated Megan's thoughtful selections; she said "Specifically with the book *Goodbye Vietnam*, [Megan] and I talked and we thought some of the Karen and Burmese kids in this classroom that would really resonate with them." Like the Vietnamese family in the book, many of the families of the refugee students in the classroom had to leave their country for life in a new place and they shared thoughtful insights during the discussions. The fifth grade teachers' attention to the lived experiences and assets of ELLs was central to their collaboration.

In some ways, Alice was still developing her skills for engaging in more in-depth cultural discussions and linking these discussions to literacy lessons. In this collaboration, Alice depended on Megan's knowledge of ELLs' families and backgrounds. One morning, Sara, a Karen student, wore traditional makeup from her country. When I asked Alice she said, "I think it has something to do with her country, but [Megan] will know more." Later that morning, Megan was reading with Sara in a small group, and Sara shared that the makeup made from a tree and wearing it is special tradition in her country. Megan asked Sara if they could search for more information online about the topic. This became a small "teachable moment" about the powder made from bark, called Thanaka, used for its healing and aromatic purposes by Karen women. The anecdote showed that Alice depended on Megan for finding out about cultural traditions that could be used for engaging students in literacy activities. She was still reliant on Megan's work in the partnership to build and integrate deep cultural connections.

In both partnerships, the teachers aligned in their beliefs and efforts to use literacy instruction to promote positive perspectives about the value of the immigrant experience and cultural diversity in the United States. ELLs were engaged in these projects and texts connected to their backgrounds. At higher levels of collaboration (convergence and creative co-construction), teachers *shared* underlying visions and beliefs about teaching and learning (Davison, 2006). When teachers' visions are not aligned, partnerships are much more strained (Davison, 2006; Peercy & Martin-Beltran, 2012). Megan and Kathy were able to use more transformative, critical literacy practices because of their shared vision of teaching and learning. This was not evident to quite the same extent in fifth grade, yet it was emerging because of Megan and Alice's interest in leveraging ELLs' cultural and linguistic diversity.

Having a "Sounding Board" to Discuss Teaching Challenges

The collaboration in both pairs was effective because of how much they respected the insights of their partners. Teachers in both classrooms valued their partner's opinions and expertise, depending on one another as what Alice called a "sounding board" in resolving daily and long-term planning challenges.

In the fourth grade partnership, the teachers checked in with each other about "big picture" plans at regular meetings and daily planning was more informal, chatting over lunch in Kathy's classroom. Often Megan and Kathy talked specifically about how each ELL was doing with the current text or writing project, but also more holistically. For example, they worried about Beza, an ELL from Ethiopia because she struggled with participation in class activities at the beginning of the year. Kathy wondered how to help her to "seem more satisfied and engaged" in class writing activities. With Megan, she critically examined factors related to the students' disengagement (i.e., missing home country, concerns about family members). After problem solving with each other and the student, they decided to encourage the student to use more digital tools – such as voice-to-text features – to help her with writing. Beza could use the technology that she loved using for meaningful activities such as researching her home country of Ethiopia and sharing her projects with the class. The teachers also helped her enroll in afterschool and mentoring programs to help with the social–emotional struggles she was dealing with. As the year progressed, this ongoing collective problem solving helped the student become a much stronger participant and, often, she was eager to share her writing ideas with classmates.

In the fifth grade partnership, the sharing of ideas to meet individual student's needs was often more related to concrete strategies and methods. When describing her partner, Alice said, "[Megan] knows these strategies. She's my sounding board and we have all these ideas." She explained that their informal planning and consulting check-ins helped her understand what strategies to implement. For instance, when students were struggling to understand summarizing, Alice and Megan developed a lesson using different-sized notecards so students could have a visual showing how the author's ideas could be condensed. When organization of persuasive essays proved challenging for Sara and Jo, two ELLs, the teachers spent their limited planning time creating graphic organizers with sentence starters for the thesis, main points, supporting details, and counterclaims. Both ELLs responded well to these tools, pulling them out from their writing folders as they worked on their essays.

In effective partnerships, teachers can navigate the complexities of teaching ELLs during their co-teaching and co-planning process. Instructing ELLs not only involves understanding the process of English language development, but also factors like cultural differences. Megan was able to use her skillset to meet both classroom teachers where they were in their planning and problem solving. In fifth grade, Megan was more of a consultant for ESL strategies that would work for many students (use of visuals, graphic organizers). Alice was at the stage of collaboration where she was looking for these types of ESL strategies. This is a characteristic of the accommodation stage (level 3), where there is a willingness by the classroom teacher to implement strategies and techniques, but not yet collaborative critical reflection. With Kathy, who already had the expertise in modifying assignments and delivery of instruction, the pair could engage in more critical reflection on individual students' progress in literacy. The results of these actions went beyond literacy, improving students' confidence and achievements across the curriculum. This, according to Davison's (2006) framework is exemplary of the highest level of collaboration, creative co-construction (level 5), where teachers have a strong respect and trust for one another and use their partnership as an apparatus for reflection to improve students' learning. Both partnerships learned from each other, trusted, and respected their partners' expertise which is essential in effective collaboration (Davison, 2006).

Sharing the Role of Providing Language Support

Both classroom teachers wanted to be prepared to meet the language needs of their students and did not see that as solely Megan's job. With consideration to their different backgrounds in teaching ELLs, this commitment transpired uniquely in each partnership. From her extensive experiences studying literacy, teaching ELLs, and working with refugee families, Kathy started off the year with a classroom full of linguistic supports (i.e., bilingual word walls and texts, sentence frames, digital tools) while Alice was learning from Megan and developing her scaffolding skills as the year progressed.

In the fourth grade partnership, Megan did not see herself as the only ESL teacher in the room. Megan commented that, when she, herself, was absent, she did not worry about the ELLs because Kathy *was an ESL teacher*. Together, they attended professional workshops on supporting ELLs (i.e., scaffolding and differentiation in multilingual classrooms). Both teachers' competency in teaching linguistically diverse learners led to more interchangeable roles in co-teaching. For example, Kathy often led the class's whole group activity while Megan floated around and supported students, individually or in small groups. But the roles were fluid, and sometimes Megan taught or co-taught whole group lessons. All students were able to receive the support from both teachers in the space.

Kathy was skillful in promoting oral discourse by leveraging the linguistic resources in her classroom. The fourth grade partners discussed intentional partnering variations, discourse moves (i.e., "Can someone restate what our friend just said?"), and use of students' first language. In lessons, Kathy developed language support partners. As Kathy described, "[Anna] can translate for [Eh Tah]…in Karen, in English, sometimes just in a more kid-friendly way than I can." Kathy also frequently researched technology available to support ELLs' language development. When reading informational texts, she used online sources that allowed students to select the reading level, language translation, and use of audio. This way, ELLs could access the same content as their peers while building their language skills. These language supports were in place when Megan was co-teaching and when Kathy was teaching by herself.

Alice's role in providing linguistic support was still evolving in fifth grade. While Alice was teaching, Megan was usually floating around the room supporting ELLs individually or working at the back table with a group of ELLs. Alice took responsibility for ELLs' language development when she was teaching solo but was often unsure of her ability. She frequently shared self-doubt about her ability to provide language support for ELLs, yet she hoped to learn more from Megan. Megan is "teaching me everything right now." Alice eagerly implemented the strategies Megan suggested even when Megan was not in the fifth grade classroom. As discussed, Megan created tools for Alice to utilize when she was not with the students (i.e., graphic organizers with visual supports, sentence starters, and models).

At times, Alice learned crucial lessons about ELLs and the need for language support in her solo teaching moments. During a poetry writing session, Alice noticed that Jo, an ELL from South Korea, was not getting much done. He was trying to write poetry with rhyme but struggling to come up with the needed vocabulary for the task. She decided to show Jo how to use a rhyme dictionary online and spent much of the class reviewing the concept of rhyming with him. Later in the week, he was using the online rhyming dictionaries independently and completing more poems. When reflecting on the needed language support in lessons, Alice said "I never realized what a good command of English a student needs to have to be able to do rhyming patterns in poetry." This anecdote shows Alice's capability for reflection on students' language skills and her willingness to support language development.

Vintan and Gallagher (2019) found that often classroom teachers feel the task of providing language support is for the ESL teacher. This misconception can cause tension in collaborative partnerships and reduce the experiences for ELLs. Both Alice and Kathy were committed to providing language support alongside Megan or when teaching solo. At the highest levels of Davison's (2006) model, teachers' roles can be thought of as interchangeable and the fourth grade partnership demonstrated this consistently. Kathy and Megan communicated through the language of ESL terminology (i.e., oral language development, discourse, and scaffolding) and they were able to be flexible in their roles in the fourth grade classroom. Alice had not had the opportunity to build her knowledge of teaching linguistically diverse learners, so the teachers' roles were still separate at times as described in Davison's (2006) lower stages. Alice took advantage of opportunities to learn from Megan and the ELLs themselves, building a new "toolkit" of ESL strategies and methods that she could use more independently in the future.

Negotiating the Limited Time with ELLs

The two partnerships were hindered by schedule interruptions and limitations. The obstacles were more visible in fifth grade. One challenge was the limited amount of time in Megan's schedule for working in fifth grade – 30 minutes a day compared with the 90 minute language block in fourth grade. Megan explained,

> There's more need for support at the lower level [fourth] and schedules are different. Fifth grade schedule is very limited and so there is only a very short amount of time that I can work with my students in fifth grade.

The limited time was most problematic in the fifth grade partnership. Alice, being new to supporting ELLs, depended heavily on Megan's ideas. Alice said "We need more Megans." Since Megan was only in fifth grade classroom for 30 minutes, so they decided to use that time mostly for meeting with reading groups. However, Megan felt that since the ELLs also struggled in writing, having additional teacher support would allow more time for one-on-one writing conferences. Megan and Alice struggled to meet with all the students and felt her students needed more individual support.

However, the teachers negotiated the limited time with ELLs. Even though Megan's physical presence in the room was lacking during much of ELA, she was a support to Alice as she co-planned for literacy activities. Megan also read students' papers on Google Docs and made comments about what ELLs were doing well and what they could work on. Megan referred to herself as a "consultant" for fifth grade since her presence was not always there, but she could still advise. Brief and very informal meetings also happened daily. For example, Megan stopped by in between her other classes to mention to Alice: "I gave Sara feedback on her paper…we still need to work on run-on sentences."

The fourth grade adapted differently to the challenge of the limited time Megan had with the class. In the fourth grade partnership, Kathy and Megan were able to find ways to prioritize time so that ELLs would get the most understanding out of the texts. When reading *The Secret School* (Avi, 2003), Megan was working with a small reading group of ELLs. During a lunch planning session with Kathy, Megan shared "We are not going to have time to write." That made sense to Kathy. It was the text discussion and oral language development during their co-teaching time that mattered to both of them. Kathy knew that she could reinforce students' writing skills during content lessons. During *The Secret School* discussion, Amira, an ELL from Iraq, used posted sentence frames (e.g., "I agree with [classmate's] idea, and I wanted to add that….") to share her ideas. Eh Tah connected the book's theme of access to education for girls to his own family, saying "My mom had to leave Burma and never went to high school." These meaningful texts discussions took place in part because of the planning conversations the teachers held where they reflected on shared goals about oral language development for ELLs. This reflects the collaborative goal setting at Davison's (2006) advanced levels.

Research on collaboration often discusses ESL teachers having to support too many students in too many classrooms (Peercy & Martin-Beltran, 2012; Vintan & Gallagher, 2019) like Megan did. Often, another limitation is the need for more common planning time between the ESL and classroom teachers. This did not come up in this study as a challenge in these partnerships, perhaps because Megan found ways to work planning time into her schedule by eating lunch with Kathy and checking in with Alice before or after school.

Discussion

Davison (2006) states that the collaboration needed to benefit ELLs' learning can be "rare and extremely difficult to sustain" (p. 458). This study provides the possibilities in building and sustaining these "rare" effective collaborative partnerships and making them more common. Because of the teachers' respect and positive attitude toward collaboration, the ESL teacher was able to negotiate her role differently in each classroom to support ELLs. Both classroom teachers recognized and prioritized their own role in ELLs' learning. As both partnerships continue to develop, these practices will have lasting effects.

Megan, the ESL teacher, was able to adjust her work in each collaboration based on the needs of not only the ELLs, but also the classroom teachers. That meant Alice needed more support in learning about working with students from different cultural and linguistic backgrounds, starting with more concrete techniques. Alice's recognition and support of Megan's specialization allowed them to provide more culturally responsive texts and lessons as well as scaffolding for students. Partly because of Kathy's strong background in ESL and their familiarity in co-teaching, the fourth grade partners were able to take their work beyond strategies and lesson delivery to developing socially consciousness through literacy. This was important at a time of continued marginalization toward immigrant and other minority groups in the United States.

In many settings, instead of an egalitarian partnership, classroom teachers held more power to determine instruction (George, 2009; Peercy & Martin-Beltran, 2012). This asymmetry in power undermines teaching and weakens learning potential. In contrast, in these two pairings, Megan was clearly respected as an equal and an expert in co-constructing meaningful teaching and learning (Davison, 2006). This equality, built on mutual trust and respect, made it possible for the teachers to make decisions about ELLs together. Vintan and Gallagher (2019) discuss the importance of recognizing the difference between deep-rooted collaboration and surface collaboration, limited to planning for strategies and lesson delivery. Many interactions in the fifth grade partnership could be considered surface collaboration, but taking into consideration the growth trajectory based on Alice's interest in "learning everything" from Megan, it is clear that a deeper partnership was evolving.

This study sheds light on challenges in collaboration for ELLs, mainly the lack of co-teaching time for ESL teachers supporting many learners. Still, positive attitudes about collaboration, shared priorities, and flexibility – all characteristics of Davison's (2006) advanced partnerships – helped to offset Megan's limited time in each classroom.

Implications and Suggestions

This study provides implications and related suggestions for both teacher educators and researchers as well as teachers and school leaders.

Teacher Education Faculty

While faculty in the fields of elementary, TESOL, and literacy education are often separate in their departments and research communities, the future teachers they are instructing will soon be collaborating on a daily basis. Keeping this in mind while planning research and teaching collaborations between researchers is essential. Studies have described teacher educators who have merged their methods courses so ESL and classroom teacher candidates can plan units together (e.g., Dellicarpini & Gulla, 2009). This work allows future classroom teachers to be prepared for the complexities of teaching ELLs before they begin co-teaching. In this study, both classroom teachers felt they began their teaching careers with limited knowledge to meet the needs of ELLs.

Also, there is a need for more research on the factors that lead to successful partnerships between ESL and classroom teachers. Studies with a larger number of teachers could look specifically at factors related to each teacher (language background, experience, and education) and the factors related to the partnership dynamics (years working together, teaching styles, and planning time).

Teachers and School Leaders

School leaders can encourage classroom spaces that belong to classroom teachers, ESL teachers, and all learners. Since ESL teachers are now sharing classroom teachers' previously solitary space, the sign on the door should include both names, as it did for Kathy and Megan's truly shared space. Also, teachers can make use of virtual classroom tools to make sure ESL teachers are including in assessing students' work when they are not able to be present. This helped with Megan's limited time in fifth grade.

Another suggestion is to have a focus on shared professional development opportunities for ESL and classroom teachers. Schools can provide school-wide trainings on culturally responsive practices and ESL methods so all teachers are able to support ELLs. This will build the school's capacity for teaching culturally and linguistically diverse learners, so that teachers and students are not dependent on ESL teachers. The professional development opportunities afforded to Kathy and Megan enabled more fluidity in their roles.

Conclusion

Many of these findings show the potential impact collaboration can have on student learning. Educators can come together to share wisdom, solve problems, and deliver stronger lessons than they could alone. This study shows ESL and classroom teachers' mainly positive experiences with collaboration. Yet, any time teachers are working toward equitable practices for ELLs, they will encounter barriers. Just like teaching culturally and linguistically diverse learners in general, there are no easy answers.

According to Bartolome (2009), there are no "one size fits all" solutions. Teaching multilingual students is not as simple as teaching a set of strategies and techniques; it is quite complex. Teachers need to be aware of the history of mistreatment and discrimination in the United States that has led to schools' devaluing of immigrant students' cultural knowledge and assets. To combat decades-long deficit view of ELLs requires commitment of classroom teachers and ESL teachers (Bartolome, 2009). To get to the place where both teachers' names are on the door outside classrooms across America, the work toward collaborative partnerships must be bold. The collaboration between ESL and classroom teachers, with the goal of improved equity for this growing group of students, can transform education.

References

Avi. (2003). *The secret school.* Boston, MA: Houghton Mifflin Harcourt Publishing.

Bartolome, L. (2009). Beyond the methods fetish: Toward a humanizing pedagogy. In A. Darder, M. Baltodano, & R.D. Torres (Eds.), *The critical pedagogy reader* (pp. 339–355). New York, NY: Routledge.

Batt, E. G. (2008). Teachers' perceptions of ELL education: Potential solutions to overcome the greatest challenges. *Multicultural Education, 15*(3), 39–43.

Corbin, J. & Strauss, A. (2015). *Basics of qualitative research: Techniques and procedures for developing grounded theory.* Thousand Oaks, CA: Sage Publications, Inc

Davison, C. (2006). Collaboration between ESL and content teachers: How do we know when we are doing it right? *International Journal of Bilingual Education and Bilingualism, 9*(4), 454–475.

DelliCarpini, M. & Gulla, A. (2009). Creating space for collaboration. *English Journal, 98*(4), 133–137.

Dykes, F., Gilliam, B., Neel, J., & Everling, K. (2012). Peeking inside Pandora's box: One university's journey into the redesign of teacher education preparation. *Current Issues in Education, 15*(2), 1–8.

Evans, C., Arnot-Hopffer, E., & Jurich, D. (2005). Making ends meet: Bringing bilingual education and mainstream students together in preservice teacher education. *Equity & Excellence in Education, 38*(1), 75–88.

George, C. (2009). Marginalization or collaboration: First year ESL teachers and the middle school context. *Middle Grades Research Journal, 4*(1), 25–52.

National Center for Education Statistics. (2017). *English language learners in public school.* Washington, D.C.: Institute of Education Sciences. Retrieved from https://nces.ed.gov/programs/coe/indicator_cgf.asp.

Nieto, S. (2009). Bringing bilingual education out of the basement and other imperatives for teacher education. In A. Darder, M. Baltodano, & R.D. Torres (Eds.), *The critical pedagogy reader* (pp. 469–482). New York, NY: Routledge.

Peercy, M. & Martin-Beltran, M. (2012). Envisioning collaboration: including ESOL students and teachers in the mainstream classroom. *International Journal of Inclusive Education, 16*(7), 657–673.

US Department of Education & US Department of Justice. (2015) *Dear colleague letter: English learner students.* Washington DC: US Department of Education. Retrieved from http://www2.ed.gov/about/offices/list/ocr/letters/colleague-el-201501.pdf

Vintan, A., & Gallagher, T. L. (2019). Collaboration to support ESL education: Complexities of the integrated model. *TESL Canada Journal, 36*(2), 68–90.

Vintan, A., & Gallagher, T. L. (2020). Effective collaborative practices in *ESL education Education Canada, 60*(2), 41–43.

Whelan, G. (1993). *Goodbye Vietnam.* New York, NY: Random House, Inc.

Yoon, B. & Uliassi, C. (2019, December). *"Researcher-As-Instrument" in qualitative literacy research.* Paper presented at the conference of Literacy Research Association, Tampa, Florida.

4 Reflections on Co-Teaching and Collaboration

Communication, Flexibility, and Congruence

Heeok Jeong and Laura Eggleston

It's not just the individual co-teaching relationships, but it's our overall relationship. We're all working together to successfully meet the needs of the students and it's working because of us. I'm not saying that other people couldn't be a part of a team, but one thing that's very important to me is that you often hear that ELL teachers, it's like a marriage and it takes years. It is, like Anna said, it took, it's a lot for myself, from my experience as a classroom teacher, I appreciate these women so much because they relinquish some of the control. They're saying, you know, Laura, I trust you. You can affect the way we teach our students.

Laura (the participant teacher) shared this statement at a meeting with classroom teachers that was held at the end of semester in order to discuss successes, challenges, and what needs to be improved for English language learners' (ELLs) learning. I (Heeok, the researcher and author) was at the meeting as a researcher, learning how teachers presented their ideas about co-teaching ELLs. As indicated in Laura's statement, Laura believes that highly effective co-teaching does not appear instantly nor fully formed, but it develops through reflection and accommodation over time. The collaboration between Laura and the three classroom teachers grew out of what Hargreaves and O'Connor (2018a) have termed "collaborative professionalism" which will be explained in detail below.

Laura is a white female ENL teacher (English as a New Language, also known as English as a Second Language (ESL)) whom I met through an educational association. While talking with Laura, she shared that her work with classroom teachers had been successful. I was curious about what factors are involved in her success with the classroom teachers. So, I decided to visit Laura's classroom to conduct research on teacher collaboration and co-teaching in order to provide insights and approaches for highly effective teacher co-teaching and collaboration practices through the lens of teachers. Many teachers do not feel that they are prepared to teach ELLs and collaborate with ENL teachers (Miller, 2011; Rumberger & Gándara, 2005); therefore, in order to explain what made the 4 years

DOI: 10.4324/9781003058311-6

of co-teaching and collaboration between Laura and three classroom teachers so highly effective and what kinds of challenges they might have faced, this study aims to answer the following two questions:

1   What are the teachers' views of the essential components of effective collaboration and co-teaching for ELLs' learning?
2   What are the teachers' views of the possibilities and challenges of collaboration and co-teaching?

Theoretical Perspectives

This study is grounded in the theoretical construct of *collaborative professionalism* (Hargreaves & O'Connor, 2018a). Hargreaves and O'Connor distinguished collaborative professionalism from professional collaboration. They noted that "collaborative professional relationships are more rooted in positive and trusting relationships among people involved" (Hargreaves & O'Connor, 2018a, p. xv) because "success with the solidity of the design depends on solidarity among teachers" (Hargreaves & O'Connor, 2018b, p. 23). In order to develop collaborative professionalism, collaborative professional relationships "need better tools and deeper trust, clearer structures and stronger cultures, expertise and enthusiasm, knowing what to do and how to be with each other—both solidity and solidarity (Hargreaves & O'Connor, 2018b, p. 21)." Hargreaves (2019) concluded that both solidity and solidarity are essential for collaborative professionalism based on his 30 years of research on teacher collaboration. Both expert knowledge and strong collegial relationships are needed for effective collaboration. Expert knowledge is related to professional capital.

Professional capital includes three components, that is, human capital, decisional capital, and social capital (Hargreaves & Shirley, 2020). Human capital indicates the ability of a teacher to connect knowledge about curriculum, pedagogy, and assessment with practice in real classrooms. Decisional capital is related to making a professional judgment in the teaching and collaborating situation. Social capital is associated with leading, supporting, collaborating, and co-teaching collegially among teachers for the improvement of pedagogical practices. Collaborative professionalism, characterized by solidity with solidarity and professional capital, does not appear fully formed, but rather it grows gradually over time through "solidarity among colleagues and a solid grounding in research, expertise, and well-designed tools and protocols" (Hargreaves & O'Connor, 2018b, p. 24).

Hargreaves and O'Connor (2018a) categorized four different forms of collaboration: emerging, doubt, design, and transformation. In the past, teaching was presumed to be an individual act without much collaboration. Later, research results demonstrated the positive impact of teacher collaboration on student learning, and teacher collaboration began emerging as an alternative to the previous individualistic para-digm. Initially, in the stage of doubt, teacher collaboration was per-formed with contrived collegiality in order to conform with top-down mandates. At this stage, numerous discussions occurred about how to collaborate in education, but not much *real* action. In the design stage, diverse terminologies related to collaborative structures were created, such as professional learning community (PLC), teams, and collaborative action research. Then, finally, collaborative professionalism paved the way for the transformation stage of teacher collaboration, and observ-able changes began to take place.

To date, little research grounded in collaborative professionalism has been conducted on the essentials, possibilities, and challenges of teacher co-teaching and collaboration, particularly, the collaboration between ENL and classroom teachers at the primary school level through the lens of the teachers. Most research on teacher collaboration and co-teaching has focused on teachers' shared learning (de Jong, Meirink, & Admiraal, 2019; Martin-Beltran & Peercy, 2014) and the positive effects of teacher collaboration on student academic achievement (Goddard, Goddard, & Tschannen-Moran 2007). Hence, this study seeks to understand what components, possibilities and challenges teachers view as conducive to highly effective teacher collaboration based on their reflections about what they experienced while collaborating and co-teaching over a period of 4 years.

Methods

Context of the Study

This study was conducted at Stewart Primary School (pseudonym) with students from kindergarten to second grade. 45% of students were eligible for free or reduced lunch, which would categorize this school as a high needs school. The school is located in Adams (pseudonym, as are all other names in this chapter) in the northeastern region of the United States. Adams is home to over 29,000 residents who take pride in their commu-nity and boast about the success of its citizens. Stewart Primary School has 663 students, 44 teachers, and 27 ELLs. The parents of the students that Laura (the teacher introduced at the beginning of this chapter) teaches work mainly in the service industry, and many of the student's families only have one parent working outside of the home. In the majority of families, the parent who is the most proficient in English is the parent who enters the workforce. The home languages of the ELLs in this study were Spanish, Arabic, Chinese, Vietnamese, Chuukese, Farsi, and Polish.

In a classroom setting, Laura worked with 27 ELLs: 21 who were mandated to receive ENL support and 6 who were not. Their families spoke a heritage language at home and benefited from the extra support that Laura provided. Laura had a stand-alone period each day with each grade level. Laura also provided her ELLs with reading intervention services. Laura's kindergarten stand-alone group consisted of 6–7 children, her first-grade group consisted of 4–5 children, and her second-grade group consisted of 6–7 children. During her stand-alone time, she provided guided reading instruction, language practice, and support in all academic content areas.

Laura worked with three classroom teachers: Anna, Joy, and Michelle. Laura co-taught Writer's workshop with Anna to the seven kindergarten students in Anna's classroom, Writer's workshop and Envisions math with Joy to the six first grade students in Joy's classroom, and Eureka math with Michelle to the 8 second grade students in Michelle's classroom. Laura and the classroom teachers team taught, taking turns teaching components of lessons as detailed by each curriculum unit. Laura joined the three classroom teachers' classrooms four times a week for 45 minutes each time. More detailed information about each teacher's profile follows in Table 4.1.

Participant Teachers

Laura, the main participant in this study, was a 47-year-old ENL teacher with TESOL and reading specialist certifications. Laura had 22 years of teaching experience at Stewart Primary School, including 16 years as a classroom teacher, 2 years as a reading specialist, and 4 years as an ENL teacher. The other participants were the three classroom teachers. Anna, a 44-year-old kindergarten teacher, had 20 years of teaching experience. Joy, a 37-year-old first grade teacher, had 16 years of teaching experience. And Michelle, a 41-year-old second grade teacher, had 20 years of teaching experience.

All of the participating teachers were white, female, and spoke only English, which is typical of the American teacher population (National Center for Education Statistics, 2019). Anna and Joy each had a master's degree in elementary education and Michelle had a master's degree in special education. Each of the participants were certified to teach elementary grades. More detailed information about the participant teachers can be found in Table 4.1.

Data Sources

The primary data of this study are interviews that I (Heeok, the researcher and author) conducted, which include three in-depth, 2-hour interviews and frequent informal interviews with Laura, one group interview with the participant teachers, Laura's reflection journal, classroom observation, and researcher's journal. All interviews with the participant teachers were conducted virtually via Zoom, audiotaped, and transcribed

Table 4.1 Teachers' Profiles

Name	Age	Ethnicity	Language	Content	Highest level of education	Years of teaching	Number of ELLs	Number of total students	Co-teaching content
Laura	47	White	English	ENL	MS in elementary ED	22	27	27	TESOL reading
Anna	44	White	English	Kindergarten	MS in elementary ED	20	7	23	Writer's workshop Envisions math
Joy	37	White	English	1st grade	MS in elementary ED	16	6	25	Writer's workshop Envisions math
Michelle	41	White	English	2nd grade	MS in special ED	20	8	26	Eureka math

verbatim. The interview questions were mostly about the essentials, possibilities, and challenges of effective co-teaching that the teachers have experienced or found based on their 4 years of collaboration and co-teaching experience.

Also, any suggestions for better education of ELLs were requested by asking, "Would you have any suggestions for better ELL education, such as ELL program, collaboration, administrative support, instructional strategies, and assessment, etc.?" Regarding classroom observation, I observed four classrooms once, but the observation was interrupted because of the COVID-19 pandemic, which could be considered a limitation of this study. While observing the classrooms, I wrote field notes as a non-participant observer, sitting in the corner of the classroom.

Data Analysis

The data were analyzed using constant comparative approach (Charmaz, 2006) with five coding procedures: (a) open coding through reading the data multiple times word by word and line by line; (b) focused coding through connecting frequent codes within and across multiple data sets; (c) axial coding through mapping core categories with relationships and dimensions; (d) conceptual coding through the internal inductive and deductive dialogues; (e) theoretical coding through triangulating and examining the relationships between and among the emerging concepts in all the data sources with the theoretical framework of this study (i.e., Hargreaves' collaborative professionalism).

In the recursive process of data analysis, I shared my interpretations of the data with Laura for the purpose of the clarification of my analysis through member checking (Yin, 2009). The rigor of this study was accomplished through the iterative processes of data mapping, multiple sources of data, and member checking.

Researcher's Position

In qualitative research, the researcher is considered as an instrument of the research (Marshall & Rossman, 2006) because "we construct our grounded theories through our past and present involvement and interactions with people, perspectives, and research practices" (Charmaz, 2006, p. 10). Thus, it is important to indicate my position as a researcher for this study.

I (Heeok) am a teacher educator and educational researcher in the field of language and literacy education. My goal in teaching and conducting research is to find ways to provide equitable opportunities to learn for *all* students, particularly linguistically, culturally, racially, and historically marginalized multilingual and multidialectal students, including ELLs. In my journey to explore the ways that minority students can learn in an equitable learning environment both in and out of the classroom context, I became interested in co-teaching pedagogy. When I met Laura, she told me that she had been co-teaching with classroom teachers successfully for 4 years; so I expanded my queries to investigate the essentials, possibilities, and challenges of effective co-teaching practices between Laura and three classroom co-teachers.

As an English teacher, teacher educator, and researcher from Korea, I can see the educational structures, discourses, processes, and situations through the lens of diverse students from non-dominant communities. Hence, it can be said that this research is constructed through my experiences, perspectives, and perceptions as a transnational, multilingual, and multicultural teacher and teacher educator, from the beginning stage of data collection, analysis, and to the final stage of writing.

Findings

Four major themes emerged as the elements of effective collaboration between Laura and three classroom teachers: communication, flexibility, congruence, and an ENL teacher's professional capital. Teacher collaboration was most effectively established through frequent communication within a trust relationship, utilizing flexible forms of collaboration in response to individual student's diverse needs, congruence between language and content, and Laura's professional capital. Collaborative planning and co-teaching were found to be beneficial for teachers, students, and parents in terms of mutual learning, equitable evaluations, provision of diverse learning experiences and perspectives, and positive academic outcomes for ELLs. Challenges included incongruence of teaching styles, division of behavior management, and time constraints.

Essentials for Effective Collaboration and Co-Teaching

Communication. Communication between Laura and the classroom teachers about the roles, purposes, and perspectives of each teacher's instruction was maintained through weekly planning, pre-planning, small talk in hallways, and discussions during lunch. In these meetings, Laura and her co-teachers shared their ideas, perspectives, and different teaching styles. Most of all, all participant teachers emphasized that they share mutual responsibility for *all* children. The open communication in the formal weekly planning meetings and reflection time after class is crucial for quality co-teaching. As Joy, the 1st grade teacher, mentioned:

> I know the planning piece is so important for Laura and me. And just thinking about the upcoming writing lessons, the overall theme for the week and just sharing those ideas. And then the reflection piece afterwards, not only talking about how the lesson went and if we do

have to re-teach, but more specifically how the children are doing in the large group as well as in more stand-alone time.

Laura also stated the importance of sharing information about students and contents:

> Another very important aspect of co-teaching is having time for co-planning. Due to a supportive administration, I am able to meet with each of my co-teachers for half an hour a week. This is important to us because we are able to plan together and be prepared for the following week. We are able to discuss learning objectives and plan who will create the visuals (anchor charts and posters, etc.). This time also provides us with an opportunity to discuss our shared students. We are able to discuss instructional strategies and how they can be used in lessons within all content areas. We discuss how we can utilize graphic organizers to promote active learning and engagement.

The centrality of effective communication for quality collaboration was also confirmed by the research on high school teachers' perceptions about co-teaching between special and general education teachers. Keefe and Moore (2004) found that open communication is essential not only from the beginning stage but also in the course of co-teaching instruction for the positive relationship building between co-teachers. Honigsfeld and Dove (2016) also emphasized the importance of communication in the collaborative instructional cycles of co-planning, co-teaching, co-assessment, and reflection based on their decades of research on co-teaching practices between ESL and general education teachers.

Trust. During their interviews with me, all the participant teachers strongly emphasized the importance of trust for effective collaboration and co-teaching instruction. As Laura stated, "It was important that we were effective communicators and respected each other's ideas and thoughts." The mutual respect between Laura and her co-teachers paved the way for the foundation of a trusting relationship, which was strongly emphasized as an essential element of effective collaboration in Laura's reflection journal:

> A trusting relationship was essential. It was important that my co-teachers felt assured that my instruction would be at the caliber that they wanted for their students. They needed to trust that I would put in the effort to be prepared and that I would come into their classroom ready. This is a very important aspect of co-teaching. TRUST.

Research has also established the importance of trust in effective co-teaching: "The importance of the relationship between the co-teachers appeared to be the most important determinant in how successful the teachers viewed co-teaching and how likely would be to continue to co-teaching (Keefe & Moore, 2004, p. 86).

Flexibility. Flexibility means changing the forms of collaboration in response to the individual ELL's needs in the situated classroom context. Some possibilities include alternating leading roles, team teaching, parallel teaching, alternate teaching, pre-teaching, and re-teaching. All the classrooms in the current multilingual and multicultural society are linguistically, culturally, and racially diverse and complex spaces with multiple variables to be considered. In accordance with these diverse needs, depending on the situation, Laura and her co-teachers utilized the six types of co-teaching practices proposed by Friend and Bursuck (2009): (a) one teach, one observe; (b) one teach, one assist; (c) parallel teaching; (d) station teaching; (e) alternative teaching; and (f) team teaching.

For example, Laura and Anna often alternated leading roles. As the lesson went on and they saw a group of students who needed extra support with certain tasks, they directed those students to the back table in a small group. One teacher worked with that group while the other continued teaching the rest of the class. When Laura and Michelle co-taught Eureka math lessons, they utilized the team-teaching approach. They planned which aspects of each lesson each of them would lead by reviewing the objectives, considering how to differentiate instruction, and discussing how to best utilize their time to effectively provide the support. In this way, they felt confident about contributing to the instruction when the other teacher was leading. The combination of the six types of co-teaching practices occurred either simultaneously or separately in the mainstream classrooms in accordance with the individual ELL's diverse needs.

Laura pre- and re-taught in her stand-alone class based on her observation of those needs, as Michelle shared how she works with Laura:

> Laura and I mostly teach math together this year, cause that's where the need was the most for my class. So, Laura often does a lot of pre-teaching in the morning with my class and then when she, or with her students during her stand-alone, so that when she come to my class, they have a little bit of knowledge of what we're doing that day. And they always alternate roles. We take turns, we divide the lesson up so that there isn't one primary teacher for that lesson. We take turns the whole time of who's a lead role and who's walking around helping. And then they have an independent practice time, that's when both of us will take a smaller group.

This kind of flexibility within a trusting co-teaching relationship is essential. The teaching that takes place is a direct result of co-planning and open-mindedness built on this relationship. It is critically important that teachers feel confident in their co-teachers' abilities to effectively teach their students. Laura feels extremely fortunate to co-teach with such excellent co-teachers who are open to sharing their classrooms with her. Also, flexibility includes the acceptance of co-teacher's different perspectives, values, and approaches to teaching, which allows every teacher to be the way he or she is. As Laura mentioned, "I feel my team is very, very flexible. This flexibility allows each other to be the teacher that we are."

Congruence. Another important element for effective teacher collaboration that I found from the study is congruence. Congruence means the alignment of language, content, and teaching style, which results from coordination among content area teachers. Laura stated how she worked with classroom teachers to make language and content be aligned:

> I think helping my students to develop their expressive language and have them understand the lecture, so their learning or teaching is accessible to them. All of what I do, I take the content and overall focus on language. All students are encouraged to use correct grammar and complete sentences. That is my goal and focus. The way that the classroom teachers present the content is slightly different from mine. Because I focus on language. When I am doing my instruction, I expand the conversation to include more language and vocabulary. You know what is your favorite animal? Classroom teachers just move on. I pause and give them more language and support them. I stop and I model how to say it, like "My favorite animal is a cat. What is your favorite animal? I model them and expand the conversation.

These statements that Laura shared with me at an interview show that both Laura's role as an ENL teacher and her pre- and re-teaching in her stand-alone class aligned with the content ELLs learned in the regular class. This made it possible for her students to connect the content with language and to express their thoughts in more complete sentences. The alignment of content and concept with language provided a strong foundation of knowledge for students. As Laura mentioned, "We align that our students can have the most exposure to the same concept so that they build their foundation. We do a lot of congruence."

Professional capital. Professional capital includes human capital, decisional capital, and social capital. As previously mentioned, human capital is related to teacher's knowledge about curriculum, instruction, and assessment. In co-teaching settings, teacher's knowledge about how to co-teach is an important aspect of professional capital. All the participant teachers participated in professional development courses about teacher collaboration and co-teaching, as stated by the kindergarten teacher, Anna: "We've taken a lot of classes to learn about working with the ELL population and we're very invested in working with that particular group. And I think the training on how to co-teach was very helpful."

Laura's human capital and decisional capital, which include 22 years of teaching experience and three teaching certifications (i.e., elementary school teacher, reading specialist, and ENL teacher), and her social capital–Laura's ability to lead, support, and encourage teachers in terms of the development of individual teacher's pedagogical practices in school–played an important role in effective co-teaching, as stated by Laura:

> I believe that my experience as a classroom teacher (kindergarten for 6 years and first grade for 10 years, reading specialist for 2 years, and ENL teacher for 4 years) had a very positive impact upon my ability to immerse myself within each classroom and offer ideas in a way that did not cause stress to my co-teachers. I understand to be a classroom teacher because I was a classroom teacher for a long time. I am always eager to teach and offered to plan and gather resources for lessons to take some of the aspects of planning that a classroom teacher faces "off of their plate." I familiarized myself with the curriculums. I did a lot of reading and I was diligent about preparing to implement lessons with my co-teachers.

It can be said that Laura's extensive and prolonged teaching experience (i.e., her professional capital) is what made the highly effective collaborative instruction provided by Laura and the classroom teachers possible. This confirms the results of previous research on high school teachers' perceptions about co-teaching: "Another general education teacher recollected that her co-teacher, '…was more of a hindrance than a help in the room because it was another person who did not know her material'" (Keefe & Moore, 2004, p. 83). This quality collaboration, built on Laura's expertise, mutual understanding, and trust, allowed her ELLs to acquire grade-appropriate language and content, and finally to achieve learning outcomes similar to or better than native English-speaking students, as demonstrated in Laura's 4 years of classroom observation. The school district supervisor, Mr. Johnson, also emphasized the positive effects of teacher collaboration on students' academic achievement at Stewart Primary School.

Possibilities of Co-Teaching

Mutual learning. The teachers shared that co-teaching brings more possibilities than teaching alone. The enhancement of mutual learning about ELLs, content, and language occurred through collaboration by sharing knowledge, experiences, thoughts, ideas, and perspectives and finally met the diverse needs of ELLs:

> Anna, the kindergarten teacher: I think co-teaching is definitely better than teaching independently because I think that we get to share our expertise with one another and we each have different skill sets and it allows for us to really better meet the needs of the children.

Michelle, the 2nd grade teacher: I can go to Joy and Anna and talk to them about things that I'm seeing in grade and ask how it was in K and one, and relying on their prior knowledge that way.

Laura, the ENL teacher: The possibilities are endless…We are able to do so many more things with our students because there are two of us, in terms of re-teaching, pre-teaching, and weekly planning.

As stated above by teachers, the co-teaching model ensures that ELLs have access to the curriculum. In a co-taught class, ELLs develop their skills and confidence as they grow in their ability to meet grade level expectations. Students have the opportunity to master the curriculum through differentiated instruction. Due to the fact that there are two teachers in the class, the same material can be taught in two or more different ways. The ENL teacher can anticipate student needs and, in planning lessons with the classroom teacher, prepare alternative lesson materials and assessments to help ELLs meet grade-level objectives. Also, Laura stated that, through co-teaching ELLs, she learned from her co-teachers who she is as a teacher.

Equitable evaluation. This study shows that co-teaching provides more equitable learning opportunities, diverse perspectives, and social and emotional support. When teachers share opinions and perspectives about students, they can provide for students and parents more equitable feedback and evaluations, and diverse learning experiences and perspectives. Anna supports this theme by stating:

Collaborating and ability to discuss what we're seeing, you know, as far as the student's progress and needs. Laura sees things differently in the small group setting. So, she's able to share what cause sometimes find, especially in kindergarten when you're getting a new child who doesn't maybe have a lot of English, they're more apt to be communicating in the smaller group setting. So, it helps to know what she's seeing so that I can target my instruction to the child's needs.

Laura, the ENL teacher: Another aspect of co-teaching is a shared understanding of our students. Today, Joy (a 1st grade teacher) and I had a meeting with a parent who is considering retention for his daughter. Joy and I are aligned in our thoughts about the needs of this student. Because we have had many conversations and shared our noticing about how the student performs in different settings (classroom vs. ENL classroom during stand-alone/reading instruction). We both take anecdotal notes and share information with each other about our observations. We actively problem solve how we can collaboratively best meet the needs of our students.

As shown above, sharing observational notes and information about students allowed parents to receive synthesized and combined opinions, and evaluations about their child, which was beneficial to parents.

Social and emotional support. Regarding social and emotional support, I observed that an ELL student who is "very smart but benefits from wait time, rephrasing, and restating" (Laura's expression) can get social and emotional support from an ENL teacher in a regular classroom through teach/one assist co-teaching. When Michelle was demonstrating how to add three-digit numbers using the Eureka math method, a really cute little boy named Jun from Chuuk Islands suddenly put his head on his desk and cried, but Michelle was so concentrated on teaching 26 students that she could not recognize his struggles in solving the math problems. Laura came to recognize he was crying, went to his desk, and gave him a hug. Jun then stopped crying and continued to do his work. Laura's emotional support in this co-teaching class demonstrates that "teachers' understanding of ELLs' cultural and social needs and their responding to the needs in a more active manner promotes the students' interactive processes" (Yoon, 2008, p. 515).

Positive learning outcomes. The positive learning outcomes of successful collaboration and co-teaching instructional practices are evidenced by ELLs' grade level or higher than grade level academic achievement, as also stated by Anna:

> We had a little girl. She spoke zero English and had no prior schooling when she came in because she came from other state and her birthday was in September. And the cutoff is September. So, she can't be with us. She started January with zero English. By the end of the year, she was reading at a level B and writing sentences.

Laura also reflected upon instances of students demonstrating academic success in her reflection journal. She wrote the following:

> It is so amazing to me how quickly some students' receptive and expressive language abilities develop. It is extremely gratifying to observe students who began kindergarten with very limited English proficiency achieving and surpassing grade level expectations in all academic areas. The past four years that I have been teaching ENLs have been some of the best years of my career. It is so meaningful as an educator to know that I played a role in children developing their ability to communicate in a second language.

The increased academic achievement of ELLs owing to collaborative instruction aligns with the results of a 3-year collaboration between ESL teachers and classroom teachers in a midwestern urban elementary school (York-Barr, Ghere, & Sommerness, 2007) and in a New York City elementary school (Bauler & Kang, 2020).

Challenges of Co-Teaching

Time constraints. Time constraints were one of the biggest challenges to both Laura and the classroom teachers. This result aligns with research result on co-teaching practices between ESOL and classroom teachers in an elementary school, "More than any other perceived challenge across the three years was lack of planning time" (Bauler & Kang, 2020, p. 349). All the participant teachers mentioned that they wished they had more planning and co-teaching time together:

> Anna, the kindergarten teacher: I wish that there was more time for the collaborative part of teaching because, I think, it's so important and so beneficial to students.
> Joy, the 1st grade teacher: As far as challenges, really just having more time together is the biggest challenge.
> Michelle, the 2nd grade teacher: Having time to talk is really important. We do have that once a week co-planning time, which is amazing, but I would love Laura every minute that I could have her.
> Laura, the ENL teacher: It is not easy to co-teach. It is a balance issue. You need to strike the balance. Classroom teachers are there all day, but I am there only for 45 minutes or 1 hour per day.

Research has evidenced that lack of co-planning time impedes effective co-teaching instruction (Baecher & Bell, 2017; Bauler & Kang, 2020). But this study shows that the teachers wanted more time for both co-planning and co-teaching, whereas previous research indicated that ESL teachers preferred stand-alone class to co-teaching format because of the imbalanced power dynamics between ESL and content teachers (Bell & Baecher, 2012). This preference by the participant teachers in this study for co-teaching classes rather than for a stand-alone format demonstrates how successfully Laura and her co-teachers had been collaborating to teach ELLs.

Incongruence of teaching styles. Incongruence of teaching styles was a challenge when Laura first started to co-teach: "One early challenge was not wanting to overstep in terms of boundaries and roles within the classroom." The teaching style clash issues were gradually resolved over time through frequent communications and seeing both "as being teachers," and finally "we've been able to actively co-teach," as Laura stated:

> One early challenge was not wanting to overstep in terms of boundaries and roles within the classroom. I wanted to be sure that my co-teacher was comfortable with the amount of teaching that I wanted to do. Also, I didn't want to follow their lead, but I want to teach. And they knew that I wasn't ever happy, like sitting back, like from day one, I wanted to teach. With my co-teachers, we've been able to actively co-teach so that we both are viewed as being teachers.

Division of behavior management. The division of behavior management sometimes became a challenge because of the dynamically changing class-room situations. "Behavior management was a concern. In terms of who would be disciplining children. It took time for some teachers to release control. Have to strike a balance." Laura stated that she and Joy, the 1st grade co-teacher, had similar teaching styles: "I should be on top of every-thing in the classroom." So, at first, it was not easy for Joy to release her control in her class. But over time, Laura and Joy learned how to co-teach by sharing their thoughts and understandings of the equal responsibility for each student during their pre-planning and post-instruction reflection time. Laura comments on this topic:

> A challenge of co-teaching is having to relinquish control of your classroom. When I am integrating into classrooms, my co-teachers and I have established an understanding with our students that we are both equally responsible for the class in terms of discipline (we both implement behavior plans, provide permission to use the bathroom, etc.). This creates a sense of value within the co-teaching relationship.

The "sense of value within co-teaching relationship" is needed to make co-teaching instruction effective and sustained. For example, Keefe and Moore (2004) found that high school special education teachers were viewed as educational assistants by general education co-teachers and students because of the special education teacher's ill-defined role in the co-teaching class and their lack of content knowledge. Also, research has found that ESL teachers and their diverse students felt marginalized in mainstream classrooms where the roles and participation structures between ESL teacher and general education teacher are not equally dis-tributed (George, 2009; Lo, 2014; Whiting, 2017).

Discussion and Implications

The results of this research confirm the centrality of collaborative profes-sionalism, that is, solidity with solidarity for effective teacher collaboration and co-teaching. The essential elements of the solidity necessary for col-laborative professionalism include communication, flexibility, congruence of content with language and teaching styles, and professional capital. The solidity of teacher collaboration can be actualized within trusting relation-ships, that is, solidarity. The possibilities and challenges of highly effective teacher collaboration at any particular school will depend on the degrees of solidity and solidarity in the professional culture. The relationships among challenges, collaborative professionalism, and possibilities for effective co-teaching pedagogy are intertwined, interconnected and can be understood as continua of co-teaching pedagogy, as represented in Figure 4.1:

Figure 4.1 Continua of Co-Teaching Pedagogy: Challenges, Collaborative Professionalism, and Possibilities.

The continua of co-teaching pedagogy explain how the challenges can be overcome through solidity in solidarity and finally accomplish the possibilities of quality teacher collaboration and co-teaching. For example, this study demonstrates that a trusting relationship among co-teachers beyond the co-teaching relationship allowed open and frequent communication regarding how to teach ELLs to occur in both weekly meetings and any momentarily available places (i.e., hallways, cafeteria, classrooms, parking lot, etc.), as stated by Anna: "I think when you have really good rapport, um... personal experience with the person you're working with, it makes a huge difference." This solidarity enhances the possibilities for successful collaborative co-teaching practices; that is, the provision of diverse perspectives and equitable evaluations, positive academic outcomes for ELLs, and mutual learning of teachers and students. Solidity in teacher collaboration may not be very effective if there is not solidarity among teachers because "trust is a quality that makes both relationships and knowledge robust and enduring" (Raider-Roth, 2005, p. 35).

If we think of the opposite situation where solidarity exists without solidity, quality co-teaching cannot occur although co-teachers may have established a strong bond and personal relationship with each other. This is because they do not have enough knowledge about how to teach ELLs (e.g., professional capital) nor do they communicate about their roles, perspectives, and ideas about how to teach ELLs. Also, consider the situation where there is an ENL teacher without professional capital. One of the advantages of teacher collaboration is flexibility, but adopting different teaching models (e.g., parallel teaching, team teaching, one teach/one assist, etc.) most appropriate for the situated classroom context might not be possible if the ENL teacher and the classroom teachers are not compatible or comfortable working together, or if there is no ENL teacher with professional capital.

This study shows that when Laura, a highly qualified ENL teacher with professional capital, co-taught ELLs with content-area teachers (i.e., Anna, Joy, and Michelle) within a trusting relationship, the challenges to collaboration (e.g., teaching style clashes or difficulties of release of control in class) were resolved through frequent open communications in solidarity. Thus, "sustainable improvement requires both solidarity among colleagues and a solid grounding in research, expertise, and well-designed tools and protocols" (Hargreaves & O'Connor, 2018b, p. 24). In this study, the data show that in order for successful co-teaching pedagogy to occur, communication, flexibility, congruence, and professional capital were essential within the context of trusting relationships and in the process of co-planning, co-teaching, co-assessing, and co-reflecting, along with co-responsibility for *all* students' learning and development.

Implications for Teachers and Teacher Educators

Quality collaborative and co-teaching instruction have beneficial impact on both increased academic achievement and equitable learning opportunities for *all* students including ELLs, and the professional growth of teachers (Ronfelt, Farmer, McQueen, & Grissom, 2015). Thus, it is strongly recommended that teachers create a culture of community with mutual respect, open mindedness, and responsibility for *all* students by engaging themselves together in the cycles of co-designing, co-instructing, co-assessing, and co-reflecting within a trusting relationship. Additionally, teachers need to remember that solidity combined with solidarity can make it possible to overcome the challenges to effective co-teaching, and finally accomplish collaborative professionalism. This study shows that the essential elements of solidity are communication, flexibility, congruence, and professional capital. Solidity leads to teacher's professional growth, positive academic outcomes, and equitable learning opportunities when built in mutual trusting relationships. The challenges to effective co-teaching such as time constraints, teaching style clash, and behavior management issues can be overcome through solidity in solidarity.

We recommend that teacher educators include the epistemological and practical issues related to teacher collaboration and co-teaching practice in teacher education programs. For example, inclusion of co-teaching courses in teacher education programs could be beneficial to both instructors and their teacher candidate students in terms of mutual professional development, learning about how to differentiate instruction more effectively, and learning how to value different perspectives (Graziano & Navarrete, 2012). Those programs could provide inquiry space to answer the questions of why collaborative co-teaching is necessary, what should be taught during co-teaching instruction, and how co-teaching can be accomplished effectively, along with hands-on practical strategies including various co-teaching models. Those questions could be answered by referring to this research study.

Implications for Administrators

This study demonstrates that high quality collaborative co-teaching practices need leadership support. Thus, we suggest that administrators (e.g., principals and superintendents) encourage and organize school systems and cultures for more robust teacher collaboration and co-teaching. Professional development needs to be ongoing, continuous, dynamic, and embedded in teacher's daily lives (Lieberman, 1995; Loucks-Horsley et al., 1998); so teachers need interrelated learning opportunities and communities in school that will allow them to construct the generative change they need, to appropriate their personal pedagogical knowledge, and to adapt their knowledge in order to collaborate and co-teach with other teachers, including ENL teachers, within and across disciplines in diverse situated classroom contexts.

In the current US public school context, more than 50% of students are students of color who speak languages other than English or non-dominant varieties of English at home (National Center for Education Statistics, 2019), so "the school is no longer about *my* student. It is about *our* students" (Hargreaves & O'Connor, 2018a, p. 15). All the participant teachers in this study stated, "No ELLs, immigrant students, or native English-speaking students exist. *All* students are *our* students." Collaborative education "entails sharing, talking, trusting, co-teaching, and learning. But it also values other verbs, such as challenging, critiquing, including, empowering, and debating" (Hargreaves & O'Connor, 2018a, p. 15).

In conclusion, in order to provide quality and equitable learning opportunities to *all* students and to enhance the positive learning experiences and academic outcomes of *all* students, the creation of collaborative professionalism, characterized by teacher collaboration and co-teaching based on trusting relationships and a supportive school culture, is profoundly essential.

References

Baecher, L., & Bell, A. B. (2017). Opportunity to teach: Push-in and pull-out models of English learner instruction. *Journal of Education and Culture Studies*, *1*(1), 53–68. doi:10.22158/jecs.v1n1p53

Bauler, C. V., & Kang, E. J. S. (2020). Elementary ESOL and content teachers' resilient co-teaching practices: A long-term analysis. *International Multilingual Research Journal*, *14*(4), 338–354. doi:10.1080/19313152.2020.1747163

Bell, A. B., & Baecher, L. (2012). Points on a continuum: ESL teachers reporting on collaboration. *TESOL Journal*, *3*(3), 488–515. doi:10.1002/tesj.28

Charmaz, K. (2006). *Constructing grounded theory: A practical guide through qualitative analysis*. Los Angeles, CA: Sage.

de Jong, L. Meirink, J., & Admiraal, W. (2019). School-based teacher collaboration: Different learning opportunities. *Teaching and Teacher Education*, *86*, 1–12. doi:10.1016/j.tate.2019.102925.

Friend, M., & Bursuck, W. D. (2009). *Including students with special needs: A practical guide for classroom teachers* (5th ed.). Columbus, OH: Merrill.

George, C. (2009). Marginalization or collaboration: First year ESL teachers & the middle school context. *Middle Grades Research Journal*, 4(1), 25–52. Retrieved from https://web.a.ebscohost.com/ehost/pdfviewer/pdfviewer?vid=2&sid=855ec282-999b-40a4-acdc-113c362afd75%40session mgr4008

Goddard, Y. L., Goddard, R. D., & Tschannen-Moran, M. (2007). A theoretical and empirical investigation of teacher collaboration for school improvement and student achievement in public elementary schools. *Teacher College Record*, 109(4), 877–896. Retrieved from https://education.illinoisstate.edu/downloads/casei/collaboration_studentachievement.pdf

Graziano, J. K., & Navarrete, L. A. (2012). Co-teaching in a teacher education classroom: Collaboration, comprise, and creativity. *Issues in Teacher Education*, 21(1), 109–126. Retrieved from https://files.eric.ed.gov/fulltext/EJ986819.pdf

Hargreaves, A. (2019). Teacher collaboration: Thirty years of research on its nature, forms, limitations and effects. *Teaching and Teachers: Theory and Practice*, 25, 603–621. doi:10.1080/13540602.2019.1639499

Hargreaves, A., & O'Connor, M. T. (2018a). *Collaborative professionalism: When teaching together means learning for all*. Thousand Oaks, CA: Corwin.

Hargreaves, A., & O'Connor, T. M. (2018b). Solidarity with solidity: The case for collaborative professionalism. *Phi Delta Kappa*, 100(1), 20–24. doi:10.1177/0031721718797116

Hargreaves, A., & Shirley, D. (2020). Leading from the middle: Its nature, origins and importance. *Journal of Professional Capital and Community*, 5(1), 92–114.

Honigsfeld, A., & Dove, M. G. (2016). Co-teaching ELLs: Riding a tandem bike. *Educational Leadership*, 73(4), 56–60. Retrieved from http://www.ascd.org/publications/educational_leadership/dec15/vol73/num04/Co-Teaching_ELLs@_Riding_a_Tandem_Bike.aspx

Keefe, B. E., & Moore, V. (2004). The challenge of co-teaching in inclusive classrooms: At the high school level: What the teacher told us. *American Secondary Education*, 32(3), 77–87. Retrieved from https://www.jstor.org/stable/41064524

Lieberman, A. (1995). Practices that support teacher development: Transforming conceptions of professional learning. *Innovating and evaluating science education*, 95(64), 67–78. Retrieved from https://www.nsf.gov/pubs/1995/nsf95162/nsf_ef.pdf#page=58

Lo, Y. Y. (2014). Collaboration between L2 and content subject teachers in CBI: Contrasting beliefs and attitudes. *RELC Journal*, 45(2), 181–196. doi:10.1177/0033688214535054

Loucks-Horsley, S., Hewson, P. W., Love, N., & Stiles, K. E. (1998). *Designing professional development for teachers of science and mathematics*. Thousand Oaks, CA: Corwin.

Marshall, C., & Rossman, G. B. (2006). *Designing qualitative research*. Thousand Oaks, CA: Sage.

Martin-Beltran, M., & Peercy, M. M. (2014) Collaboration to teach English language learners: Opportunities for shared teacher learning. *Teachers and Teaching*, 20(6), 721–737. doi:10.1080/13540602.2014.885704

Miller, J. (2011). Teachers' work in culturally and linguistically diverse schools. *Teachers and Teaching, 17*, 451–466.

National Center for Education Statistics (2019). *Common core of data (CCD): Public elementary/secondary school universe survey.* Washington, DC: U.S. Department of Education.

Raider-Roth, M. (2005). *Trusting what you know.* San Francisco CA: Jossey-Bass.

Ronfelt, M., Farmer, O. S., McQueen, K., & Grissom, A. J. (2015). Teacher collaboration in instructional teams and student achievement. *American Educational Research Journal, 52*(3), 475–514. doi:10.3102/0002831215585562

Rumberger, R. W., & Gándara, P. (2005). Seeking equity in the education of California's English learners. *Teachers College Record, 106*(10), 2032–2056. doi:10.1111/j.1467-9620.2004.00426.x

Whiting, J. (2017). Caught between the push and the pull: ELL teachers' perceptions of mainstreaming and ESOL classroom teaching. *NABE Journal of Research and Practice, 8*(1), 9–27. doi:10.1080/26390043.2017.12067793

Yin, K. R. (2009). *Case study research: Design and methods.* Thousand Oaks, CA: Sage.

Yoon, B. (2008). Uninvited guests: The influence of teachers' roles and pedagogies on the positioning of English language learners in the regular classroom. *American Educational Research Journal, 45*(2), 495–522. doi:10.3102/0002831208316200

York-Barr, J., Ghere, G., & Sommerness, J. (2007). Collaborative teaching to increase ELL student learning: A three-year urban elementary case study. *Journal of Education for Students Placed at Risk, 12*(3), 301–335. doi:10.1080/10824660701601290

5   Reimagining Collaboration

Exploring How ESL Teachers and Technology Coach Perceive Collaboration to Improve ELLs' Language Skills

Ana Vintan and Tiffany L. Gallagher

With the teachers that I've had the opportunity to work with, [...] it comes down to tools and strategies that teachers all want to get to, and be able to do by themselves, but there's not enough time in the day to do all the things that you need to do. Collaborating, it's a lot of fun, but at the same time, you know that it's needed. Once you do that a few times, the tools and strategies that the teachers are using are without really thinking about it anymore.

(Caroline, ESL Teacher, Interview)

Flexibility was very important in learning how to teach ELLs with technology. Using digital resources has been a collaborative situation, not just with me but with my ELL students and teaching staff. That was not part of my role as an ESL teacher, but I got involved because I could reach out and pull people together.

(Sally, ESL Teacher, Interview)

These English as a second language (ESL) teachers' voices demonstrate their experiences in collaborating with classroom teachers and a technology coach. Possibilities and challenges of collaboration within ESL education illustrate ways in which English language learners (ELLs) are being supported by all educators. ESL teachers' voices are portrayed within the analysis throughout this chapter to show how digital resources can be meaningfully integrated to support ELLs in the classroom.

Background and Theoretical Framework

ELLs comprise one of the fastest growing subsets of the student population in Canada. An advocacy group, People for Education (2017), reported 72% of Ontario English elementary schools included ELLs, a statistic that is expected to rise in this large Canadian province. Given the diverse cultural and linguistic landscape of the student demographic in today's classrooms (Cheng, Klinger, & Zheng, 2009; Molle, 2013), there

DOI: 10.4324/9781003058311-7

is a dire need to explore the collaboration among classroom and ESL teachers and support staff such as coaches, to understand the opportunities and challenges faced by educational professionals in using instructional resources (digital and/or non-digital) to promote oral and written language instruction with ELLs.

Educators are well-aware that their ELLs face numerous challenges, including that of learning English in addition to learning the curriculum content. Similar to proficient English-speaking students, ELLs have unique talents and skills, and make academic progress when given appropriate learning opportunities and focused support. Dove and Honigsfeld (2010) state that, "an ESL program should enhance student understanding of English while learning classroom content, as well as offer English-proficient peers to serve as language models" (p. 9). When teachers spend time mapping out successful learning strategies for ELLs, and communicate these strategies to all educators involved, there is potential for effective pedagogical support for students. Indeed, Dove and Honigsfeld (2010) highlight the importance of fostering teacher collaboration in ESL education, "with carefully planned and sustained training and long-term planning that gets all stakeholders on board, [then] schools will be better able to establish a new culture over time, which supports collaboration … and allows teacher leadership to emerge" (p. 19).

In Canada, education is governed by the provinces and territories that each adopt curriculum and policy documents. In the Province of Ontario, where this study was situated, the Ontario Ministry of Education (OME) created the *STEP: Steps to English Proficiency: A Guide for Users* (2011) to support ESL and classroom teachers in the planning of targeted activities for ELLs to develop the English literacy skills. The *STEP* document (OME, 2011) is comprised of grade-specific literacy proficiency descriptors with specific observable language behavior (OLB) criteria designed for educators to gauge ELLs' development and it outlines a continuum of concepts and skills derived from the Ontario curriculum with modification or accommodations specifically for ELLs. Each OLB is customized according to the language learning level or *STEP* (OME, 2011) that the student is working on. Additionally, the *STEP* document outlines initial as well as continuing assessment with an emphasis on ongoing classroom-based assessment for ELLs. This resource, which is shared between the ESL teacher and the classroom teacher, is designed to aid in instructional planning as well as tracking students' language acquisition. The practical applications of this document for ESL and classroom teachers were examined as part of this study's data collection.

Our research documented the possibilities and challenges reflected in the ways that ESL teachers worked together with classroom teachers and with a technology coach to develop, share, and implement educational resources to address ELLs' learning needs. With the aim of contributing to the growing research on ESL collaboration, this chapter will present a collective case study of how five ESL teachers and one technology coach describe collaboration to use resources to promote oral and written language instruction with ELLs. Accordingly, our study explored the following research question:

How do ESL teachers collaborate with classroom teachers and a technology coach to use instructional resources (digital and/or non-digital tools) and modify their instructional practices to support ELLs' language skills?

Literature Review

The following literature provides a backdrop for the research featured in this chapter. There is a summary of the common collaborative practices within ESL education and professional learning as well as a review of how ESL teachers collaborate when using technology in order to make an impact on their instruction.

Collaboration within ESL Education

Collaboration among ESL teachers and classroom teachers is not static, and often dependent on various factors, including common needs of ELLs, teachers' schedules, shared lesson/unit plans, and unforeseen events that affect the flow of classroom activities. In navigating these factors, flexibility is required on the part of both educators to co-create a collaborative relationship. Hoffman and Dahlman (2017) define teacher collaboration in ESL education as occurring on a continuum, including in-class collaboration for delivering and monitoring pedagogical tasks, as well as scheduled collaboration outside the classroom to monitor and plan learning goals for the ELLs. This comprehensive and flexible conceptualization of a collaboration continuum within ESL instruction was adapted for the scope of the research project.

To support the inclusion of ELLs in the classroom, ESL teachers must be familiar with the classroom tasks and plans created by the classroom teacher as they work with the ELLs. To foster collaboration among ESL teachers and classroom teachers, they need to (a) communicate about the achievements and educational needs of the ELLs; (b) co-plan instructional strategies and resources; (c) identify modifications and accommodations necessary for the ELLs; and (d) co-create literacy objectives, educational milestones, and long-term learning goals (Calderón, Slavin & Sánchez, 2011; Hoffman & Dahlman, 2017). Dieker (2001) draw a parallel between special education and ESL teachers who both need to work cooperatively with classroom teachers. Classroom teachers, special education, and ESL teachers need to have a common familiarity with curriculum objectives and pedagogical goals. Dieker discusses how special education teachers navigate their role of focusing on student accommodations and modifications in combination with a mutual understanding with classroom teachers regarding planning for integrating students with special needs into the classroom. In the current study, ESL teachers navigated their role in a manner similar to special education teachers combining their knowledge of curriculum expectations to facilitate collaboration with classroom teachers with regard to instructional resources used to enhance ESL education.

Further, our study explored possibilities and challenges in how these educators collaborate to use digital and/or non-digital tools within instruction for ELLs. Diallo (2014) contends that tablets and apps are instructional tools that are changing English language pedagogy. The Ontario Ministry of Education (2008a, 2008b) outlines instruction that effectively uses information technology as a way of supporting ELL instruction. While there is a mandate in educational policy for educators to employ various mediums in ESL instruction, including technological resources, educators are often challenged in utilizing these resources in ESL instruction.

Teacher Collaboration Using Technology

A contemporary investigation on how teachers collaborate to support their ELLs using technology is a very timely pursuit in the mid-pandemic era of distance learning in education. There is a precedence for facilitating student motivation and learning through the use of technology within ESL instruction (Bahrani & Tam, 2012). Turgut (2011) found that educators who used laptops in ESL instruction reported motivational benefits for students from the use of visuals to transcend language barriers for new vocabulary and the use of online literacy-based games. ELLs also engaged more with their peers as a function of working on the laptops. In instructional planning, teachers focused on ELLs' learning strengths rather than weaknesses and were able to track and share ELLs' work and assessment data with other educators. Thus, collaboration among educators of ELLs can be enabled with technology. The current research project included ESL teachers' experiences collaborating with a technology coach to specifically integrate digital resources to support ELLs.

ESL teacher collaboration with the use of technology often does not come without challenges. Previous research has documented that educators express practical concerns regarding their comfort levels in addressing technical issues that arise when facilitating learning activities using technology, which impeded the use of devices to their full potential (Turgut, 2011). Thus, there is an ongoing need for professional development for educators to establish effective methods for teacher partnerships, leadership roles, and ways of professionally addressing conflicts that occur in the collaborative process of integrating technology into ESL instruction. While much of the research shows possibilities of supporting ELLs when teachers collaborate to implement technological tools, our research focuses specifically on how ESL teachers and a technology coach use technology as they collaborate with classroom teachers to support ELLs.

Professional Development for ESL Teachers

Given that ELLs spend the majority of their school day in the general education classroom, it is critical for their classroom teachers to possess the knowledge and skills needed to provide them with effective instruction. Professional development and effective coaching have been demonstrated to be effective when delivered via technology, such as webcam technology to schools that may otherwise not be equipped to support teachers (Amendum, Vernon-Feagans, & Ginsberg, 2011). Additionally, research suggests that with the aid of professional learning, ESL teachers develop innovative multimodal representations to engage their ELLs to be more technology literate while simultaneously enhancing students' oral and written literacy (Dalton & Smith, 2012). While ESL teachers are willing to integrate technological platforms to enhance instruction, it has been noted that "teachers' preference for using technology [is] to enhance existing goals and curriculum" (Dalton & Smith, 2012, p. 22). Thus, this study sought to explore ways in which ESL educators collaborated with classroom teachers to establish effective instructional methods using technological tools and experts such as a technology coach.

A technology or digital coach can assist educators who experience difficulties with technology integration (Lynch, 2014). An integral part of this professional learning process is the active participation of teachers in authentic experiences in a collaborative environment, with guidance, support, and feedback (Ansyari, 2015). A technology or digital coach can provide instructional scaffolding for improving teachers' ability to integrate technology in pedagogically meaningful ways (Doering, Koseoglu, Scharber, Henrickson, & Lanegran, 2014). Moreover, benefits have been documented when teachers work together in a community of practice to transfer technology knowledge to instructional and curricular integration (Courduff & Szapkiw, 2015).

Ciampa and Gallagher (2016) discuss the importance of teachers' reflective practice on collaboration when integrating technology into their instruction. Collaborative relationships are established and students experience cohesive instructional methods when educators, including ESL teachers, reflect on challenges and successes not only as by-products of particular teaching styles, but also of teaching approaches. Designated planning time is a supportive factor in collaborative reflective practices. As well, teachers express a need for shared repositories to curate exemplary instructional resources (digital and non-digital) to support their students (Ciampa & Gallagher, 2016). We considered how this finding applies to ESL teachers and classroom teachers.

Cunningham (2019) found that technological portals or repositories offered efficient means for educators to provide meaningful and timely feedback to ELLs. Additionally, the use of digital communication platforms developed meaningful interpersonal relationships between educators and students and were beneficial for educators to coordinate their roles and work closely with a number of ELLs. However, the quality and confidentiality of digital communication platforms must be considered as they pertain to education. Technological tools range in complexity and effectiveness and are arguably useful tools when they are carefully and thoughtfully selected. Vanek (2017) argues that effective use of technology, "requires engaging, highly interactive online resources that require use of creativity and critical thinking" (p. 62). While these tools may prove effective, it is the ongoing responsibility of educators to work in collaboration to ensure that tools facilitate differentiated and targeted instruction, while also being culturally appropriate for ELLs.

The perceptions of the families of ELLs regarding the impacts of technology in education, as well as the availability of devices in the homes of ELLs, is also an important factor to consider in ESL education. Gallagher, Di Cesare, and Rowsell (2019) discuss some of the perceptions and barriers experienced by newcomer families regarding use of technology including uncertainty of the pedagogical benefits of technology tools, as well as concerns related to internet safety. These authors have found that a collaborative working relationship among educators at a variety of levels supports the digital literacy of ELLs' families. Educators need to be aware of the diverse ways that technology is utilized outside of the classroom, while simultaneously building a collaborative relationship among ESL teachers, technology coaches, parents, and community partners to foster digital literacy.

It is opportune to consider the intersection of collaboration, professional learning, and technology use in ESL education. This chapter will describe the possibilities and challenges experienced by ESL teachers as they collaborate with classroom teachers to use instructional resources (digital and/or non-digital) to promote oral and written language instruction with ELLs. As well, herein, we describe the benefits and challenges perceived when an ESL teacher collaborates with a technology coach to integrate digital resources to support ELLs and to evoke change in classroom teachers' practices.

Study Context for Teacher Collaboration

In this chapter, we present a subset of data from a larger case study which explored collaboration among classroom and ESL teachers, as well as a technology coach who collaborated with an ESL teacher. While the larger study explored the multifaceted nature of collaboration, this chapter will focus on the challenges and possibilities that arose as ESL teachers collaborated with in-school teams of educators, including a technology coach, to use instructional resources (digital and/or non-digital) to promote oral and written language instruction with ELLs.

School Districts' Context

The two, publicly funded school districts where data were collected are located in a diverse suburban community in Southern Ontario, Canada. At the time of the data collection, the ideology of ESL education in both of the school districts was an integrated approach to ESL instruction in accordance with the Ontario Ministry of Education's guidelines (OME, 2011). The integrated approach is one in which the ESL teacher supports the ELLs as they engage with activities within the classroom. In some schools, the ESL teacher also provides instruction for other student support services (community liaison, reading interventions, special education, etc.). Typically, in these school districts, ELLs receive ESL instruction in their grade-level classroom, with the ESL teacher as well as the classroom teacher working together. Most schools also have itinerant technology coaches who provide recommendations to ESL teachers and classroom teachers regarding best practices integrating technology into instruction.

Participants

Four site-based ESL teachers, one itinerant ESL teacher, and one technology coach participated in the data collection aspect of this research project (classroom teachers that they worked with did not contribute to the data collection). All of the ESL teachers, four female teachers and one male teacher, had previous teaching experience outside of the realm of ESL education.

   Two of the ESL teachers worked in the publicly funded, non-denominational school district, and three (including the itinerant ESL teacher) worked in the publicly funded Catholic school district. Two ESL teacher participants taught in the elementary school grades (Lauren and Nicole; grades 1–6), one ESL teacher participant taught in the elementary and middle school grades (Grant; grades 1–7), and one ESL teacher participant taught in the middle school grades (Caroline; grades 6–8) (Note: In Ontario, where this research took place, "middle school grades" are grades 7 and 8). ESL teachers' experience level in ESL education ranged between 1 and 18 years. The ESL itinerant teacher, Sally, circulated among eight elementary (K–grade 8) schools in a region within the school district; her role was to support all of the classroom teachers in these schools with their instructional practice with ELLs. Sally has been an educator for 25 years in this school district. The technology coach, Helen, was responsible for supporting the professional learning of teachers in 40 different elementary-middle schools in the district. She worked with other classroom teachers and the itinerant ESL teacher. Helen has 18 years of experience in two different school districts holding various roles from classroom teacher to curriculum specialist (science). In the school district where Sally and Helen work, the typical ELL student population is approximately 5% of the total school population. All names used in this chapter are pseudonyms.

Data Collection and Analysis

Data collection occurred between November 2017 and May 2020. Our primary data collection sources included semi-structured interviews with the ESL teachers and technology coach, observations of these participants interacting within classroom teachers and with their in-school teachers and structured analysis of teaching-related artifacts provided by the participants. Each participant was interviewed for 30–75 minutes. The interviews focused on the participants' backgrounds, experiences with co-teaching, opportunities ESL teachers had for collaboration, how ESL teachers are professionally supported to integrate resources (digital and/or non-digital) within classroom instruction, as well as teachers' understandings and apprehensions about using technology to support literacy instruction for ELLs. The interview with the technology coach similarly explored how she supported the instructional practices of the ESL itinerant teacher and the students within the caseload of this teacher.

Four of the ESL teachers were shadowed by the first author, Ana, and the itinerant ESL teacher and technology coach were followed by the second author, Tiffany, as they collaborated with other educational professionals during their assignments. Semi-structured observational notes were recorded during the observations with each of these ESL teachers; this ranged from 3 to 30 hours per teacher. For the observations of the four ESL teachers, the CIERA Observation Scheme (Taylor, Pearson, Peterson, & Rodriguez, 2005) and CQELL protocol (Goldenberg et al., 2012) were used. The focus of the observations was on the challenges and possibilities that arose as ESL teachers collaborated with in-school teams of educators including a technology coach and classroom teachers to use digital resources to promote instruction with ELLs. Additional data came from a collection of teaching artifacts (e.g., daybook plans, lesson plans, professional readings, instructional resources) provided by ESL educators and technology coach, with the data analysis focusing on the ways these artifacts served as tools for the collaborative relationships to enhance the impact of the ESL education.

The qualitative data collected (interview transcripts, field notes with observation protocols, artifacts) were coded by each of the authors for emergent themes using an inductive analysis approach (Ezzy, 2002). For the field notes, the code levels used on the CIERA Observation Scheme protocol (Taylor et al., 2005) complemented the generic lesson elements observations made on the CQELL protocol (Goldenberg et al., 2012). For the artifacts, coding occurred for examples of professional collaboration in regard to lesson preparation, learning strategies used, technology integrated, and notes regarding how these were established. Axial coding of these data utilized the sequence of steps in thematic analysis (Strauss & Corbin, 1990). These codes included collaboration amongst ESL educators and other teachers, sharing of ESL resources (digital and non-digital), and spontaneous collaboration. Nodes pertaining to each theme were compiled, and direct quotes from the primary source data were used in the analyses. This systematic approach (Ezzy, 2002) allowed for focused coding and emergence of three robust themes: collaborating to use resources, effective practices to maximize ELLs support, context driven engagement with other educators, and technology coaching binds a teacher collective. The authors cross-confirmed their findings with each other and then peer debriefers were used to establish credibility of the emergent themes. This entire inductive analysis procedure was facilitated with the qualitative data analysis program, NVivo 10.0 (QSR International, 2014).

Major Findings

What we learned from engaging with these educators is that collaboration is a process that can act as a catalyst for professional learning and enhanced practices in ESL education. This major lesson is supported by four thematic pillars that we describe below: collaborating to use resources, effective practices to maximize ELLs support, context driven engagement with other educators, and technology coaching binds a teacher collective.

Collaborating to Use Resources

All ESL teacher participants talked about collaborating with classroom teachers to share resources for ELLs. Caroline, Nicole, and Lauren sought to supplement ESL specific resources to accompany the unit plans that classroom teachers had designed. Sally stated that:

> Ongoing collaboration at the start of a unit of study was essential in allowing ESL teachers to see the envisioned unit progression that classroom teachers had in mind. From this baseline, ESL teachers can spend time researching resources that could aid ELLs in achieving the curricular objectives and support their literacy development.
>
> (Sally, ESL Teacher, Interview)

ESL teacher participants talked about collaborating with classroom teachers as well as other ESL teachers to find and share digital and non-digital learning tools for ELLs. Overall, the majority of these tools provided either visuals, or leveled modifications to promote oral and written language instruction with ELLs. This is one example of the process of collaborative practices between and among teachers. Our research observations documented that a collaborative relationship is an on-going, malleable relationship, one which requires both formal as well as informal check-ins among educators. This was accomplished by weekly opportunities to communicate. We observed how it was crucial for classroom teachers to communicate with ESL teachers and technology coaches about their long-term educational plans in order for ESL teachers to be able to supplement ESL specific resources to support ELLs; in this way, both the amount of communication and quality of it was important to the collaboration. ESL teachers and technology coaches had a repertoire of ESL specific resources pertaining to different content areas that the classroom teachers could integrate into their instruction. These resources supported ELLs, but also had potential of providing accommodations for other learners in the classroom. ESL teachers also talked about collaborating with other ESL teachers to develop and share resources for ELLs:

> As a team [we worked] to create this list of strategies. These goals come from the OLB that direct our program and our support...There has been some collaboration as an ESL team to also do documents and programming that we think is needed, for example the support plan, because we found this would be helpful to record part of the student's background, to record modifications that were being used, and the goals that we collaborated with the classroom teacher to work on.
>
> (Lauren, ESL Teacher, Interview)

ESL teacher participants made use of technology as a resource in working with ELLs. Grant talked about taking a Chromebook to every one of his assigned classrooms to help with English translation as well as providing visuals for ELLs. This was consistent within the observations of all four of the ESL teacher participants, as technology was used either as a translation device, or to provide visuals. Yet, it is interesting to note that technological tools for ELLs such as apps or websites were not observed and there were no codes on the CIERA observation protocol (Taylor et al., 2005) relating to digital materials used in instruction for ELLs. This suggests that technology was used exclusively as an aid for translation and visualization.

The Google Drive was a frequently mentioned as a resource that all of the participants used to collaborate in sharing resources with other educational professionals. Observations were made of the technology coach guiding ESL teacher, Sally to various shared folders within a common Google Drive. Grant talked about an ESL education specific resource folder:

It's a Drive that's shared with our ESL team; we can see initial assessment, parent resources, Ministry [of Education Ontario] documents, and some slideshows. These are ways of supporting students. So that would be something we would collaborate with the classroom teacher on, helping them with the tips, and the reality is, for me at this school, I'm here twice a week, between 3-4 periods, the classroom teacher has that ELL student for the rest of that time. So, it is a lot of sharing, shared resources. We worked together, with the scope and sequence to distinguish between the different *STEPS* (OME, 2011), and the different levels. Our meeting schedule is on the Drive.
(Grant, ESL Teacher, Interview)

This shows the commitment on the part of ESL teachers to support classroom teachers by utilizing this technological tool to support and supplement ESL specific instructional resources despite time and scheduling constraints. Caroline talked about substituting hard or paper copies of learning materials with electronic copies on the Google Drive:

If teachers have a quiz or a test they're going to be giving, they can send that to me in the Drive, I can make a copy of it, alter it for the language learner, share it back, and it saves me driving all over. I find using the Drive has been amazing for myself, and I think for supporting teachers that I don't get to see all that often. And it's also great for sharing resources. I shared this graphic organizer with three teachers here, even though it was in Persian, I did one in Arabic and then I shared it with them and said, "Add onto it as needed."
(Caroline, ESL Teacher, Interview)

Caroline described a collaborative relationship with a classroom teacher which occurred mostly on the Google Drive. Rather than arranging time to meet in person, Caroline and the classroom teacher began by co-developing a unit plan. From there, Caroline took the initiative of creating leveled activities to support her ELLs in the class, as well as other learners who required literacy accommodations. In the process, Caroline had developed a bank of resources that she was willing to share with any teacher that could use them:

The beautiful thing about the Drive is, once you get it organized, it's there for you. So next year, I don't necessarily have to do that again, I can just pull it out and add or adapt what I need to do.
(Caroline, ESL Teacher, Interview)

Lauren also utilized the Google Drive as a tool to help her provide instant and meaningful resources to classroom teachers. She talked about the benefits of accessibility by being able to draw on any resources she had saved on the Google Drive to supplement ELL instruction. These examples have implications related to classroom teachers' long-term instructional planning. ESL teachers aided classroom teachers in developing a bank of resources to use with ELLs as they progressed through the STEP levels, and these tools and resources were conveniently available for classroom teachers to use with future ELLs via a digital repository on a Google Drive.

Observations show how both Sally and Helen, the technology coach, used the Google Suite of resources extensively as this was a most efficient means for Helen to bring together groups of teachers that taught at similar levels (e.g., grades 1, 2, 3). These teachers had a common need to learn about these digital tools, but they were also viewing this as a means to support early elementary classroom teachers.

The majority of the professional planning artifacts shared by ESL teacher participants reflected the nature of the spontaneous collaboration that occurred between educators. Some of these artifacts were tools that ESL teachers had saved on their own Google Drives, such as graphic organizers and sentence frames. Grant provided copies of accommodations that he frequently used with ELLs which had been developed from a resource that summarized best practices in ESL education and included items such as a checklist of pedagogical strategies aimed at oral, reading, and writing strategies co-developed by ESL teachers, as well as a template for ELL/teacher support plans regarding ELLs' literacy benchmarks. These tools were readily available and easily adaptable to fit students' task specific needs.

Effective Practices to Maximize ELLs Support

Findings from the interview data, observations, and information derived from professional artifacts (lesson plans, support plans, instructional strategies, unit plans, worksheets) indicated that the ESL teacher participants had methods of sharing effective practices with other educational professionals, particularly related to ELLs' *STEP* level (OME, 2011). These participants noted that by sharing these practices, there was a positive impact on the level of collaboration with classroom teachers to develop and implement digital and non-digital learning tools for ELLs.

The educators came to appreciate that some of their ELLs might need direct support with digital resources. The technology coach, Helen, stated:

> I have been working with [newcomer] ELL students and their teacher who kind of knows them. We had to get them technology and we've had to teach them how to use the technology. We have had to do this in the evenings because that's when the parent is not working. Teaching a student how to use this technology and what he needs to do so is an interesting aspect that hadn't happened before [in my practice].
>
> (Helen, Technology Coach, Interview)

From Helen's recount, it was apparent that technology was being accessed for supporting not only the language learning needs of the ELLs, but also the family as a whole. She provided this support in collaboration with the ESL teacher, Sally.

ESL teacher participants talked about mixed level ELLs, who often demonstrated stronger OLBs (OME, 2011) in oral language than in reading or writing. This created an interesting dynamic in which ESL teachers collaborated with classroom teachers on ways of incorporating ELLs' strengths into designing learning opportunities within ELLs' zone of proximal development (ZPD) (Vygotsky, 1978) to bridge oral, reading, and writing literacy skills. Lauren talked about collaborating with classroom teachers who had ELLs working at lower *STEP* levels (OME, 2011) by providing them with tools such as apps, websites, and dictionaries to assist in basic communication with the ELLs. Lauren recalled an example of collaborating with a classroom teacher:

> She got a brand new *STEP 1* student who knew absolutely no English. My next visit, I had told her about the translate app and she put the translate app on her own phone, so she was able to communicate with the student.
>
> (Lauren, ESL Teacher, Interview)

This type of collaboration was beneficial for the classroom teacher as it provided her with best practices to address an immediate concern, and the ELL became more comfortable in the classroom. Our observation data showed that ESL teachers aided classroom teachers with both immediate concerns as well as strategies that classroom teachers could implement for long-term success of ELLs. In particular, ELLs who were working at lower *STEP* levels required immediate resources for classroom integration on a daily basis. Learning key words such as "washroom," "lunch," and "water" were challenges that could be solved with the use of translation apps. Establishing such resources that both classroom teachers as well as ESL teachers could both use with ELLs provided a collaborative solution to the immediate as well as long-term communication needs of the ELLs.

ESL teachers' beliefs about infusing ELLs' pre-existing literacy skills within the development of the English literacy knowledge aligned with the goals of the Ontario Ministry of Education instructional resources that they were using (e.g., *Many Roots, Many Voices: Supporting English Language Learners in Every Classroom* (OME, 2005)):

> They're [ELLs] thinking in their first language, so just let them write it in their first language, and then, we'll worry about translating it after. And giving the kids the freedom to do that I think is a huge strategy. And some of them will resist for a period of time, but then

they actually think, okay, this is going to help me, cause then I'll have time to have a good solid answer, as opposed to two sentences.

(Caroline, ESL Teacher, Interview)

Caroline talked about motivating ELLs to use their first language (L1) to demonstrate literacy competency and boost confidence and make ELLs aware of their strengths and literacy skills, albeit these being in a different language. This is an example of the moment-to-moment collaboration between educators in planning lessons and in utilizing instructional tools for ELLs.

Interestingly, ESL teacher participants believed that ELLs' *STEP* level (OME, 2011) had an influence on the level of collaboration. Nicole talked about the time required to determine the ELLs' literacy skills in all areas of reading, writing, and oral skills for students at lower *STEP* levels. Lower *STEP* level indicators are associated with a limited ability to demonstrate understanding of written or oral English proficiency. For Lauren, collaboration was essential with classroom teachers and special education resource teachers using the integrated approach to support ELLs who were at these lower competency levels. Nicole was also concerned with aligning her teaching goals with those of the classroom teachers and special education resource teachers. Once all educators had established how the ELLs' learning goals fit into the unit plan, Nicole would work in conjunction with these educational professionals to create learning tasks for the ELLs. Following is an example of the ESL teacher participant commenting on the influence that ELLs' *STEP* levels (OME, 2011) had on collaboration:

If there are students that are of higher needs, you're most likely to find that time to collaborate because you know those kids are not going to survive if you don't. The bonus is there's probably kids in there that are those higher levels that are going to benefit from that collaboration. Whereas, if there are students that are sort of middle of the spectrum, they're not *STEP 1*, they're not *STEP 6* which would be native speaker, but they're *STEP 3*, they can kind of bumble through and that's where you need that academic vocabulary support. Because they can hold a conversation, they can listen to what's going on in the class, and are aware and sort know what's going on, but their reading and writing is still really not at grade level. They still really need a lot of support, but they're not getting that support, cause we have to focus on those students that are at *STEP 1* and 2.

(Caroline, ESL Teacher, Interview)

Caroline talked about the inner conflict that arose from needing to prioritize time spent on collaboration for ELLs based on their academic levels. Caroline comments on this being a challenge for collaboration, "So it's this, you know, you never feel like you're doing the job." Caroline was hopeful that collaborating with educational professionals was a way of maximizing support for ELLs who did not receive their needed attention in ESL education:

> There's not enough of us [ESL teachers] and so, you kind of hope that when you're collaborating with the [classroom] teacher for these other language learners, and the tools and strategies that you're using, these other kids are going to benefit. You have to try and be optimistic, otherwise, you would leave the job rather quickly.
>
> (Caroline, ESL Teacher, Interview)

These views of Caroline might be interpreted as her perspective on the instrumental nature and importance of collaboration between ESL and classroom teachers.

Lauren provided a copy of a unit plan that she had collaborated on with a classroom teacher to create. This was a unit of study about helpers in the community (e.g., nurses, fire fighters, police) composed of several learning tasks and modifications established for the ELLs. This artifact exemplified the less frequent long-term collaboration that occurs between ESL teachers and classroom teachers. Such planning is beneficial in allowing the ESL teacher to be more instrumental in classroom activities, and to have opportunities to find resources for the ELLs.

Overall, ESL teachers collected and curated instructional resources to promote the oral and written language instruction in ESL education and were eager to share these with other educational professionals to support ELLs. Overall, however, we observed that the ESL teacher participants did not use digital tools often; when digital tools were employed, they were mostly used to provide visuals and to aid in translation of material. The artifacts collected reflected the spontaneous collaboration among educators and the relative lack of long-term collaborative planning for ELLs.

Context Driven Engagement with Other Educators

The visibility of the ESL teacher in the classroom through an integrated approach also created opportunities for ESL teachers to support several learners in the class. This primarily included ELLs, but also extended to other struggling students. Several participants discussed ways of maximizing support, as Lauren said, "There have been instances where I've worked not only with my ESL student, but I've worked with other students that have that same need."

In this way, ESL teachers also acted as educational assistants and collaborated with educators in finding and sharing resources to support numerous learners:

When I approach a teacher, I need to gently find out, "Okay, what are you working on in class?" and then, "Oh, look, I have this reading that's at the students' grade level, maybe you can use it for other students in your class that are not reading at grade level. Or I created this graphic organizer, and this is going to help students answer these questions. Would these resources be useful for the other students? I can share them on the Drive." Then they [the classroom teachers] think, "Oh, wow, I have this awesome extra set of hands that can create this graphic organizer or can find what I need." And then they say, "Oh, you know, I'm going to be doing this unit next." And then you think to yourself, "Sweet, I'm in!"

(Caroline, ESL Teacher, Interview)

Collaboration was encouraged by demonstrating to classroom teachers how beneficial the support of the ESL teacher could be. This suggests that classroom teachers need context-embedded examples of how collaboration with an ESL teacher can positively impact on their practices.

Still collaboration within a teaching staff is not always easily enacted despite concerted efforts to do so. Sally recognized that not all classroom teachers reached out for her assistance in ESL programming or Helen's technology support for their ESL instruction:

We had good discussions about how to give opportunities to other teachers. For some reason, they are too busy to engage or to get the support. We tried different things, I would approach different teachers and get them to tell me what they want. Gradually, we got more teachers on board to sign up by a period and come into the collaborative work.

(Sally, ESL Teacher, Interview)

Both Lauren and Grant shared a list of ELL learning strategies as an artifact that modeled collaboration within the ESL team. These strategies included oral, reading, and writing accommodations for ELLs. Lauren discussed using these strategies with non-ELLs who benefited from individualized accommodations. After developing these strategies together as an ESL team, teachers collaborated with administrators to share progress made in ESL education. It became apparent to us as researchers that classroom teachers need time to build trust and rapport and affirm the utility of working with ESL teachers.

As an ESL teacher, Sally assumed a leadership role among the eight schools and all of the classroom teachers that she supported. In her capacity, Sally needed a streamlined way to coordinate with the classroom teachers' instruction and the ELLs learning; she describes this:

We (Sally and Helen) created an ESL Google classroom. I said to her, I need it for me. It is too hard for me to go into every teacher's class to assign work or review things. I didn't know how to do it. So, we created a primary (grades 1–5) and intermediate (grades 6–8) ESL Google classroom. First, I worked with two students at each of my schools going through the Google classroom and programs. Then I included and shared access to this with the classroom teacher.

(Sally, ESL Teacher, Interview)

This was a strong example of an ESL teacher that accessed both digital and human resources to assertively draw in classroom teachers to see the benefits of collaborating on a platform.

Technology Coaching Binds a Teacher Collective

The findings point to the instrumental role of a technology coach for eliciting collaboration among classroom and ESL teachers. In this school district, we observed how this additional educator was dedicated to the professional learning and support of technology in ESL education. In this way, we saw how an effective technology coach who becomes an active school staff member, may act like a linchpin, coordinating collaboration among all of the teachers and administration. Sally, who also acted in an itinerant role described the technology coach role:

She (Helen) was part of our school improvement planning meeting. We [all teachers] met for the morning and divided into groups, we had the plan and went through it to determine how to support teachers, their questions, how to walk through different apps and websites, how to do things in Google classroom. It was very beneficial, we looked at what the school needed to do to support staff and students. Having her support was important and the administration saw this. It informs us about where we need to go and working collaboratively.

(Sally, ESL Teacher, Interview)

When working with ELLs, the teachers' connection with the family is essential and often educators find that they are providing support and instruction for more than just the ELLs. This demands a level of collaboration among the ESL teacher, classroom teacher, and often others such as an administrator or support staff. Sally enlisted the assistance of Helen, the technology coach to liaise with families of ELLs that were using digital resources from the classroom in the home:

Through Helen's support, we have been able to connect with families through Google Meets (video conference platform) who have just arrived in Canada. Their kids didn't have any exposure to technology, it was problematic. Through the schools, technology has been distributed but even if families had a device, there were kids who had not seen a Chromebook and had no idea what to do with it. So, through Helen's help, we collaborated and held individual family sessions so they could see how to access the ESL Google classroom and how to log in. Their classroom teacher also showed them the classroom work and I showed them how to [use] speech to text programs (Google Read and Write) and the translator even if they wrote it in their own language.

(Sally, ESL Teacher, Interview)

During the pandemic when schools were not open, but distance learning was taking place, Helen's collaborative skills were invaluable and she found that out of necessity that she was working with ESL families, classroom teachers, ESL teachers, and principals:

I have worked with Sally for a while and now at one of her schools there was a situation that the principal needed help with an ESL family and technology at home. Sally recommended me, so now I formed a new relationship with the principal and the classroom teacher. So now the teacher is reaching out to me to help that ELL child in his class which is great.

(Helen, Technology Coach, Interview)

The needs of the ESL school community require a level of collaboration among educators that is of a distinct nature. Not always are educators prepared or available to orchestrate this level of collaboration to provide for the technology learning needs of all of its students and their families, especially when the English language might be a barrier. One of the significant findings from this study is the realization that an additional educator such as a technology coach might be the binding agent that supports collaboration within a teacher collective:

I was working with a family that felt badly because they couldn't do all the homework with their own ESL. I respected that and that was my reason for saying that the most important task is reading that I am assigning now. If there was anything else they needed, we were here to help. It has been a triangle: me, Helen and parents. Helen is a bond or glue keeping us together.

(Sally, ESL Teacher, Interview)

In this way, the technology coaching acts as the glue that binds the teacher collective including the classroom teachers, ESL teacher, and, in many schools, the administrator as well.

Implications and Suggestions

Our major findings highlight the role of collaboration among ESL educators as a vehicle that can drive effective instruction using resources to meet the needs of ELLs. The ESL teacher participants utilized the digital and non-digital resources available to them and collaborated when they needed additional approaches to maximize support for their ELLs. At times, there was not the technological or experiential capacity present and teachers needed to make do. We found that ESL teachers supplemented non-digital resources with pre-established resources created by classroom teachers. In this way, collaboration was not focused on the tools, but rather the goals of educational plans for ELLs, and resources to support ELLs in achieving these goals in a holistic way (Dove & Honigsfeld, 2010).

One aspect of collaboration that these ESL teacher participants valued was sharing resources with other classroom teachers and special education resource teachers as a way of optimizing the time of educators. This is a major finding of our research project in reinforcing the important role that ESL educators play in professional collaboration within the scope of supporting ELLs. Consistent with the results of the present study, research (e.g., Baltus & Belhiah, 2013; Ahmed, Horan, & Lewis, 2016) shows that teachers express the ongoing need for teaching resources from departments of education to assist in the planning of curriculum modifications for ELLs. With the addition of itinerant teachers and technology coaches, the relationship between educators and families is strengthened to support ELLs through a cohesive, streamlined approach (Calderón et al., 2011). The present project has demonstrated how all three types of educators (ESL teachers, classroom teachers, and technology coaches) collaborate to use instructional resources (digital and/or non-digital tools) to support ELLs' language skills.

Additionally, this research project highlights the potential for teacher collaboration as facilitated by educators sharing expertise in collaborative relationships. Some specific examples include ways in which the ESL teacher participants in the current research project who had specific teaching specializations talked about an increased desire to further their content knowledge in these areas with an ESL specific focus. Consequently, possibilities exist in how ESL teachers engaged with other educational professionals in different ways, depending on school community context, the type of ELLs they were working with, and the accessibility of instructional tools and other educators' expertise. Possibilities for engagement between educators include collaborating to use resources: effective practices to maximize ELLs support, context driven engagement with other educators, and how technology coaching binds a teacher collective.

Challenges prevail, as there are times when teachers are likely to need support during collegial discussions regarding technological tools that are effective in ESL education (Dagenais, Fodor, Schulze, & Toohey, 2013).

When available, the role of the technology coach mobilized collaboration of in-school teams of teachers (Doering et al., 2014). The resulting collaboration shows possibilities for influencing the development of accommodations that are differentiated for ELLs and utilize specific ESL instructional strategies. Thus, it was apparent that the combination of content specific knowledge, ESL specific pedagogical strategies, and the knowledge that each educator had about individual ELLs resulted in unique approaches to meet ELLs' needs (Dieker, 2001). In light of this finding, future research may explore how ESL teachers with and without pedagogical content knowledge describe opportunities for collaboration in ESL education.

Due to the small sample size of educators in the present study, there is potential for the emergence of distinct patterns in the experiences and pedagogical practices of a particular group of educators. A larger sample could provide more generalizable results and broader themes and anomalies regarding how in-school teams of educators collaborate to provide support for ELLs and use instructional resources. However, the benefit of a small sample is that it allows for more time to develop a relationship between the researcher and educators, and to obtain a rich, contextual picture of the practices of this targeted group of educators, as well as to establish credibility. In addition, having collected data from two different school boards allows for variety in the educational aims that ESL teachers have, which inevitably influence the ways in which they interact with other educators and develop their pedagogy to serve ELLs.

Finally, this project, which looked at the distinctive ways in which ESL teachers work with classroom teachers of ELLs, has highlighted that there was some surface level collaboration that occurred in relation to the use of technological platforms in ESL education. The majority of collaboration with regard to sharing technological resources was limited to sharing websites and pass codes for translation or leveled texts. ESL teacher participants perceived the benefits of using technology to aid ELLs, but the collaboration with other educational professionals about utilizing technology in planning for ELLs occurred infrequently, unless there were additional support staff members, such as a technology coach, in place. The role of the technology coach was a neutral one, binding the collaboration of all in-school teams of teachers. The implication that this finding has for practice, is to seek ways for educators to continue to collaborate on integrating instructional technology in ways that promote critical thinking and problem solving to guide students to meaningful learning (Bahrani & Tam, 2012; Kivunja, 2014).

Future longitudinal research in the area of collaboration in ESL education may seek to capture how collaboration to use instructional resources changes over time between groups of educators. Our research study has described the nature of this collaboration over a certain period of time, but it is likely that given the dynamic nature of resource and technology develop and the need for instructional methods to be responsive, continued research is warranted. The ESL specific knowledge that teachers accumulate over time, as well as the natural evolution of collaboration with other educational professionals, may provide a more conclusive account for the development of collaboration. It would be interesting to explore the ways in which collaboration is influenced by ELLs' literacy progress and how educators collaborate to set learning goals and gather resources for ELLs on a continuum. These implications are important for teacher education programs to consider, particularly, the need to know how to integrate differentiated instruction to support ELLs and diverse learners. Additionally, consideration of the role of ESL teachers and the partnerships between classroom teachers and technology coaches may be an important topic of discussion and consideration in teacher education programs.

References

Ahmed, H. A., Horan, D.A., & Lewis, M. A. (2016). Redefining 'community' through collaboration and co-teaching: A case study of an ESOL specialist, a literacy specialist, and a fifth-grade teacher. *Teachers and Teaching, Theory and Practice*, 22(8), 927–946. https://doi.org/10.1080/13540602.2016.1200543

Amendum, S. J., Vernon-Feagans, L., & Ginsberg, M.C. (2011). The effectiveness of a technologically facilitated classroom-based early reading intervention: The Targeted Reading Intervention. *The Elementary School Journal*, 112(1), 107–131. https://doi.org/10.1086/660684

Ansyari, M. (2015). Designing and evaluating a professional development programme for basic technology integration in English as a foreign language (EFL) classrooms. *Australasian Journal of Educational Technology*, 31(6), 699–712. https://doi.org/10.14742/ajet.1675

Bahrani, T., & Tam, S. S. (2012). Audiovisual news, cartoons, and films as sources of authentic language input and language proficiency enhancement. *Turkish Online Journal of Educational Technology*, 11(4), 56–64. Retrieved from https://files.eric.ed.gov/fulltext/EJ989255.pdf

Baltus, R., & Belhiah, H. (2013). Teaching practices of ESL teachers in Ontario. *International Journal of Language Studies*, 7(3), 89–118.

Calderón, M., Slavin, R., & Sánchez, M. (2011). Effective instruction for english learners. *The Future of Children*, 21(1), 103–127. Retrieved from https://www.jstor.org/stable/41229013

Cheng, L., Klinger, D. A., & Zheng, Y. (2009). Examining students' after-school literacy activities and their literacy performance on the Ontario secondary school literacy test. *Canadian Journal of Education*, 32(1), 118–148. Retrieved from http://files.eric.ed.gov/fulltext/EJ843991.pdf

Ciampa, K., & Gallagher, T. (2016). Collaborative inquiry and vertical team teaching: Implications for literacy instruction. *The Teacher Educator*, 51(2), 153–174. https://doi.org/10.1080/08878730.2016.1152156

Courduff, J., & Szapkiw, A. (2015). Using a community of practice to support technology integration in speech-language pathologist instruction. *Journal of Special Education Technology*, 30(2), 89–100. https://doi.org/10.1177/0162643415617373

Cunningham, K. J. (2019). How language choices in feedback change with technology: Engagement in text and screencast feedback on ESL writing. *Computers & Education*, *135*, 91–99. https://doi.org/10.1016/j.compedu.2019.03.002

Dagenais, D., Fodor, A., Schulze, E., & Toohey, K. (2013). Charting new directions: The potential of Actor-Network Theory for analyzing children's videomaking. *Language & Literacy: A Canadian Educational E-Journal*, *15*(1), 93–108. https://doi.org/10.20360/G2KG6V

Dalton, B., & Smith, B.E. (2012). Teachers as designers: Multimodal immersion and strategic reading on the internet. *Research in the Schools*, *19*(1), 12. Retrieved from http://www.msera.org/docs/rits-v19n1-complete.pdf#page=17

Diallo, A. (2014). *The use of technology to enhance the learning experience of ESL students* (Master's thesis). Concordia University, Portland, OR. Retrieved from http://files.eric.ed.gov/fulltext/ED545461.pdf

Dieker, L. A. (2001). What are the characteristics of "effective" middle and high school co-taught teams for students with disabilities?. *Preventing School Failure*, *46*(1), 14–23. https://doi.org/10.1080/10459880109603339

Doering, A., Koseoglu, S., Scharber, C., Henrickson, J. & Lanegran, D. (2014). Technology integration in k–12 geography education using TPACK as a conceptual model. *Curriculum and Instruction*, *113*(6), 223–237. https://doi.org/10.1080/00221341.2014.896393

Dove, M., & Honigsfeld, A. (2010). ESL co-teaching and collaboration: Opportunities to develop teacher leadership and enhance student learning. *TESOL Journal*, *1*(1), 3–22. https://doi.org/10.5054/tj.2010.214879

Ezzy, D. (2002). *Qualitative analysis: Practice and innovation*. London, UK: Routledge.

Gallagher, T. L., Di Cesare, D., Rowsell, J. (2019). Stories of digital lives and digital divides: Newcomer families and their thoughts on digital literacy. *The Reading Teacher*, *72*(6), 774–778. https://doi.org/10.1002/trtr.1794

Goldenberg, C. Coleman, R., Reese, L., Haertel, E., & Rodriguez-Mojica, C. (2012). *Classroom Quality for English Language Learners (CQELL) in Language Arts Instruction Observation Protocol*. Retrieved from https://people.stanford.edu/claudeg/sites/default/files/observation_protocols_0.pdf

Hoffman, P., & Dahlman, A. (2017, September). Together we are better. *Compleat Links*, *4*(3). Retrieved from https://www.tesol.org/read-and-publish/journals/other-serial-publications/compleat-links/compleat-links-volume-4-issue-3-(september-2007)

Kivunja, C. (2014). Do you want your students to be job-ready with 21st century skills? Change pedagogies: A pedagogical paradigm shift from Vygotskyian social constructivism to critical thinking, problem solving and Siemens' digital connectivism. *International Journal of Higher Education*, *3*(3), 81–91. https://doi.org/10.5430/ijhe.v3n3p81

Lynch, M. (2014). Ontario kindergarten teachers' social media discussions about full day kindergarten. *McGill Journal of Education*, *49*(2), 329–347. https://doi.org/10.7202/1029423ar

Molle, D. (2013). *Implementation of the English language proficiency standards across the WIDA Consortium (WIDA Research Report)*. Madison, WI: WIDA Consortium.

Ontario Ministry of Education. (2005). *Many roots, many voices: Supporting English language learners in every classroom. A practical guide for Ontario educators*. Toronto, ON: Queen's Printer for Ontario.

Ontario Ministry of Education. (2008a). *Supporting English language learners: A practical guide for Ontario educators Grades 1 to 8.* Toronto, ON: Queen's Printer for Ontario.

Ontario Ministry of Education. (2008b). *Supporting English language learners with limited prior schooling: A practical guide for Ontario educators.* Toronto, ON: Queen's Printer for Ontario.

Ontario Ministry of Education. (2011). *STEP: Steps to English proficiency: A guide for users.* Toronto, ON: Queen's Printer for Ontario.

People for Education. (2017). *Language support.* Retrieved from https://people-foreducation.ca/research/language-support-2017/

QSR International. (2014). *NVivo 10 for Windows: Getting started.* Retrieved from http://download.qsrinternational.com/Document/NVivo10/NVivo10-Getting-Started-Guide.pdf

Strauss, A., & Corbin, J. M. (1990). *Basics of qualitative research: Grounded theory procedures and techniques.* Newbury Park, CA: Sage.

Taylor, B. M., Pearson, D. P., Peterson, D. S., & Rodriguez, M. C. (2005). The CIERA School Change Framework: An evidenced-based approach to professional development and school reading improvement. *Reading Research Quarterly, 40*(1), 40–69. https://doi.org/10.1598/RRQ.40.1.3

Turgut, G. (2011). A case study on use of one-to-one laptops in English as second language classrooms. *Turkish Online Journal of Qualitative Inquiry, 3*(4), 28–47. Retrieved from https://files.eric.ed.gov/fulltext/ED537755.pdf

Vanek, J. (2017). Response to "Expanding access to learning with mobile digital devices". *Journal of Research and Practice for Adult Literacy, Secondary, and Basic Education, 6*(2), 59. Retrieved from https://coabe.org/wp-content/uploads/2019/09/Summer2017JournalInteractiveFINAL.pdf#page=61

Vygotsky, L. (1978). *Mind in society.* Cambridge, MA: Harvard University Press.

6 "Leadership Roles at Different Points"

Collaborating to Plan for and Teach ESL Students in a Secondary Social Studies Classroom

Amanda Giles

In this chapter, I present my qualitative case study that focuses on the process of collaboration between a middle school social studies teacher (Kassie, pseudonym as are all other names) and me, as an English as a second language (ESL) teacher, for ESL students' successful learning. The excerpt below shows the dialogue that we shared during our collaborative planning session in an eighth grade social studies classroom:

> We really focus on Joan of Arc, and there's kind of a debate on her," explained Kassie to me on an early Wednesday morning before the beginning of the school day. Kassie said, "I want to break the class into two parts based on the conflicting perspectives of Joan of Arc. I want students to debate her influence and character.
>
> "Okay, but how do you want to provide students with enough information to be able to debate her character?" I questioned, as Kassie shared her ideas for our next collaborative teaching session.
>
> "We'll give them information about her and divide the class into positive and negative characteristics and have them convince each other. That's kind of my vision. It breaks up the monotony of lecture and notes and forces them to speak to explore the controversy surrounding Joan of Arc. I can make handouts that ask students to write down three points, listen to the other side, write down the opposing viewpoints, and then choose an opinion based on the facts," Kassie continued as she solidified the content objective for the collaborative lesson.
>
> "Now we'll have to create sentence frames so that the ESL students can speak and write about this historical figure," I added to remind Kassie of the importance of making the content and language accessible to ESL students. "We'll give them an exit slip to form their own opinion. Let's make it very structured for language so that they can use the sentence frames to either speak or write their opinion. Do you see what I'm saying?" I asked. Without giving Kassie a chance to reply, I continued, "Yeah, and then we could find a video that introduces Joan of Arc that kind of shows both her positive and

DOI: 10.4324/9781003058311-8

negative qualities. Then it would be really interesting if we could pair students up and have them debate like you said. I love the idea of putting them in pairs so that …"

"…Students have a specific role and responsibility in the debate," Kassie broke into my explanation to affirm my suggestions.

"Yeah, exactly!" I said excitedly as I nodded my head ready to begin the lesson design. "I'll share a Google document with you, and we'll get started," I added.

As shown in this excerpt, our dialogue exemplifies how Kassie, the content teacher, specified the content objective (e.g., explain the historical controversy of Joan of Arc's character) and how I designed a lesson activity to help ESL students access and master the established content objectives through graphic organizers and sentence frames. Kassie and I also wanted to create opportunities for students to engage in performance-based activities (e.g., debate) and collaborate with their peers to discuss this historical figure so that ESL students could participate in the social studies content area classroom in relevant and authentic ways. To accomplish these aims, Kassie and I drew on our respective expertise and previous experiences to assume leadership roles at different points during the collaborative process, which ultimately worked to provide learning opportunities for Kassie, me, and the ESL students in the collaboratively taught social studies classroom.

Background of the Study

Recent attention in second language teaching and learning calls for such collaborative partnerships like my collaboration with Kassie and emphasizes how this collaboration can work to create equitable educational outcomes for ESL students in content area classrooms (Dove & Honigsfeld, 2018; Peercy, 2018). Given the tremendous possibilities for teacher and student learning outcomes (Dove & Honigsfeld, 2018; Giles & Yazan, 2020), it is important to explore the collaborative planning and teaching processes as teachers plan for and teach ESL students, particularly in secondary schools where such partnerships can be more difficult to sustain (DelliCarpini, 2018; Peercy, 2018). Rigid content area departments can cause the ESL teacher to feel isolated from the school community without a specific content or subject area to claim (Arkoudis, 2003). There is also often only one ESL teacher to work with all ESL students across multiple grades, which can pose additional challenges to initiating and sustaining collaborative partnerships in secondary schools (Baecher, Rorimer, & Smith, 2012).

Yet, when secondary ESL and content area teachers navigate the challenges, they report that such collaboration can produce many benefits, such as teacher camaraderie (Peercy, Ditter, & DeStefano, 2016), strengthened collegial relationships (Baecher, Rorimer, & Smith, 2012; Peercy, 2018), and opportunities for professional growth as teachers strive to increase ESL students' outcomes (Giles, 2019, 2020; Peercy & Martin-Beltrán, 2012).

Building on the literature about teacher collaboration, this chapter reported on a study that examined how I, as an ESL teacher, collaborated with a social studies teacher. This chapter focused on the collaborative process of how the social studies teacher and I planned for and taught ESL students in a collaboratively taught eighth grade social studies classroom in the Southeastern region of the United States. This chapter begins with the theoretical framework that guided this study, presents the relevant literature, and explains this study's methodology. This discussion is followed by the study's findings, and then concludes with practical suggestions for initiating and sustaining collaboration in content area classrooms.

Research on Teacher Collaboration

This study on teacher collaboration is guided by a sociocultural learning framework. Teacher collaboration can become a generative space for teachers' professional learning and development. Framed by a sociocultural learning understanding, teachers participate in multiple instructional activities to refine their pedagogical beliefs, assume different identities, and transform their instructional practices to impact student outcomes (Freeman & Johnson, 1998; Johnson & Golombek, 2016). Applying this social learning lens to ESL and content teachers' collaboration means that collaborating teachers learn when they grapple with content curricula, "co-construct knowledge" (Martin-Beltrán & Peercy, 2014, p. 1), experiment with new teaching roles (Giles, 2019), and enact multiple professional identities (Giles & Yazan, 2020) to work toward the shared purpose (Peercy & Martin-Beltrán, 2012) of making the content and language accessible to ESL students (DelliCarpini, 2018; Peercy, 2018).

Such sociocultural learning theories align with research on teacher collaboration, yet, research on teacher collaboration between ESL and content teachers occurs primarily in elementary schools (Ahmed Hersi, Horan, & Lewis, 2016; Peercy, Ditter, & DeStefano, 2016) and less frequently in secondary schools (See e.g., Arkoudis, 2003; Creese, 2002; Giles, 2018, 2019; Giles & Yazan, 2020). Earlier studies on teacher collaboration in secondary schools emphasized how different pedagogical beliefs hindered collaborative partnerships between ESL and science teachers (Arkoudis, 2003). Collaborative partnerships in secondary schools can also worsen the ESL teacher's status within the school community (Creese, 2002). More specifically, Creese (2002) examined nonbilingual content area teachers who instructed subjects across the curriculum and found that students considered ESL teachers as classroom assistants and less like "proper teachers" (p. 605).

Despite such challenges, more recent studies report how the ESL teacher's leadership, agency, and perseverance can work to strengthen the ESL teacher's role within the school community (Giles, 2018, 2019; Giles & Yazan, 2020). For example, in my previous study (Giles, 2018) on collaborative work with a secondary social studies teacher, I found that the misuse of planning time and the misunderstanding of collaborative teaching notions were two challenges in collaboration. For most of the planning sessions in the study, the collaborating social studies teacher and I discussed assignments unrelated to our collaborative lesson. The social studies teacher defined his ideal collaboration as having the ESL teacher assist in the social studies classroom. The challenges were evident. However, my lead planning and teaching role helped to navigate such challenges in addition to my agency and perseverance to sustain collaboration with the social studies teacher. As a result, our navigation bolstered my role as the ESL teacher within the school community.

Additional earlier studies that involved secondary teachers working with ESL students reported that teachers' positioning (Giles & Yazan, 2020; Yoon, 2008) and teachers' limited training and unpreparedness (Rubinstein-Avila & Lee, 2014) influence how content teachers work to plan for and teach ESL students. While teachers' unpreparedness and limited training involve teachers of all content areas, Duff (2001) specifically found that the secondary social studies teacher's references to pop culture and the content demands of the social studies content, in general, made it difficult for ESL students to access and master the content area standards. Further, social studies teachers can rely heavily on informational texts laden with academic-specific vocabulary that can prove challenging for ESL students (Giles, 2018, 2019). Such content-specific challenges point to the need to explore how these teachers initiate and sustain such partnerships in secondary schools. To this aim, the current study examines how the social studies teacher and I co-plan and co-teach ESL students in a collaboratively taught eighth grade social studies classroom.

Study Context for Teacher Collaboration

Given the content-specific challenges of social studies and the possibility for teacher and student learning outcomes, this qualitative case study answered the following research question: What possibilities and challenges do ESL and content teachers encounter as they plan and teach ESL students in a collaboratively taught eighth grade social studies classroom in the Southeastern United States?

This section explains the study's context beginning with the school site and participants. Following this information, this section concludes with the study's data collection methods and analytic procedures.

School Site

Starcreek Middle School (pseudonym) was the school site in this study. Situated in a large suburban school district in Alabama, Starcreek instructed students in sixth, seventh, and eighth grades. There were 41 students receiving English language services, and 11% of the student body indicated an additional language on a home language survey at registration during the 2017–2018 school year. State and district guidelines specified that any student who marked an additional language take the World-Class Instructional Design and Assessment (WIDA) Screener to assess their English language proficiency. If students made a qualifying score (i.e., 4.9 or lower), they typically received English language services taught in a pull-out English language 50-minute class period taught by me, the ESL teacher. The district required that ESL teachers follow an ESL instructional model for language services and use the WIDA English Language Development Standards to guide their instructional activities. The district also mandated ESL students[1] to take the ACCESS for ELLs 2.0 English Language Proficiency Assessment annually until a satisfactory score (i.e., 4.8 or above) was reached to exit the English language program.

The Collaborating Social Studies Teacher

Kassie was the collaborating social studies teacher in this study. She was a white female in her mid-twenties. She had her Bachelor of Science in Secondary Education with an emphasis in social studies. She began her teaching career at Starcreek 3 years prior to this study, which took place during the 2017–2018 school year. She eagerly agreed to participate in this study because she positioned me, the researcher, as "invested in helping these students," so much so that she exclaimed that it only took one collaborative planning session to convince her that I was willing "to do whatever it [took] to do this lesson" based on the language and social studies standards. While this study reported our collaborative experiences over one academic semester, Kassie collaborated with me as early as her first year of teaching at Starcreek when she admitted to feeling unprepared to teach the beginning ESL students in her social studies classroom. She reported that she spoke some Spanish from taking courses in high school, yet this beginning level of Spanish was insufficient to help bilingual students master the social studies standards. Despite her lack of training, Kassie's energy and enthusiasm for life were contagious and helped her make friends easily with her colleagues at Starcreek.

During the 2017–2018 school year, Kassie taught five ESL students in her social studies content area classroom. Of the five ESL students in Kassie's social studies classroom, four students agreed to participate by signing the parental assent form. Three students identified Spanish as their home language, and one student identified Mandarin Chinese as her home language. The three ESL students who spoke Spanish entered kindergarten at an elementary school in the same school district as Starcreek and were placed in the ESL program at that time. These students were considered long-term ESL students because they spent the majority of their schooling as ESL students. The student who identified Mandarin Chinese enrolled in Starcreek during her eighth-grade year. Her parents adopted her from China when she was 5 years old and enrolled her in a private school until her eighth-grade year. Her parents marked Mandarin Chinese on the home language survey, and her mother indicated that she thought she might need language assistance because she believed her child struggled with content specific vocabulary words. With her mother's approval, I administered the initial language assessment, and the student made a qualifying language score. As such, the 2017–2018 school year was this student's first year in the ESL program.

My Dual Role as the Researcher and Participating ESL Teacher

My role for this study was a participant-researcher. I am a white female and was in my early thirties at the time of this study. Beginning my career at Starcreek in 2010, I taught eighth grade English/language arts. I have undergraduate degrees in English and Spanish and a master's degree in Secondary Education with an emphasis in English/language arts. The study's state allowed for any teacher who held certification in either secondary English/language arts or an additional language to teach ESL, of which I held both certifications. When I taught English/language arts, I used Spanish frequently to help my students access and master the Common Core State Standards for language arts. In 2015, I transitioned into my current role as ESL teacher and part time Spanish teacher. In this new role, I learned that collaboration with content teachers needed to be a crucial part of my new role if ESL instruction at Starcreek were going to be a shared responsibility. I began a PhD program that same year because I wanted to focus on second language teaching and learning, and more specifically, I sought to research ESL and content teachers' collaborative partnerships. I began to initiate collaborative partnerships with teachers who had the highest number of ESL students. I selected Kassie as the social studies teacher participant because she taught the greatest number of ESL students in the eighth grade, and she agreed to participate in this study.

My own epistemological beliefs about research influenced how I collected and analyzed the data. In this way, I believe that effective ESL instruction involves collaborative planning and teaching (Dove & Honigsfeld, 2018). In assuming the role as research-participant, I relinquish claims of objectivity and accept the biases that I bring to the collaborative process with the social studies teacher (Denzin, 2016). I also believe that practitioners and researchers must be willing to blur these lines and engage in activities that work toward equitable learning outcomes for ESL students in their local communities (Kamberelis & Dimitriadis, 2005). While I admit that my biases are unavoidable in the data collection, analysis, and reporting of this study, I attended to issues of trustworthiness to strengthen the research study's quality. I specified my own epistemological beliefs about research that discussed my own interests and involvement in this study. I additionally discussed my methodological procedures with a critical friend throughout each stage (e.g., data collection, analysis, reporting) to ensure transparency (Merriam & Tisdell, 2016).

Data Collection Methods and Analysis

The data from this study were drawn from a larger study (see Giles, 2019, for my dissertation research). For this particular study, data collection methods included three audio-recorded interviews with Kassie, four video-recorded collaborative planning sessions, two video-recorded collaborative teaching sessions, two audio-recorded collaborative viewing sessions, and two reflective journals authored by Kassie. The data methods spanned two collaborative cycles; each cycle consisted of planning and co-teaching a lesson based on the social studies and language standards.

The first collaborative cycle began with an interview where I asked Kassie to discuss her previous training and experiences working with ESL students and to explain her expectations for collaboration. After the first interview, she and I met to plan a lesson on the five pillars of Islam. We taught this lesson together after the two collaborative planning sessions. Following the collaborative teaching session, Kassie and I watched the teaching video together and discussed Kassie's renewed understandings related to ESL instruction. Kassie reflected further on these learning opportunities in a journal, and afterward, I interviewed Kassie a second time to clarify her responses. This second interview ended the first collaborative cycle and began the second cycle. Data methods continued similarly during the second cycle. In this second lesson, Kassie and I planned and taught a lesson about Joan of Arc's historical significance and contribution to the Hundred Years' War.

Data analytic procedures included grounded theory techniques (Charmaz, 2006; Glaser & Strauss, 1967) aligned with a qualitative case study research design (Merriam & Tisdell 2016). This case study sought to describe the collaborative challenges and possibilities that Kassie and I encountered in collaboration. To examine the collaborative processes between Kassie and me, I used in-vivo and descriptive codes (Saldaña, 2013) during the initial coding cycle. During the second coding cycle, I focused specifically on the challenges and possibilities in collaborating to plan for and teach ESL students. Finally, during the third coding cycle, I created theme statements from the categories, which became the findings. The theme statements will be explained in the next section.

Findings and Discussion

The findings showed how unequal planning responsibilities during the first cycle led to the creation of an instructional activity that did not align completely with the lesson objectives. Despite this misalignment, collaborative reflection led to opportunities to re-teach parts of the lesson in order to solidify ESL students' mastery of the lesson objectives. Such reflection also created the possibility for Kassie's increased leadership and renewed understanding related to planning for and teaching ESL students in the collaboratively taught secondary social studies classroom. In this section, I will discuss the unequal planning responsibilities and the instructional misalignment as the collaborative challenges. After this explanation, I will discuss how collaborative reflection helped Kassie and I navigate the challenges, and how this navigation worked to create Kassie's increased leadership and learning outcomes as the possibilities in this collaborative planning and teaching process.

Unequal Planning Responsibilities

Unequal planning responsibilities were challenges in collaboration. Kassie established the lesson objectives based on the social studies standards during the first collaborative planning session. She stated that she wanted to teach a lesson on the five pillars of Islam, which meant that students would read an informational text on the five pillars, answer guiding questions, and discuss this text in collaborative groups. Kassie's only nonnegotiable during the first cycle was that we use a specific informational text on the five pillars. When I asked Kassie how she and I would divide planning responsibilities, she drew on our past collaborative experiences and asked, "How about we do what we've done in the past where you've just kind of figured out what we're going to do?" Kassie's response indicated that she wanted me to assume primary responsibility for the lesson design, and she also stated her desire that I design a similar activity to an earlier lesson that we co-planned and taught together. This meant that she wanted me to divide the reading into smaller sections and design guided reading questions without much of her input.

While I began to think aloud how I intended to design the lesson, Kassie remarked, "I just liked how, because you're so much better at thinking through this, the words are going to trip them up. This is how we need to organize it. Don't you think?" In response, I agreed that there were "vocabulary words that we needed to teach in the lesson," yet, my response did not contest the fact that Kassie wanted me to design the lesson entirely. Kassie shared a Google document with me, e-mailed me the informational text on the five pillars, and inserted a table to compare and contrast the three world religions (e.g., Islam, Christianity, and Judaism), which served to introduce the lesson. She also acknowledged our unequal planning responsibilities, and yet again, I agreed to designing the lesson entirely on my own:

KASSIE: If you want to set up, like however you decide we should do the pillars, like I don't expect you to do this for all five. So, if you do the first one and second one, I can do one or two of them, like you don't need to feel like you have to set up the entire document. I can follow your lead.

AMANDA: Okay, yeah. Generally, though, once I get one started, the rest goes pretty quickly. I don't mind doing it. So, but yeah, but if I need you, I'll let you know.

As shown in these dialogues, instead of giving Kassie an opportunity to learn how to break the reading into smaller sections and design her own reading questions, I assumed the lead role in designing the first lesson.

In reflecting on my own design, I wrote that I did not challenge Kassie's delegation of responsibility because I knew how to divide the informational text without Kassie's assistance. I also feared that Kassie might not want to collaborate with me on future lessons if I asked her to do additional work that was not required. My fear originated from the fact that the school district nor the school required that content and ESL teachers collaborate to plan for and teach ESL students. Knowing this, I was always cognizant of the fact that content teachers could decide at any time to end the collaborative process. If this happened, then my efforts to promote a shared responsibility for ESL instruction through collaboration would not be realized. Notwithstanding my fear, in agreeing to design the lesson without Kassie's assistance, I constrained Kassie's learning opportunities related to planning for and teaching ESL students. Designing the entire lesson without Kassie further created unequal planning responsibilities, which created more work for me to do in addition to my other responsibilities in the school community.

Despite the unequal planning responsibilities, Kassie and I planned to equally share teaching roles in our second planning session. We agreed that Kassie would introduce the lesson activity by showing the video and briefly compare and contrast the three religions by reviewing the table that she included. Afterward, I would explain the model and language objective, which was that students write their answers in a complete sentence using a subject and a verb. We would then facilitate the discussion in collaborative groups by walking around to answer questions and check on students' progress. The teaching session would conclude with an exit slip that would serve as a formative assessment on the students' initial understanding of the five pillars of Islam. For this purpose, I designed an exit slip where students matched the pillar to its appropriate description.

Misaligned Instructional Activities

The unequal planning responsibilities led to the second challenge in the collaborative process. In analyzing the results on the formative assessment, we learned that students "zoned out" during the whole-group discussion. When students completed the exit slip, many students were only able to match their group's pillar to its description. Three of the four ESL students missed two or more questions out of the five questions on the exit slip. The fact that students missed the majority of the questions indicated that our instructional activities did not align with the formative assessment (i.e., exit slip). Our instructional activities required students to specialize in one pillar, yet the formative assessment assessed students' understanding of all pillars. The instructional activities did create space for a whole group discussion, but Kassie and I did not provide students with a tool (e.g., guided notes or gist statements about each pillar) for students to listen actively during the whole-group discussion so that students could identify all pillars on the exit slip.

Consequently, this formative assessment showed that students did not master the content objective to explain the five pillars of the Islam. Had I allowed Kassie a stronger role in the planning session, Kassie and I might have resolved this misalignment before the actual teaching session. During our planning session, Kassie did ask, "How are we getting them to know about the four pillars that they don't have? Just read over the answers that the other groups do?" Kassie's questions pinpointed our instructional misalignment prior to the teaching session. In responding to Kassie's questions, I did not realize the significance of Kassie's questions because I explained that students would discuss the additional pillars. Kassie did not challenge my response or discuss her concerns in more detail. Had Kassie taken a stronger role in planning the lesson activity initially and/or explained her concerns in more detail in this specific conversation, we might have resolved this instructional misalignment prior to co-teaching the lesson.

Reflective Collaborative Teaching

Kassie and I navigated and resolved this misalignment when we reflected on our collaborative instructional practices during the first collaborative viewing session. Such reflection on our collaborative teaching played a crucial role because this reflection was the catalyst that paved the way for the possibilities in our collaborative encounter. When Kassie and I reflected on our instructional practices, we surmised that the formative assessment did not accurately reflect our instructional activities. Put another way, we acknowledged that we assessed students' knowledge of all the pillars when students only had the opportunity in class to become experts in one pillar. Since students had the Google document during the whole-group discussion, they did not have to listen to their classmate's discussion. I questioned our pedagogical choices by saying:

> I mean I created the exit slip, so this is on me, but I wonder if the slip accurately reflected how we taught the lesson because students only did their one pillar, which made me wonder if they were really engaged enough during that discussion.

By taking responsibility for the misalignment, I hoped to create a space where Kassie would freely challenge my decision. In turn, Kassie agreed that the lesson delivery limited students' ability to pay attention during the discussion. Such reflection allowed us to confront and change our instructional practices for the remainder of this collaborative cycle. To this aim, we decided to reteach the pillars during the next teaching session. Our reteaching ultimately led to students' mastery of the content objective, which was the goal of our collaboration. As shown in Figure 6.1, the ESL student confused two of the three pillars on the exit slip following the first instructional activity. After Kassie and I retaught the information, all ESL students matched correctly the pillars on the exit slip, which showed that they mastered the content objective.

Kassie also showed leadership when she too acknowledged and resolved to make changes during the second collaborative cycle. In doing

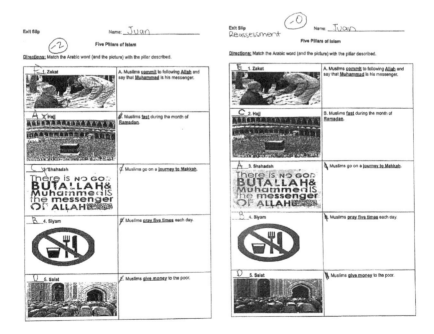

Figure 6.1 A Student's Exit Slip before and after Reteaching.

so, Kassie noted the changes she wanted to make in the second cycle by articulating that she wanted to make guided notes in the following excerpt:

> I would make each student responsible for taking notes while other people were presenting the answers. Because the entire class worked on one shared document, it was easy for the students to zone out when it was not their turn because they knew the answers were already on the document. I would like to have them have more responsibility and ownership in knowing the information.

Kassie's reflection shows that we both mutually agreed that we could increase students' participation if we made instructional changes during the second collaborative cycle. Her resolve to make changes also strengthened her leadership role during our collaborative encounter. Her acknowledgment and resolution underscored her vested interest in changing our instructional practices to ensure that students master the content objectives. While this misalignment was initially a challenge, it ultimately generated opportunities for Kassie and me to reflect on and change our collaborative instructional practices moving into the next collaborative cycle.

Kassie's Increased Leadership in the Second Cycle

Despite the fact that Kassie did not actually create the lesson activity in the second cycle, she did take a stronger leadership role in articulating her own vision for the second collaborative lesson. In doing so, Kassie established the content objectives for the lesson by stating that she wanted students to evaluate Joan of Arc's historical significance to the Hundred Years' War. To accomplish this, students would read primary sources that showed Joan of Arc's positive and negative attributes. Kassie explained, "We could break the class into two and have one perspective not like her at all and have their reasons why and kind of debate it, and then have those who do like her." Following Kassie's intention to have a debate on Joan of Arc's character, we discussed that students would work in pairs.

At the beginning of the class, students would work independently to read about Joan of Arc's character using the primary source documents. One student in the pair would document Joan of Arc's positive characteristics, while the other student would document her negative characteristics. In a debate activity, the students would share their perspective, while the other student took notes. In an effort to ensure that we repaired the misalignment in this teaching session, Kassie insisted, "That was kind of the vision I had for this because I think it, I just don't want us to get in the thing again where they kind of tune each other out." I accepted Kassie's "vision" and stated that we needed to consider that ESL students might need a language strategy to write and speak about Joan of Arc with their partner, by saying, "Let's make the activity very structured for language so that they can use the sentence frames to either speak or write about her." After this discussion, we attempted to divide planning responsibilities. Kassie agreed to "make the base scaffold" for the lesson, and I would "edit it to make sure the language" was accessible to ESL students.

Yet, when I looked at the lesson activity the night before our next planning session, I noticed that Kassie did not make the original scaffold as she intended during the previous session. I proceeded to scaffold the lesson activity and make the language accessible so that Kassie and I would still be able to teach the lesson on the specified date. During the follow-up planning session, Kassie showed appreciation for my contribution. As I explained the lesson activity, I also pointed out where I made the language more accessible to ESL students. For example, on the introductory chart about Joan of Arc, I stated:

> I simplified the language here a little bit. Instead of "deluded peasant," I said "crazy peasant." Instead of "shrewd," I said "wise," probably it would be wise and strong, something like that. Instead of "devout," I said "committed" just because here you're not really worried about, oh, do they understand what "shrewd" means, you really want them to know that one side of the argument is that she was a wise leader.

After I discussed the lesson activity and explained the changes I made to help the ESL students access and master the content standards, I asked Kassie if she wanted to simplify the language in the primary sources for the ESL students. In doing so, I expressed my concern that ESL students might not be able to read the primary sources. Kassie responded that she wanted students to be able to read primary source documents, so she preferred that we retain the language in the original documents. I assented to Kassie's wish as long we clarified students' confusion on difficult words as students worked in pairs during the collaborative teaching session. We discussed teaching roles, agreeing that Kassie would introduce the lesson, and I would explain the chart that summarized the opposing viewpoints of Joan of Arc. Kassie and I modeled how each student pair would carry out their respective tasks by giving them a positive and negative characteristic of Joan of Arc's historical contribution. We then facilitated independent work in pairs by circling the room, answering questions, and helping the ESL students access the language in the primary sources.

During the collaborative teaching session, Kassie took a leading role in using language strategies (e.g., gist statement) to help a particular ESL student access the language in the primary sources in the following:

> I'd ask what small segment of this best summarizes or backs up the character trait that they said. And they'd point to a small little part or half of a sentence or a whole sentence, and I'd underline that part,

just so we could again kind of getting out all the different kind of fluff and zeroing in on what was most important. So, I think just breaking it down like that in steps helped them understand the goal more.

By asking the students to point to and/or retell the gist of the primary source in their own words, Kassie illustrated how she helped accommodate the dense language during the students' independent work time. In doing so, Kassie showed her own awareness of language strategies (e.g., summaries, gist statement, underlining key words) and her ability to use them to simplify the language in the primary sources. After students had sufficient time to find information about Joan of Arc's character, they shared this information and evaluated their partner's claims. After students engaged in this debate, they wrote down a final evaluation about Joan of Arc's character.

Figure 6.2 shows an ESL student's exit slip, which shows that this student met the lesson objectives by evaluating Joan of Arc's character and evidencing this evaluation with three supporting details. In this way, Kassie and I exhibited leadership roles at different times, and we contributed our expertise based on our job title and past experiences. As the content teacher, Kassie specified the content objective and her vision for the lesson, and as the ESL teacher, I scaffolded the lesson with sentence frames and paragraph scaffolds to help ESL students access and master the content and language objectives.

YOU DECIDE: EXIT SLIP

Directions: Now that you've heard both sides, what do you think about Joan of Arc? Is she a positive or negative historical figure? You must pick a side!

Which side do you agree with more? (Highlight one!)

visionary from God		visionary from devil
groundbreaking feminist		troubled youth
dedicated patriot/warrior	😇 😈	disloyal traitor
wise leader	OR	crazy peasant
self-sacrificing saint		self-serving manipulator
committed Christian		evil-doing rebel

Explain your choice.

Joan of Arc is a negative historical figure because she worships the devil, she wore men's clothes, she was a witch.

Figure 6.2 A Student's Exit Slip from the Second Collaborative Cycle.

Kassie's Renewed Understanding of ESL Instruction

Our collaborative encounter created opportunities for Kassie's perceived learning outcomes related to planning and teaching ESL students. In the final interview, Kassie responded that this collaborative process renewed her understanding related to making the vocabulary accessible to ESL students and forced her to reflect on collaboration as an effective model for language instruction. She stated:

> This was the first time that I've really done like a pure co-teaching where we both take leadership roles at different points, and so I think that was a good experience, and I learned how to collaborate and meet beforehand and work with someone who has a different perspective, but we have the same goal in mind.

For Kassie, our shared leadership roles occurred when she and I shared teaching roles during the collaborative teaching sessions. Having no previous experience engaging in collaborative planning and teaching, Kassie developed a greater awareness and began to actually implement collaborative planning and teaching in practice. It is important to note that Kassie's previous experiences with collaborative teaching included working with teachers in special education. Despite the fact that she, in theory, collaborated with them, she admitted that these experiences were not indicative of true collaboration because they did not involve collaboratively planning or teaching shared lesson objectives where "both [took] leadership roles." For the first time, Kassie experienced collaborative planning, teaching, and reflection, which increased her own learning outcomes related to planning for and teaching ESL students.

Even though I perceived the unequal planning responsibilities in our collaborative process, Kassie did not perceive any challenges in collaboration because, in her mind, our collaborative experience more accurately aligned with her notions of collaborative planning and teaching. There were unequal planning responsibilities for me, but collaborative reflection helped us resolve our instructional misalignment and ultimately created space for increased ESL students' outcomes and Kassie's learning outcomes related to planning and teaching ESL students in the secondary social studies classroom.

Implications and Suggestions for Future Collaborative Efforts

This study showed the process by which Kassie and I collaborated to plan for and teach ESL students in a collaboratively taught eighth grade social studies classroom. This study's findings support earlier studies on teacher collaboration that show that collaboration can serve as professional development for teachers in learning how to plan for and teach ESL students (Giles, 2019, 2020; Peercy & Martin-Beltrán, 2012).

As a novice teacher, Kassie had no formal training in college related to ESL instruction, which is consistent with earlier research on the preparation of secondary content teachers working with ESL students (Rubinstein-Avila & Lee, 2014). This study's collaboration generated opportunities for Kassie to renew her understandings about how to make the content-specific vocabulary accessible to ESL students. Such renewed understandings related directly to earlier research that implies that secondary social studies teachers might need assistance with lessons because the content-specific vocabulary can make it more challenging for ESL students to master the content objectives (Duff, 2001). As such, collaboration can be a fruitful space in creating opportunities for social studies teachers to increase their understanding of learning to plan and teach lessons to ESL students in the content area classroom.

This study is also distinct from earlier work that reports on the ESL teacher's relegated role in collaboration (Creese, 2002). Yet, my strengthened role as the ESL teacher is a similar finding in my earlier work on collaboration (Giles, 2018; Giles & Yazan, 2020). In this particular study, I assumed a leadership role planning and teaching both lessons in the social studies content area classroom. The fact that I assumed a pivotal role in creating the lesson activities contributed to Kassie's increased learning outcomes since Kassie had no training related to ESL instruction. My leadership role undoubtedly served to create lesson activities that ultimately led to ESL student's increased participation as the learning outcome in collaboration. Such consistent findings implicate the fact that unequal planning roles might be necessary at least initially to create the needed space for content teachers to envision new activities and approaches to planning for and teaching ESL students in content area classrooms. Once Kassie witnessed a different lesson activity, she did share a leading role in teaching both lessons, even after seeing the first collaborative lesson. In this way, content teachers might also need to witness multiple lesson activities before they can confidently plan and create their own lesson activities accessible to ESL students in content area classrooms.

Navigating the collaborative challenges is also necessary to create space for ESL student's increased content mastery and participation in content area classrooms. Collaborative reflection served to navigate the instructional misalignment in this study's collaboration. This refection led to ESL students' increased learning outcomes and opportunities for participation. The exit slip in Figure 6.1 exemplifies how one ESL student increased his content understanding after we realized the instructional misalignment and retaught the content objectives. The fact that ESL students could articulate Joan of Arc's historical significance and debate her character shows ESL students' content mastery (shown in Figure 6.2) and heightened participation in the second collaborative cycle. For this reason, the challenges experienced in collaboration proved necessary and beneficial in working to influence ESL students' learning outcomes in the content area classroom.

Future ESL and content teachers' collaborative efforts might aim to explore additional challenges and possibilities in collaboration with additional content area teachers (e.g., mathematics, English/language arts, and science) to increase the trustworthiness of these findings. Moreover, in reflecting on initiating and sustaining collaboration with content teachers, ESL and content teachers' collaborative efforts should be voluntary based on the teachers' preferences for collaboration (Dove & Honigsfeld, 2018). Both collaborating teachers should be committed to sustaining collaboration to completion. For example, unequal planning responsibilities can occur when planning for and teaching ESL students, so an additional session to co-construct the lesson together might work to navigate this challenge. Teachers should also explicitly agree on planning responsibilities and follow-up a second time on these responsibilities if needed. Further, these collaborative efforts should begin small (Giles, 2018) and focus on shared student-centered outcomes (Peercy & Martin-Beltrán, 2012) to navigate the challenges successfully and work to create equitable participatory outcomes in collaboratively taught classrooms.

Note

1 I am aware that the label, ESL student, is highly criticized in research on second language teaching and learning research in favor of more inclusionary terminologies, such as emergent bilinguals. This usage does not reflect my own beliefs or stance about students, but rather reflects the program model specified by the study's district.

References

Ahmed Hersi, A., Horan, D. A., & Lewis, M. A. (2016). Redefining 'community' through collaboration and co-teaching: A case study of an ESOL specialist, a literacy specialist, and a fifth-grade teacher. *Teachers and Teaching, 22*(8), 927–946.

Arkoudis, S. (2003). Teaching English as a second language in science classes: Incommensurate epistemologies?. *Language and Education, 17*(3), 161–173.

Baecher, L., Rorimer, S., & Smith, L. (2012). Video-mediated teacher collaborative inquiry: Focus on English language learners. *The High School Journal, 95*(3), 49–61.

Charmaz, K. (2006). *Constructing grounded theory: A practical guide to qualitative analysis*. Thousand Oaks, CA: Sage.

Creese, A. (2002). The discursive construction of power in teacher partnerships: Language and subject specialists in mainstream schools. *TESOL Quarterly, 36*(4), 597–616.

DelliCarpini, M. (2018). Administrative issues in collaborative teaching. In J. Liontas, M. DelliCarpini, G. Park, & S. Salas (Eds.), *TESOL encyclopedia of English language teaching* (pp. 1–9). Hoboken, NJ: Wiley.

Denzin, N. K. (2016). *The qualitative manifesto: A call to arms*. New York, NY: Routledge.

Dove, M., & Honigsfeld, A. (2018). *Co-teaching for English learners: A guide to collaborative planning, assessment, and reflection*. Thousand Oaks, CA: Corwin.

Duff, P. (2001). Language, literacy, content, and (pop) culture: Challenges for ESL students in mainstream courses. *Canadian Modern Language Review*, *58*(1), 103–132.

Freeman, D., & Johnson, K. E. (1998). Reconceptualizing the knowledge-base of language teacher education. *TESOL Quarterly*, *32*(3), 397–417.

Giles, A. (2018). Navigating the contradictions: An ESL teacher's professional self-development. *TESL Canada Journal*, *35*(2), 104–127.

Giles, A. (2019). *The influences of ESL and content teachers' collaboration on teachers' learning and ESL students' participation: A case study of middle school mainstream classrooms.* (Unpublished doctoral dissertation). The University of Alabama, Tuscaloosa.

Giles, A. (2020). 'They're participating way more': The impact of ESL and content teachers' collaboration on students' participation: Selected poster presentations from the American Association of Applied Linguistics conference, Denver 2020. *Language Teaching*, *53*(4), 1–4.

Giles, A., & Yazan, B. (2020). "You're not an island": A language arts teacher's changed perceptions in ESL and content teachers' collaboration. *Research in Middle Level Education Online*, *43*(3), 1–15.

Glaser, B. G., & Strauss, A. L. (1967). *The discovery of grounded theory.* Chicago, IL: Aldine.

Johnson, K. E., & Golombek, P. R. (2016). *Mindful L2 teacher education: A sociocultural perspective on cultivating teachers' professional development.* New York, NY: Routledge.

Kamberelis, G., & Dimitriadis, G. (2005). *On qualitative inquiry.* New York, NY: Columbia University.

Martin-Beltrán, M., & Peercy, M. M. (2014). Collaboration to teach English language learners: Opportunities for shared teacher learning. *Teachers and Teaching: Theory and Practice*, *20*(6), 721–737.

Merriam, S. B., & Tisdell, E. J. (2016). *Designing your study and selecting a sample. Qualitative research: A guide to design and implementation.* San Francisco, CA: John Wiley & Sons.

Peercy, M. M. (2018). Mainstream and ESL teacher collaboration. In J. Liontas, M. DelliCarpini, G. Park, & S. Salas (Eds.), *TESOL encyclopedia of English language teaching* (pp. 4631–4636). Hoboken, NJ: Wiley.

Peercy, M. M., Ditter, M., & DeStefano, M. (2016). "We need more consistency": Negotiating the division of labor in ESOL–mainstream teacher collaboration. *TESOL Journal*, *8*(1), 215–239.

Peercy, M. M., & Martin-Beltrán, M. (2012). Envisioning collaboration: Including ESOL students and teachers in the mainstream classroom. *International Journal of Inclusive Education*, *16*(7), 657–673.

Rubinstein-Avila, E., & Lee, E. H. (2014). Secondary teachers and English language learners (ELLs): Attitudes, preparation and implications. *The Clearing House: A Journal of Educational Strategies, Issues and Ideas*, *87*(5), 187–191.

Saldaña, J. (2013). *The coding manual for qualitative researchers.* Thousand Oaks, CA: Sage.

Yoon, B. (2008). Uninvited guests: The influence of teachers' roles and pedagogies on the positioning of English language learners in the regular classroom. *American Educational Research Journal*, *45*(2), 495–522.

7 "I See Myself as Another Teacher"

Co-Teaching Practice for ELLs in a Science Class

Min Wang and Daniel Ness

Since the nascent stages of co-teaching as a paradigm in schools, specifically with the signing of the Individuals with Disabilities Education Improvement Act of 2004 as well as the No Child Left Behind initiative, the marriage metaphor has been frequently used both in the research literature and in practice. After all, when we think of co-teaching, we see two teachers in class – one general education teacher and, most often, one special education teacher; less often is an English language learner (ELL) teacher. These teachers either team teach, similar to a tag team where one teacher picks up after the other leaves off, or take turns – namely, when one teacher finishes after several minutes of teaching, the second takes over, possibly to finish the entire period. Murawski (2009) has even gone so far as to use the marriage metaphor in the very title of her book: *Collaborative teaching in the secondary schools: Making the co-teaching marriage work!* Indeed, in co-teaching classrooms, a sense of sharing exists between teachers both in terms of time engaging students and time spent preparing for lessons. Moreover, research findings suggest that equal partnership, namely parity, is an essential construct that enables the success of co-teaching among ELLs (Dove & Honigsfeld, 2010; Pratt, Imbody, Wolf, & Patterson, 2017). But in the classroom context, we question the extent to which the case of an equal partner teaching relationship actually exists, let alone a co-teaching marriage.

The purpose of this chapter is to identify the efficacy of the co-teaching model as it unfolds in a science classroom. This classroom is in a school with a very large ELL population that has content specialty or special education co-teacher dyads who serve ELLs. Because the school is in a district with a high percentage of ELLs, the district has always been in great need of ESL certified teachers. Unfortunately, these teachers have been in short supply and certified special education teachers have served in their place. As researchers, we examine how the equal partner marriage metaphor conveys the experiential realities of a pair of co-teachers in a seventh-grade science class for one academic semester. Research questions that guided the current study include: How much knowledge about co-teaching did co-teachers have?; What roles did they claim as a co-teacher?; And how did they collaborate in class?

DOI: 10.4324/9781003058311-9

Research on Co-Teaching for ELLs

Unfortunately, there is a dearth of research on co-teaching with respect to the interactions between content specialty teachers and their ELL teacher peers. Moreover, literature in this area is often bereft of research methods that tap the essence of co-teachers' feelings and emotions with regard to their teaching positions and roles. For example, while the idea of an unequal balance among ELL co-teachers is evident in the literature (Honigsfeld & Dove, 2016), the use of specific methodologies or supporting evidence in the field is often lacking. Similarly, while discussion on ELLs and co-teaching is somewhat common, it often indicates support for ELL co-teaching without data analysis or results from data collections.

Through case studies of three teachers – a Teaching English to Speakers of Other Languages (TESOL) specialist, a literacy specialist, and a general education fifth-grade teacher – who were involved in a co-teaching collaborative environment, Ahmed Hersi, Horan, and Lewis (2016) investigated the development of a professional learning community. As the authors state, "The emerging community of practice offered these teachers a space to learn and problem-solve by utilizing their specialized disciplinary knowledge of students and expanding the application of reading strategies during language arts" (p. 927). According to the authors, any opportunities for reviewing and revising the curriculum did not come to fruition because the teachers were largely unable to negotiate their roles and responsibilities that were part of a top-down administrative initiative. Consequently, the teachers were unable to reach parity or equal partnership from the perspective of both planning and teaching. Similarly, Chitiyo and Brinda (2018) studied the manner in which 77 teachers were in the process of preparing themselves for co-teaching. Their results indicate that the majority of these teachers lacked preparation for co-teaching. While 74 of the 77 teachers knew what co-teaching was – either through university coursework or a school training program, only half believed that they were confident enough to implement co-teaching into their way of teaching.

Although research on ELL learning and co-teaching is limited, there is a small corpus of literature that investigates the efficacy of co-teaching and ELLs' success in school. Bahamond (1999) seems to be one of the earliest researchers who examined data related to co-teaching in inclusive classrooms with large ELL populations. As one of the pioneering researchers to espouse the relatively novel alternative of co-teaching in bilingual education, Bahamonde has argued in favor of co-teaching as a fundamental component of ELLs' success.

Drawing on data collected from a culturally and linguistically diverse elementary school, Davison (2006) has employed questionnaires and interviews in order to examine the strengths and weaknesses of ELL student learning and co-teaching through the collaborative relationships between content and ELL teachers. Davison developed a framework that uses teacher dialogue along with critical discourse analysis to determine teacher stages of collaboration and effectiveness. She concluded that partnerships between content specialty teachers and ELL teachers are not lacking difficulties, and teacher attitudes in co-teaching vary greatly. In contrast to Davison's work, York-Barr, Ghere, and Sommerness (2007) examined the extent to which co-teaching instructional models support ELLs at an elementary school in an urban school setting. They posited that strengths in co-teaching ELLs far outweigh weaknesses. Their results from field notes, conversations, and classroom observations indicate that ELLs' academic achievement increased noticeably and that teachers found co-teaching worthwhile.

Dove and Honigsfeld (2017) and Honigsfeld and Dove (2008, 2016) have contributed a relatively large body of research on co-teaching in the ELL student context. Like Honigsfeld and Dove (2008), York-Barr, Ghere, and Sommerness's (2007) earlier work has supported the contention that co-teaching increases the academic success of English language learners and increases the potential of meeting national, state, and regional standards. In their later work, Honigsfeld and Dove (2016) have argued that co-teaching is analogous to riding a tandem bike, and, more often than not, the content teacher takes the front seat. They claim that content teachers and ELL teachers must maintain a level of trust and suggest that both teachers must engage in co-planning and co-assessment efforts if co-teaching is to be successful.

Drawing on social constructivism in connection with cooperative learning, Norton (2013) concluded that while openness, flexibility, and the ability to differentiate instruction were strengths in the co-teaching process, both content and ELL teachers can improve co-teaching by gaining skills in each other's areas of expertise. Employing interpretive inquiry and cross-case analysis, Martin-Beltran and Peercy (2014) also have supported the idea that co-teaching successfully increases ELLs' academic abilities. Martin-Beltran and Peercy suggested that institutions of teacher education should include learning experiences that emphasize collaborative teaching as part of their programs for preparing more qualified teachers to teach culturally and linguistically diverse student populations.

Beninghof and Leensvaart (2016) examined the co-teaching roles of an English language arts teacher with an ELL teacher in a district whose ELL student population has increased considerably. They, too, found that co-teaching, supported by co-planning and co-assessment, greatly increased ELL student success. Bauler and Kang (2020) discovered that while co-teaching can be a successful teaching model for ELLs through sharing and implementing ideas, barriers, such as insufficient time for co-planning and constraints in the curriculum, hampered co-teaching to fully succeed.

Of the few studies that examine co-teaching using case studies, Pappamihiel's (2012) work in an elementary school with a large ELL student population has supported the conclusion that strong administrative and faculty support can yield benefits for ELLs in classes with co-teachers. Cramer, Liston, Nevin, and Thousand (2010) reported on findings from two studies that utilized surveys, interviews, and observations. Based on their analyses of these studies, they concluded that co-teaching is a beneficial method for improving student success. The authors also base their conclusions on the putative need for co-teaching as indicated in teacher education standards. However, in each of these studies, there is little, if any, conclusive evidence that co-teaching actually provides positive outcomes not only for ELLs, but also for the co-teachers themselves.

Theoretical Framework

The current study on co-teaching is guided by positioning theory (Harré & van Langenhove, 1998). Positioning refers to locating oneself and being located by someone else with rights and obligations in and through language, such as conversations, storytelling, or narratives (Davies & Harré, 1990; Harré & van Langenhove, 1998). In social positioning research, two relevant perspectives on positioning are fundamental: (1) self-positioning and (2) other-positioning. Self-positioning refers to claiming identities for oneself. Self-positioning guides people to think about their roles and assignments, such as taking responsibilities to act in such roles. Harré and van Langenhove (1998) posit that "[w]hen a person is engaged in a deliberate self-positioning process this often will imply that they try to achieve specific goals with their act of self-positioning. This requires one to assume that they have a goal in mind" (p. 224). Other-positioning refers to assigning identities to others (Davies & Harré, 1990; Harré & van Langenhove, 1998). Through conversations, the speaker and the listener who take on various positions constantly deny each other opportunities or provide each other with the chance to say or do certain things (Kayi-Aydar, 2014). For example, when one positions another as deficient, he or she may deny that person the right to correct his or her cognitive performance; if one positions another as intelligent, he or she may allow that person the possibility for improving their performance (Harré & Moghaddam, 2003). Positioning theory has been developed as "an *analytical lens* and *explanatory theory*" (Green, Brock, Baker, & Harris, 2020, p. 119, emphasis original) to demonstrate the evolvement of learning and identities through discourse in classroom settings. Functioning as an analytical lens, positioning theory guides researchers to focus on the construction of positioning between the teacher and students through developing discourse for learning and engagement in classroom activities (Louick & Wang, 2021; Wang & Louick, 2020). Serving as an explanatory theory, positioning theory provides researchers with a theoretical guidance to investigate how participants assume or reject certain positions through discourse and classroom interactions (Green et al., 2020).

We used positioning theory as a theoretical framework and analytic tool to better understand the co-teaching practices in classroom interactions and through interview narratives. The teachers' verbal language not only demonstrated their teaching performance but also their self- and other-positioning. Also, their positioning reflected their teaching beliefs and teaching philosophy. Although the teachers' verbal language was analyzed in a detailed manner, their non-verbal language, such as their gestures and physical location, was also a central focus in understanding their positioning actions (Wang, 2020).

Methodology

Study Context and Participants

We used a qualitative case study (Yin, 2003) method to conduct the research during the spring semester of the 2017–2018 school year in a middle school located in a very large urban community in the Northeast United States. This school had a high reputation for students' performance in many disciplines. As researchers, both of us observed sixth- and seventh-grade classes once a week for a longitudinal study that examined newly arrived ELLs' classroom interactions for an entire semester. A science class was selected to report co-teaching practices because the largest population of ELLs was in this particular class. Also, both co-teachers (Ms. Dana, the science teacher, and Ms. Murphy, special education teacher) have TESOL certifications (both names are pseudonyms).

This class consisted of 33 students from multiple countries. The top five areas of origin were China, Bangladesh, South Korea, Russia (students identified as Jewish and spoke both Hebrew and Russian), and regions in South America (students spoke Spanish). At least 10 languages were spoken in the class. There were 12 females and 21 males, including 6 ELLs at the entering and emerging level, 6 students with disabilities, 6 students with disabilities in addition to language needs, and 15 general education students. In terms of student structure and demographics, the middle school utilized a cohort model in that the students from each class remained together as they moved from one classroom to the next.

Ms. Dana and Ms. Murphy participated in this study. Ms. Dana was a content specialty teacher and Ms. Murphy was a special education teacher, who also served in the capacity of aiding ELLs. Ms. Dana was Caucasian American and Ms. Murphy was African American. Although there was one ESL (Since the school still used the old term, we kept it this way out of respect) teacher in the school who implemented push-in and push-out instruction, Ms. Murphy was a certified TESOL teacher, so the ESL teacher did not participate in this study. Ms. Dana was 29 years of age and had taught for 5 years when the study began. Ms. Murphy was 35 years of age and had taught for 13 years.

Science Classroom Context

In Ms. Dana's science classroom, there were posters about earth science and life science on each of the four walls. Two big bookshelves, the tops of which had houseplants set on them, were placed on two sides of the classroom. What makes the science classroom context so important is that it seemed to demonstrate the teachers' attempt to motivate their students' interest in science and academic development. Students were sitting in groups, eight groups in total. Each group had four students in the first seven groups, but there were five students in the last group. All ELLs were sitting in different groups. This arrangement made it convenient for the teachers to provide students with assistance. They believed that doing so made it easier to accommodate ELLs' needs.

Data Sources

Data sources included class observation and interviews. The class observation took place on June 18, 2018. I (Min, first author) was sitting with one of the ELLs in the last group. Daniel (second author) was sitting with the second group on the left side of the classroom. The class was audio-recorded with the participants' consent. Both of us were taking field notes while observing the class. The class observation became the primary data source for the study.

We also conducted an interview with each of the co-teachers after the class observation. Each interview lasted for about 1 hour and 30 minutes. We audio-recorded the interviews. The type of interview utilized in the data collection process was the structured interview, whereby we developed an interview protocol of 14 questions having to do with teachers' perceptions of co-teaching from the perspectives of their co-teaching peers and their ELLs. The interview transcripts were the secondary data source.

Data Analysis

We used positioning theory as an analytic tool to analyze the data. The examination of the two teachers' interview narratives and classroom interactions was conducted through an in-depth analysis of their verbal language because when teachers talk, they intentionally or sometimes unintentionally construe themselves and others as "social beings" (Bamberg, 1997), whose positions and identities are formed and enacted (Zembylas, 2003). We paid close attention to certain lexical items (such as personal pronouns and evaluative words) and speech acts (such as stating, warning, and demanding) to understand how the teachers positioned themselves and others as well as how their positioning influenced classroom interactions. We also attended to the numbers of utterances, the frequency of turn-taking, and word choices to understand how they performed their roles while co-teaching. In addition, their non-verbal language, such as their physical location in the classroom, was analyzed. These constituents formed the classroom discourse, which provided us with necessary information to analyze each teacher's positionings and interactions.

Researchers' Positionality

As a researcher in TESOL, a teacher educator, and a former ELL, I (Min) am always interested in how "human learning and development is constructed through discourse" (Green et al., 2020, p. 121) and how language shapes one's positioning. However, since I never co-taught a class, I was not familiar with the dynamic and discourse in this co-teaching classroom. As a border crosser, I was shuttling between the familiar and unfamiliar to make my "personal and theoretical commitments visible" (Kleinsasser, 2000, p. 155). I believe that researching the co-teachers' understanding of co-teaching and their classroom interactions is necessary in order to display their teaching life from multiple positions, instead of speaking for them.

As a researcher in curriculum and instruction, Daniel has focused a great deal of attention on how both Pre-K-12 students and pre-service teachers develop cognitively, socially, and emotionally. Everyone enters the classroom with unique backgrounds and experiences that support learning. In general, the co-teaching paradigm has attempted to help bridge the gap between students who have been historically marginalized and so-called mainstream students so that all students have equal opportunity to succeed in school (Cobb & Sharma, 2015). While Daniel, too, has never co-taught, he strongly believes that it is imperative for the research community to gain a more robust understanding of co-teaching and how it can support equity in the classroom.

Findings

Findings show that the two co-teachers possessed some knowledge about co-teaching. They claimed that they were "co-actors" who supported each other in many ways, such as co-delivering lessons, co-teaching vocabulary, and paying close attention to ELLs' participation and performance. The section below reports interview data on the co-teacher's knowledge about co-teaching and how they positioned each other as co-teachers. Their understanding of co-teaching could reflect their classroom interactions and positioning actions while delivering lessons. The interview data functioned as a support for us to understand their collaboration in class.

Knowledge about Co-Teaching

Although findings show that both Ms. Dana and Ms. Murphy had some knowledge about co-teaching, the way in which each teacher described it was slightly different. For example, Ms. Murphy directly defined co-teaching as two teachers in the same classroom to meet the needs of a mixed population of students. She emphasized that the two teachers should be experts in different areas. Ms. Murphy also commented that if there was no co-planning, there was no co-instruction. She suggested that it would be ideal if two co-teachers worked together for a long period of time because they could become familiar with each other's field. This is especially beneficial to special education and ESL teachers because they will have more chance to participate in co-teaching, instead of sitting in the back of the classroom doing "reality checking." Ms. Dana did not directly give a definition of co-teaching, but introduced two approaches to co-teaching, including parallel teaching and station teaching, to explain how they co-delivered lessons on a daily basis.

Understanding of Roles of Co-Teachers

At an interview, when we asked how they perceived their co-teacher, both Ms. Dana and Ms. Murphy regarded their partner highly. Ms. Dana considered Ms. Murphy as an amazing asset and an inspiration to pursue her TESOL program. She explained,

> She [Ms. Murphy] always has her finger on the pulse. She always had really good ways of reformatting the science material to make it more approachable for the students who are struggling...She is dual[ly] certified. She can address them from the special ed. perspective and also from the language perspective, so I'm very fortunate to work with her.

Ms. Dana also valued and appreciated Ms. Murphy's expertise in classroom management, pacing the lesson, questioning, and being sensitive to students' needs. Ms. Murphy firmly believed that Ms. Dana was the content teacher. Moreover, she claimed that Ms. Dana was her "expert," but, there was neither a main character nor a supporting character because both of them were "co-actors" and they were both "supporting each other."

When we asked how they perceived themselves as a co-teacher, Ms. Dana regarded herself as a student to her co-teacher. Interestingly, Ms. Murphy did not see herself as a special education or ESL teacher, but *another* teacher. She believed that both teachers should be *teachers* – not specifically special education, ESL, or general education teachers. She explained,

> I see myself as another teacher. Not as a special ed. teacher or an ESL teacher...So, I think both teachers should be teachers...Yes, as a teacher. Not as a help...They (students) look to me just as much as they look to [the co-teacher's name]...

Ms. Murphy emphasized her role as "another teacher." She indicated that the special education teacher or ESL teacher needs to receive the same recognition from students as the general education teacher does because they were oftentimes viewed as helpers. It seems as if the label of the special education or ESL teacher is a stigma. That is why Ms. Murphy considered herself as *another* teacher.

The section below reports on the class observation data, which demonstrates how the two teachers collaboratively supported each other to deliver the lesson. We focused on the co-teachers' verbal and non-verbal language to understand their positioning actions and classroom dynamics.

Collaboration in Class

Positioning themselves as "co-actors," Ms. Dana and Ms. Murphy smoothly collaborated with each other in class interactions. Ms. Dana and Ms. Murphy delivered a lesson on reproduction, entitled "Main Structure of the Male/Female Reproductive System." Ms. Dana was standing near the white board, but Ms. Murphy was standing in the middle of the classroom. Due to the sensitivity of the subject matter, Ms. Dana started the class by telling the students general rules. While the students were copying the Focus Questions (FQ) and Do Now (DN) tasks, Ms. Dana began checking vocabulary. Below are excerpts of the classroom interactions between the co-teachers followed by analysis.

Excerpt 1

1. Dana: What is the function of a hormone?
2. Murphy: Someone tell me the answer. I am going to make some cold calls.
3. Dana: What is the function of a hormone?
[A student raises hand]
4. Murphy: What is the function of a hormone? New people?
5. Dana: Why does the body need hormones?
6. Murphy: [An ELL's name] wanna try it out?
7. Murphy: (Pointing to another student) You have something different?
8. Dana: I could not hear you.
9. Murphy: (Repeated what the student said) Hormones help us grow, she said.
10. Dana: Can you make a big sentence including all the information about hormones?
11. Murphy: Taking everything from the white board.
12. Murphy: Somebody new want to try?
13. Dana: Let's do partner chat first.
14. Murphy: It's on the board. There is no trick.
[Both teachers started chatting with students to check how they worked together]

In the excerpt above, two teachers demonstrated their collaborative engagement through the "one teach one assist or drift" co-teaching model. Ms. Dana led the class by stating the class rules and then checking vocabulary. Ms. Dana's instructional actions can be understood as her positioning acts: as the content specialty teacher she took an initiative to start the class which implied her positioning as "the leading character" on the stage of the classroom; however, with a TESOL certificate in hand, Ms. Dana grabbed the opportunity to pave the way for ELLs to better understand the content matter through checking vocabulary. She could have given the opportunity to Ms. Murphy but she saved it for herself. This event seems to show that Ms. Dana not only is specialized in science but also in teaching ELLs as well.

Ms. Murphy actively collaborated with Ms. Dana by calling on students to answer questions, giving them scaffolds when necessary, and repeating Ms. Dana's questions. For example, shortly after Ms. Dana posed the first question, Ms. Murphy responded very quickly by giving an order to the students. When she found that no one was going to offer an answer, she stated that she was going to "make some cold calls." Her statement appeared to target two types of students: those who did not pay attention to the lesson as well as ELLs who may have had difficulty understanding the content matter. Ms. Murphy's utterance seemed to function as a warning to the students, which demonstrated her power as *another* teacher, instead of a help or teaching assistant. When she saw some old-timers raise their hands, Ms. Murphy continued to encourage newly arrived ELLs by calling them "new people" to participate. Ms. Murphy noticed that an ELL was hesitant to raise her hand and asked her if she wanted to try. In line 12, Ms. Murphy motivated newcomers (ELLs) to take this opportunity for engagement by asking, "Somebody new want to try?" It is obvious that Ms. Murphy held the floor more often than Ms. Dana did. When students had difficulties in answering Ms. Dana's questions, Ms. Murphy provided the class with hints, such as "taking everything from the white board." and "it's on the board. There is no trick." Ms. Dana mainly focused on the content, but Ms. Murphy's focus was on the students, especially newly arrived ELLs ("new people"). Positioning herself as *another* teacher who was certified with both special education and TESOL, Ms. Murphy attended to the needs of ELLs and other students who needed special attention. She proactively guided and engaged the students in classroom interactions.

Although the two teachers performed their positioning acts through their verbal language, their physical presentation also indicated their positioning. For example, Ms. Dana located herself in front of the classroom, but Ms. Murphy positioned herself in the middle of the classroom. Their physical presentation, which became another kind of discourse, not only spoke to their pedagogical positioning but also their agency. Ms. Dana's physical location confirmed her leading role as a general education teacher. Interestingly, Ms. Murphy did not locate herself in the back or on the side of the classroom but located herself in the middle of the classroom. Ms. Murphy's location seems like an implicit message to Ms. Dana and the students: "I am at the center of the class. I am teaching, not just assisting." Ms. Murphy's desire for recognition was made visible through both her verbal and physical positioning.

Excerpt 2

Both teachers' self- and other-positioning was formed and shaped by their verbal and non-verbal language, which also guided and featured their classroom interactions and performance. The following interaction took place after students had a comprehensive understanding of hormones. As described in the excerpt above, Ms. Dana also led students to understand the key concepts. As before, she paid close attention to ELLs.

1   Dana: Let's talk about puberty. There is information on the white board.
2   Murphy: You guys read it.
3   Murphy: [An ELL's name], read the first box.
4   Dana: When does puberty start and end?
5   Murphy: At a given age.
6   Dana: Yes. Who can tell **us** the answer?
7   Murphy: It's on the white board.
8   Murphy: [An ELL's name], read it for **me**.
9   Murphy: Read it louder.
10 Dana: Some people start at 9. Some might start at 13 or even later, but the average age is 13.
11 Dana: When we reach puberty, our body changes.
12 Murphy: You boys can tell when you go through puberty when your voices change from a higher-pitched voice to a lower-pitched voice... Some of you still have high pitched voices and some of your voices are starting to get lower...
13 Murphy: There are also cultural issues with voice and pitch as boys grow up...
14 Murphy: [An ELL's name], read the next box for **me**.
15 Dana: How many of you have reached puberty?
[The students in the class laugh and giggle.]
16 Murphy: (classroom management) calm down. Boys, please settle down and concentrate.
17 Dana: We not only experience biological changes but also psycho-logical and emotional changes.
18 Murphy: [An ELL's name], read the next box for **me**.
19 Murphy: Shhhhh. Read it louder coz **I** cannot hear you.
20 Murphy: (engages in classroom management in order to calm the class down.)

26   Dana: Are there any questions? (Only the boys of the class ask questions. All students laugh when boys ask questions.)

The dynamic in this excerpt seems different from the previous one. In Excerpt 1, Ms. Dana started the class and led the discussion. Ms. Murphy provided adequate assistance and encouraged students to participate. The teaching model featured was "one teach, one assist." However, in this excerpt, both teachers seemed to share the equal weight on delivering the lesson. For example, when Ms. Dana changed the topic to "puberty" and hinted the class where to find relevant information, Ms. Murphy promptly chimed in by giving a demand, "You guys read it." In line 3, Ms. Murphy directly gave an ELL an order to read the information on the white board. When Ms. Dana asked the class when puberty starts and ends, Ms. Murphy added, "At a given age." Ms. Dana confirmed with her and continued to solicit answers from the students. Ms. Murphy directed students' attention to the information once again by emphasizing, "It's on the white board." This is very helpful for newly arrived ELLs since some of them had limited English proficiency. It is very easy for them to get lost.

While Ms. Dana pointed out that reaching puberty resulted in body changes, Ms. Murphy grabbed this opportunity to demonstrate her knowledge about life science. Ms. Murphy does not solely specialize in special education and ESL but is also equipped with content matter knowledge. She made her self-positioning as *another* teacher visible and audible. Ms. Murphy's classroom positioning actions were aligned with Ms. Dana's perception of the roles of co-teachers in the interview. She stated, "We're both science teachers, we're both special ed. and ESL teachers, we're both everyone's teacher." Ms. Dana's statement was verified by their classroom interactions.

In the rest of the excerpt, the interaction between the two teachers was similar to Excerpt 1: Ms. Dana asked questions and Ms. Murphy assisted students to find answers through providing them with hints or guiding them to read information on the white board. Ms. Murphy attended to newly arrived ELLs. For example, she called on several ELLs to read the information about puberty and asked them to read it loudly so that the entire class could hear them. Again, Ms. Murphy held the floor more often than Ms. Dana did.

It is also worth noting that Ms. Murphy's speech acts are different from Ms. Dana's. Her utterances, such as "read the first box," "read the next box for me," and "Read it louder," performed direct illocutionary acts (Searle, 1969). These directives carried a lot of power and authority. However, Ms. Dana expressed demand in a more indirect way. For instance, in line 6, she asked, "Who can tell us the answer?" She could have said, "Please give us the answer." But she used a question format instead. Ms. Murphy also used the first single personal pronouns "I" and "me" in her utterances, but Ms. Dana used the first plural pronoun "us," which can refer to the teachers or the teachers and the students. It indicated the community of practice, but "I" and "me" exclusively refer to Ms. Murphy. It is likely that Ms. Murphy tried to emphasize her self-positioning as a teacher instead of a helper.

Discussion and Implication

Being equipped with certain knowledge about co-teaching and considering each other as a support, the two co-teachers collaboratively engaged in co-teaching to accommodate ELLs' various needs. The teaching practice in this co-taught class demonstrated the efficacy of co-teaching, which is aligned with the literature we discussed above: Co-teaching has been proven effective to meet the needs of a mixed populations of students, especially ELLs and students with disabilities because co-teaching is mainly featured by tapping into two teaching professionals' expertise to improve student learning (Ahmed Hersi, Horan, & Lewis, 2016; Bauler & Kang, 2020; Gleeson & Davison, 2016; Russell, 2019; Whiting, 2017). However, there are continued concerns about implementing co-teaching to maximize learning, such as building equal partnerships between co-teachers, developing a sense of belonging, and recognizing and valuing co-teachers' expertise (Whiting, 2017).

We believe that the co-teachers' positive self- and other-positioning made the collaboration of co-teaching a salient feature, which highlighted the co-teacher's demonstration of equal partnership. Equal partnership has the potential to benefit all students in the classroom, especially ELLs. However, research has shown that ESL teachers in co-teaching primarily position themselves and are positioned in the observer or assistant roles because their job is considered to be supportive, thus demonstrating less parity between the co-teachers (Bouck, 2007; Flores, 2012; King-Sears, Jenkins, & Brawand, 2020; Rice & Zigmond, 2000). As soon as ESL teachers take up the supportive role in a co-taught classroom, their pedagogical expertise is not evidenced in delivering instruction (Strogilos & Tragoulia, 2013). It is unfair to the students who need the language support and special attention because they might not receive the fullest extent of support from the co-teachers. Also, the existing teaching resource does not become fully recognized, valued, and used. The fundamental rationale of co-teaching is to maximize the paired teachers' expertise to benefit all students. If one of the co-teachers serves as a teaching aide or teaching assistant, this teacher's expertise might have remained underperformed, which turns out to be a waste of resources. It can also undermine the teacher's identity construction to negotiate a sense of belonging, which can further damage her or his self-worth.

How do ESL teachers negotiate the equal partnership with their co-teachers? There are several strategies that could be helpful to solve this problem based on Ms. Dana's and Ms. Murphy's teaching practices. First, positive self-positioning can help special education teachers and

ESL teachers gain power in a co-teaching classroom. As Ms. Murphy indicated, the label of special education and ESL teachers carries negative connotations, so she avoided using this label, but positioned herself as a teacher, *another* teacher. Her self-positioning became a belief that guided her what to do and how to do it in the classroom. She actually performed as *another* teacher through scaffolding, inquiring, and instructing content matter knowledge. She took the ownership of the class and teaching, instead of seeing herself as an invited guest who does reality checking, managing classroom behaviors, and grading on the sidelines.

However, if Ms. Murphy did not possess content matter knowledge, she would not be able to act as *another* teacher. Therefore, the second strategy is to grow content matter knowledge. In effect, many special education and ESL teachers are not equipped with content knowledge. The lack of content knowledge tends to restrict their role to supporting teachers or teaching aides. When special education teachers and ESL teachers are unable to deliver instruction and do not have ownership of content knowledge, it is difficult for them to position themselves and be positioned as teachers. This is why some special education and ESL teachers have led instruction less frequently and have served as instructional support more frequently (Vannest & Hagan-Burke, 2010). Very often, these teachers are perceived as inferior to general education teachers (Flores, 2012); however, broadening their knowledge span can help them position and be positioned differently. In this respect, there are several ways to gain content knowledge, such as participating in professional development, conducting lesson co-planning, and self-learning.

In addition, general education teachers' positive other-positioning of their co-teaching partners is crucial for building an equal relationship in a real sense. If Ms. Dana did not recognize and value Ms. Murphy's expertise, Ms. Murphy would not be able to act as *another* teacher. Ms. Dana believed that Ms. Murphy was an expert in special education, ESL, and science. She used "always has her finger on the pulse" and "She always had really good ways reformatting the science material to make it more approachable for the students who are struggl[ing]" to describe Ms. Murphy as an excellent co-teacher. Ms. Dana also considered Ms. Murphy as "an amazing asset and an inspiration" and her "expert" – because she could contribute to co-teaching "from the special ed. perspective and also from the language perspective" – so Ms. Dana felt very "fortunate" to have Ms. Murphy as a co-teacher. This very positive other-positioning functioned as a foundation for Ms. Dana and Ms. Murphy's equal co-teaching relationship.

It is evident that both Ms. Dana and Ms. Murphy tried to accommodate the linguistic and academic needs of ELLs, especially newly arrived ones. They created opportunities to center them from the peripheral areas of the classroom by asking them to read information on the white board and scaffolding them to organize their own spoken language. However, Ms. Murphy's other-positioning of ELLs seems problematic. She referred to the newly arrived ELLs as "new people" or "anybody new." This label can have deleterious effects: in discouraging ELLs to be mainstreamed, in segregating the newcomers and old-timers, or even increasing the difficulty for ELLs to build a sense of belonging. In this regard, it would be better for the teachers to call their names, instead of "new people" or "anybody new." Because their names often carry very rich cultural and linguistic meanings (Kohli, & Solórzano, 2012), these ELLs have their own names, which represent the core of their identities.

Additionally, although "one teach, one assist" or "one teach, one observe" is beneficial for ELLs and students with disabilities, if teachers use this approach too often, they can do more harm than good. First of all, this approach can easily single out students who need special attention or help. The co-teaching classroom might become another place for segregation instead of integration. In addition, these approaches may place the special education and ESL co-teacher in a lower position because the content teacher or general education teacher delivers the lesson, but the special education or ESL teacher does observations, classroom management, asking and answering questions, or re-explaining concepts. This teaching model can naturally or structurally position the two teachers in a hierarchical situation. They can also make students believe that one teacher is more important than the other or one teacher is the leader, but the other is a helper. In addition, it might divert students' attention away from the other teacher's teaching and foster dependent behavior (Friend, 2014).

While co-teaching is a challenging enterprise, such as inadequate knowledge about co-teaching, limited time for co-planning, building an equal partnership, and constructing and negotiating identities as co-teachers, Ms. Dana and Ms. Murphy's co-teaching practices have shown some promising possibilities, including positive positioning actions, necessary knowledge about each other's field, and long-time collaboration. With respect to co-teaching science content, it is important to note that science instruction by both science teachers and science-teacher-ESL-teacher dyads has historically placed emphasis on the teaching of lower-order content knowledge, such as labeling and defining terms, as well as procedural knowledge. We argue that one of the most effective co-teaching environments is one in which both co-teachers emphasize conceptual knowledge and higher-order thinking skills, such as analyzing and synthesizing ideas. Greater focus on the latter skills will likely have more influence on students' motivation in science as well as other STEM subjects (Estrella, Au, Jaeggi, & Collins, 2018; Lee, 2005; Rollnick, 2000). To face the challenge and become qualified, adept co-teachers, professional development is imperative. Co-teachers should be equipped with rich co-teaching knowledge, including the basics of co-teaching, the reasons for co-teaching, the roles of co-teachers, and approaches to co-teaching. Also, co-planning should be given due attention and emphasis because no-planning means no-co-teaching.

References

Ahmed Hersi, A., Horan, D. A., & Lewis, M. A. (2016). Redefining "community" through collaboration and co-teaching: A case study of an ESOL specialist, a literacy specialist, and a fifth-grade teacher. *Teachers and Teaching, 22*(8), 927–946.

Bahamonde, C. (1999) Teaching English language learners: A proposal for effective service delivery through. *Journal of Educational and Psychological Consultation, 10*(1), 1–24. https://doi.org/10.1207/s1532768xjepc1001_1

Bamberg, M. G. (1997). Positioning between structure and performance. *Journal of Narrative and Life History, 7*(1–4), 335–342.

Bauler, C. V., & Kang, E. J. (2020). Elementary ESOL and content teachers' resilient co-teaching practices: A long-term analysis. *International Multilingual Research Journal, 14*(4), 338–354. https://doi.org/10.1080/19313152.2020.1747163

Beninghof, A., & Leensvaart, M. (2016). Co-teaching to support ELLs. *Educational Leadership, 73*(5), 70–73.

Bouck, E. C. (2007). Co-teaching... not just a textbook term: Implications for practice. *Preventing School Failure: Alternative Education for Children and Youth, 51*(2), 46–51.

Chitiyo, J., & Brinda, W. (2018). Teacher preparedness in the use of co-teaching in inclusive classrooms. *Support for Learning, 33*(1), 38–51.

Cobb, C., & Sharma, M. (2015). I've got you covered: Adventures in social justice-informed co-teaching. *Journal of the Scholarship of Teaching and Learning, 15*(4), 41–57.

Cramer, E., Liston, A., Nevin, A., & Thousand, J. (2010). Co-teaching in urban secondary school districts to meet the needs of all teachers and learners: Implications for teacher education reform. *International Journal of Whole Schooling, 6*(2), 59–76.

Davies, B., & Harré, R. (1990). Positioning: The discursive production of selves. *Journal for the Theory of Social Behaviour, 20*(1), 43–63.

Davison, C. (2006). Collaboration between ESL and content teachers: How do we know when we are doing it right? *International Journal of Bilingual Education and Bilingualism, 9*(4), 454–475.

Dove, M. G., & Honigsfeld, A. (2010). ESL coteaching and collaboration: Opportunities to develop teacher leadership and enhance student learning. *TESOL Journal, 1*(1), 3–22.

Dove, M. G., & Honigsfeld, A. (2017). *Co-teaching for English learners: A guide to collaborative planning, instruction, assessment, and reflection.* Thousand Oaks, CA: Corwin Press.

Estrella, G., Au, J., Jaeggi, S. M., & Collins, P. (2018). Is inquiry science instruction effective for English language learners? A meta-analytic review. *AERA Open, 4*(2). https://doi.org/10.1177/2332858418767402

Flores, N. (2012). Power differentials: Pseudo-collaboration between ESL and mainstream teachers. In A. Honigsfeld, & M. G. Dove (Eds.), *Coteaching and other collaborative practices in the EFL/ESL classroom: Rationale, research, reflections, and recommendations* (pp. 185–193). Charlotte, NC: Information Age Publishing.

Friend, M. (2014). *Co-teaching: Strategies to improve student outcomes.* Port Chester, NY: National Professional Resources Inc.

Gleeson, M., & Davison, C. (2016). A conflict between experience and professional learning: Subject teachers' beliefs about teaching English language learners. *RELC Journal, 47*(1), 43–57.

Green, J. L., Brock, C., Baker, W. D., & Harris, P. (2020). Positioning theory and discourse analysis: An explanatory theory and analytic lens. In N. S. Nasir, C. D. Lee, R. Pea, & M. McKinney de Royston (Eds.), *Handbook of the cultural foundations of learning* (pp. 119–140). New York: Routledge.

Harré, R., & Moghaddam, F. (Eds.). (2003). *The self and others: Positioning individuals and groups in personal, political, and cultural contexts.* Westport, CT: Greenwood Publishing Group.

Harré, R., & van Langenhove, L. (Eds.). (1998). *Positioning theory: Moral contexts of international action.* Malden, MA: Wiley-Blackwell.

Honigsfeld, A., & Dove, M. (2008). Co-teaching in the ESL classroom. *Delta Kappa Gamma Bulletin, 74*(2), 8–14.

Honigsfeld, A., & Dove, M. G. (2016). Co-teaching ELLs: Riding a tandem bike. *Educational Leadership, 73*(4), 56–60.

Individuals with Disabilities Education Improvement Act, 20 U.S.C. 1400 et seq. (2004). https://sites.ed.gov/idea/statute-chapter-33/subchapter-i/1400

Kayi-Aydar, H. (2014). Social positioning, participation, and second language learning: Talkative students in an academic ESL classroom. *TESOL Quarterly, 48*(4), 686–714.

King-Sears, M. E., Jenkins, M. C., & Brawand, A. (2020). Co-teaching perspectives from middle school algebra co-teachers and their students with and without disabilities. *International Journal of Inclusive Education, 24*(4), 427–442.

Kleinsasser, A.M. (2000). Researchers, reflexivity, and good data: Writing to unlearn. *Theory Into Practice, 39*(3), 155–162.

Kohli, R., & Solórzano, D. G. (2012). Teachers, please learn our names!: Racial microaggressions and the K-12 classroom. *Race Ethnicity and Education, 15*(4), 441–462.

Lee, O. (2005). Science education with English language learners: Synthesis and research agenda. *Review of Educational Research, 75*(4), 491–530.

Louick, R., & Wang, M. (2021). Classroom discourse and learning disability: Interactional opportunities for development of self-determination beliefs. *The Journal of Educational Research, 114*(1), 52–63.

Martin-Beltran, M., & Peercy, M. M. (2014). Collaboration to teach English language learners: Opportunities for shared teacher learning. *Teachers and Teaching, 20*(6), 721–737.

Murawski, W. W. (2009). *Collaborative teaching in the secondary schools: Making the co-teaching marriage work!* Thousand Oaks, CA: Sage.

Norton, J. C. (2013). *Elementary ESL and general education co-teachers' perceptions of their co-teaching roles: A mixed methods study* (Doctoral dissertation, George Washington University).

Pappamihiel, N. E. (2012). Benefits and challenges of co-teaching English learners in one elementary school in transition. *TAPESTRY, 4*(1), 1–13.

Pratt, S. M., Imbody, S. M., Wolf, L. D., & Patterson, A. L. (2017). Co-planning in co-teaching: A practical solution. *Intervention in School and Clinic, 52*(4), 243–249.

Rice, D., & Zigmond, N. (2000). Co-teaching in secondary schools: Teacher reports of developments in Australian and American classrooms. *Learning Disabilities Research & Practice*, 15(4), 190–197.

Rollnick, M. (2000). Current issues and perspectives on second language learning of science. *Studies in Science Education*, 35, 93–121.

Russell, F. A. (2019). ESOL and mainstream teacher collaboration: Overcoming challenges through developing routines. *NYSTESOL Journal*, 6(1), 19–33.

Searle, J. R. (1969). *Speech acts: An essay in the philosophy of language* (Vol. 626). Cambridge, UK: Cambridge University Press.

Strogilos, V., & Tragoulia, E. (2013). Inclusive and collaborative practices in co-taught classrooms: Roles and responsibilities for teachers and parents. *Teaching and Teacher Education*, 35, 81–91.

Vannest, K. J., & Hagan-Burke, S. (2010). Teacher time use in special education. *Remedial and Special Education*, 31(2), 126–142.

Wang, M. (2020). *Multimodalities and Chinese students' L2 practices: Positioning, agency, and community*. Lanham, MD: Lexington Books.

Wang, M., & Louick, R. (2020). Positioning and motivation: A discourse analysis of classroom interactions between teacher and students with disabilities. *Learning Disabilities: A Multidisciplinary Journal*, 25(2). https://doi.org/10.18666/LDMJ-2020-V25-I2-10310

Whiting, J. (2017). Caught between the push and the pull: ELL teachers' perceptions of mainstreaming and ESOL classroom teaching. *NABE Journal of Research and Practice*, 8(1), 9–27.

Yin, R. (2003). *Case study research: Design and methods*. Thousand Oaks, CA: Sage.

York-Barr, J., Ghere, G., & Sommerness, J. (2007). Collaborative teaching to increase ELL student learning: A three-year urban elementary case study. *Journal of Education for Students Placed at Risk*, 12(3), 301–335.

Zembylas, M. (2003). Emotions and teacher identity: A poststructural perspective. *Teachers and Teaching*, 9(3), 213–238.

8 Co-Taught Integrated Language and Mathematics Content Instruction for Multilingual Learners

Carrie McDermott and Andrea Honigsfeld

In this chapter, we present a single case study of one high-school co-teaching team consisting of a mathematics teacher (Mrs. Renj, pseudonym as all other names) and an English to speakers of other languages (ESOL) teacher (Ms. Luna). As researchers, we conducted this study in an integrated secondary mathematics class at a high school. Students were in grades 9–11. This chapter focuses on the effective collaborative practices used to support multilingual learners' (MLLs) core content attainment as well as language and disciplinary literacy development. To begin our in-depth discussion on the teachers' collaborative practices, we invite the reader to the integrated Algebra I class.

Classroom Context

There were 16 students in the class with language acquisition levels ranging from basic speech emergence (entering) through expanding (advanced) levels, including some identified as students with interrupted/inconsistent formal education (SIFE) (New York State School Report Card Data, 2018–2019). The co-teachers, Mrs. Renj (math) and Ms. Luna (ESOL) planned weekly to identify the core concepts students needed to understand and how they would differentiate the information and scaffold materials to ensure comprehensible input. It is important to note that at the time of the observation, this team was new and had been working together for less than 6 months.

In addition to this planned collaborative time, the team carved out time daily to discuss updates as needed to ensure student progress, understanding, and goal completion. This was often not scheduled via in-person meetings, text, a quick stop in the hallway, or an email. Prior to the observed lesson, Mrs. Renj and Ms. Luna co-planned their instruction by identifying the concepts and foundation students would need to construct meaning and accomplish their lesson objective: "I can solve multi-step equations." The planning for this lesson specifically focused on rigorous instruction with high expectations aligned with state standards focused on language development with specific consideration of

DOI: 10.4324/9781003058311-10

the academic vocabulary words students would need to know and understand (e.g., distribute, combine, solve, multiply, add, subtract, variable, etc.) in conjunction with the mathematical skills (e.g., simplifying information, combining like terms, isolating the variable, etc.) necessary to solve the equation.

The lesson was differentiated to meet the needs of the various language levels and mathematic abilities of the students. For example, students at the entering level were provided models, visual representations, and bilingual videos of the problem-solving process to solve the multistep equation. Mrs. Renj focused on the math concepts specifically, "Students need to know how to solve multi-step equations, use the distributive property, and combine like terms. This needs to be the objective." Ms. Luna considered language within the content to support MLLs.

> If we want to help our MLLs learn and understand the math, we need to support their understanding of the academic language around the concepts. Many of these kids may not have learned this stuff before they came to us and the foundation of language is critical to their success. We also want them to feel success so they are willing to take risks and figure it out.

The discussion was rich with collaborative insight on building conceptual understanding through language development. They also discussed increasing student independence in the class by providing the needed scaffolding and gradually pulling the supports away as they acquired more language and mathematical skills.

Based on our observation, Mrs. Renj and Ms. Luna also discussed their roles throughout the lesson. Mrs. Renj was primarily responsible for opening the lesson and guiding the students through the math concepts while Ms. Luna highlighted the academic language and made the learning more accessible for the students. Both teachers anticipated facilitating learning throughout the activities and identified various means of formative assessment.

In this 40-minute class, students were solving multistep equations with Mrs. Renj and Ms. Luna. The class began with students completing a "Do Now" activity where they worked independently to solve a multistep equation. As students engaged in their work, they were encouraged to explain and show how to simplify both sides of the equation to a peer. Students worked together to co-construct their understanding of the distributive property and combining like terms to make meaning of the numbers to isolate the variable, in both English and Spanish. Throughout the activity and lesson, Mrs. Renj and Ms. Luna facilitated learning and encouraged students to expand their knowledge and understanding of the mathematical concepts needed to solve a multistep equation while co-constructing language. Although materials were differentiated and provided in both the home and target languages, students were encouraged to use the target language in their student-to-student interactions as much as possible.

Once students completed the activity and discussed their work with a partner, Mrs. Renj used an iPad to annotate the answers on the SmartBoard carefully emphasizing the problem-solving process. Using this technology intentionally gave Mrs. Renj the freedom to walk around the room and check for comprehension and application of knowledge. As she used specific terms, Ms. Luna pointed to the terms on the word wall and gave an explanation in both English and Spanish to help students make connections between the mathematical content and language with home language supports. In addition, Ms. Luna checked for understanding by using a teacher-created checklist for assessment purposes to ensure students were meeting specific milestones of the objective. The teachers used the initial activity to springboard into more challenging mathematical concepts. Periodically, students used "translanguaging" to help each other through the process of solving the math problems. For example, one student asked their team, "How do I combinar this? How do I make it distribuir?" Another student showed a different way to combine the information and distribute it as someone else explained it in their native Spanish. Through "translanguaging," students were successfully able to grasp the concepts and meet learning targets in the content through language development.

The teachers worked collaboratively in a welcoming and affirming environment throughout the class encouraging students to navigate their learning by using linguistic supports and scaffolded materials. Teachers took time to explain or revisit concepts and check for understanding. The pedagogy, curriculum, and assessment were inclusive and culturally responsive which helped make the algebra content accessible for the students in the class.

The co-teaching team encouraged the use of a home language in the classroom. They understood many of the students had limited exposure to the type of math they were learning due to the former education and curriculum in their country of birth. To encourage newcomers including SIFE, entering, and emerging students to participate in the class, the co-teachers used a ticket system. This gave the team an opportunity to encourage and evidence learning. Through this system, students could potentially gain enough tickets to earn up to five points on an upcoming exam.

Purpose of Research

This work aims to deliberately reconnect communities by bringing policy makers, institutes of higher education, teachers, and school leaders together through collaboration, in education problem solving to meet the needs of all students in secondary mathematics classrooms. More specifically, this chapter explores how a co-teaching team collaborates to support "innovative linguistic, literate, and cultural practices" (Paris & Alim, 2014, p. 86) in integrated mathematics and language instruction to offer MLLs opportunities to develop conceptual or grade-appropriate mathematics content and core standards.

The broad-based objective of this chapter is to ascertain how one co-teaching team supported MLLs in secondary mathematics in mastering core content while also developing language proficiency and acquiring disciplinary literacy skills in English through the Culturally Responsive-Sustaining (CR-S) Framework (NYSED, 2019). A more narrowly defined objective is to deconstruct the core understandings and actions of the collaborative team as they co-construct their role as co-teachers of academic language and disciplinary literacy within a collaborative service delivery model.

Theoretical Perspectives

Culturally Responsive-Sustaining Framework

The theoretical framework that has guided our study has recently emerged from a combination of multiple theories. The CR-S framework is based upon decades of research related to culturally responsive and sustaining pedagogy. It has evolved to both challenge and build upon culturally sensitive and culturally relevant pedagogies, both of which had previously critiqued the Euro-centric or color-evasive approaches to curriculum and instruction (Annamma Jackson & Morrison, 2016; Foldy & Buckley, 2014; Gay, 2002; Ladson-Billings, 1995, 2006; Paris & Alim, 2017).

Many researchers (Au & Kawakami, 1994; Erickson, 1987; Gay, 2000, 2002; Ladson-Billings, 1990; Sealey-Ruiz, 2011) have concluded that all educators need to develop cultural competencies to work with diverse student populations with the goal of maximizing the students' learning experiences and providing them with an equitable education. Culturally sustaining pedagogy, first introduced by Paris (2012), offered a new theoretical lens that invites researchers and practitioners to foster linguistic and cultural pluralism. Paris not only carefully reviewed and critiqued decades of research on culturally responsive (Ladson-Billings, 1995, 2014) or proficient pedagogy, but he also argued that they fall short on fully engaging the MLL population. Instead, he proposes culturally sustaining pedagogy defined as "supporting multilingualism and multiculturalism in practice and perspective for students and teachers. That is, culturally sustaining pedagogy seeks to perpetuate and foster—to sustain—linguistic, literate, and cultural pluralism as part of the democratic project of schooling" (Paris, 2012, p. 93). Paris and Alim (2017) went further and translated this research into a comprehensive set of practical applications for the K-12 school and classroom context.

CR-S education (NYSED, 2019) is identified through the cultural lens of human development and learning in which diversity of ability, race, social class, language, gender, sexual orientation, nationality, religion, etc., are accepted and seen as resources for teaching and learning. NYSED (2019) developed the CR-S framework in response to the needs of stakeholder communities to support student success through effective and equitable education that identifies student differences as strengths, not deficits. The conceptual understanding within the CR-S framework is based on the ability of stakeholders to co-construct:

> student-centered learning environments that affirm cultural identities; foster positive academic outcomes; develop students' abilities to connect across lines of difference; elevate historically marginalized voices; empower students as agents of social change; and contribute to individual student engagement, learning, growth, and achievement through the cultivation of critical thinking.
>
> (NYSED, 2019, p. 7)

This framework is grounded in four core principles. The first principle, a welcoming and affirming environment, is one that students are respected and feel safe, represented, and reflected. The second focus is high expectations and rigorous instruction to challenge students to grow and take risks while embracing their style of learning to encourage them to succeed. The third is an inclusive curriculum and assessment which empowers learners to be agents of change and open to other ideas and perspectives in an effort to dismantle dominant inequities. The fourth and final principle is ongoing professional learning, constantly evolving to allow learners to self-direct their outcomes through conscious self-reflection. This study focuses on all four principles to examine how the participant teachers include these components in their co-teaching for multilingual learners to have a clearer understanding of the cultural implications of teaching and how self-reflective practices impact learning for diverse populations. The CR-S framework (NYSED, 2019) is well-suited to serve as a theoretical framework for this study because the four principles are aligned to the collaborative, integrated model of instruction, which we are investigating in high school mathematics classes.

Research on Integrated Collaborative Approaches

The review of recent literature on integrated, collaborative approaches returned limited number of empirical studies. Much has been published about effective strategies general-education teachers can use to offer more culturally and linguistically responsive instruction for MLLs (Calderón & Slakk, 2018; Ferlazzo & Sypnieski, 2018; Gibbons, 2015; Singer, 2018; Staehr Fenner & Snyder, 2017). Similarly, the knowledge base on inclusive practices for students with disabilities as well as for MLLs has been expanding (Beninghof, 2020; Friend & Cook, 2012; Honigsfeld & Dove, 2010, 2012, 2014, 2019; Murawski & Lochner, 2017; Peery, 2019; Villa, Thousand, & Nevin, 2013). A considerable body of literature explores how MLLs may be best supported to acquire academic language skills; the findings consistently point to supporting language development within the context of the core disciplines. For example, Bailey (2007) defined being academically proficient as: "knowing and being able to use general and academic vocabulary, specialized or complex grammatical structures, and multifarious language functions and discourse structures—all for the purpose of acquiring new knowledge and skills, interacting about a topic, imparting information to others" (pp. 10–11), a competence that is necessary for successful academic practice and participation.

However, emerging research indicates that a substantial shift has occurred in English language development (ELD) instructional and assessment practices in recent years. Developing academic language, general content area literacy skills, as well as disciplinary literacy skills are recognized as critical for MLLs to successfully participate in academic tasks (Gottlieb & Ernst-Slavit, 2014; Zacarian, 2013; Zwiers, 2014). It is increasingly accepted that all teachers share the responsibility for engaging students in academic language practices and for building oral and written language skills closely tied to rigorous English language arts (ELA) and content standards. As Gottlieb and Ernst-Slavit (2014) noted, teaching academic discourse is particularly important for "those students for whom English is a second, third, or fourth language and for students from underrepresented backgrounds who may not be surrounded by the types of thought and academic registers valued in schools" (p. 25).

Therefore, it is essential for teachers to understand that cultural practices can impact students' readiness to learn as well as how they are accustomed to learning. For this reason, researchers at WIDA (2014) also recognized, "Given the diversity of students and teachers, no isolated theory or approach is adequate to guide the learning and teaching of all language learners" (p. 6). Purposeful teacher collaboration for the sake of MLLs holds a special promise for many reasons, including the following:

- Curriculum continuity with clear goals and objectives
- Instructional consistency that support content and language development
- Reduction in fragmented, disjointed learning experiences for students
- Less student isolation and more integration into the school community (Cohan, Honigsfeld, & Dove, 2019).

More research is needed to examine the specific attributes of integrated, collaborative approaches to serving MLLs across the core content areas. Our study is designed to fill that gap.

Integrated Language, Disciplinary Literacy, and Mathematics Instruction for MLLs

While many believe that math is a universal language (Parker Waller & Flood, 2016), both K-12 educators and researchers agree that the language of mathematics presents both unique challenges and opportunities for MLLs (see for example, Carr et al., 2009; Leith, Rose, & King, 2016; Moschkovich, 2010). In a recent comprehensive review of the literature on how MLLs fare in K-12 mathematics education, de Araujo et al. (2018) took a sociocultural perspective to highlight what discourse practices students and their teachers use to advance mathematical understanding. This theoretical stance builds on what Schleppegrell (2007) also acknowledged when stating that "each subject area has its own ways of using language to construct knowledge, and students need to be able to use language effectively to participate in those ways of knowing" (p. 140).

More specifically, Celedón-Pattichis and Ramirez (2012) identified three core principles for supporting MLLs simultaneously in their language development and mathematical content attainment. These instructional principles (engaging students in challenging mathematical tasks, developing their academic language, and encouraging multiple modes of expression and communication) parallel the dimensions of instruction recommended by National Council of Teachers of Mathematics (NCTM) (2013):

- Establish learning environments and classroom norms that support the active engagement of all students, including MLLs […]
- Identify and use instructional strategies that make content more accessible […] and consider how to implement culturally relevant pedagogy in mathematics classrooms […].
- Orchestrate classroom discussions in ways that support acquisition of mathematics concepts and language development […]
- Assess MLLs in ways that permit them to show what they know and are able to do (para 3).

One significant conclusion de Araujo et al. (2018) drew has major implications for the need for this study. They found that "teachers are located squarely at the complex intersection of language education (although often not certified or prepared for it) and mathematics curriculum and instruction" (p. 904). As such, teacher collaboration may uniquely contribute to successful integration of content and language learning in the secondary classroom.

In the past 10 years, research on collaboration and co-teaching for MLLs has expanded. Early research documented the challenges of developing effective collaborative relationships and co-teaching practices (Davison, 2006; DelliCarpini, 2008, 2009; Hurst & Davison, 2005). Documentary accounts of successful collaborative and co-teaching practices have also surfaced (Kaufman & Crandall, 2005). More recent, emerging research has documented that ELD/ESOL specialists and their general-education co-teachers continue to struggle with establishing an equitable partnership (Fogle & Moser, 2017) or with defining their roles when it comes to content and language integration (Martin-Beltrán & Madigan Peercy, 2012; Peercy & Martin-Beltrán, 2011).

Methods

Study Context

We conducted this study in 2019 at a high school located in a suburban area of New York. The MLLs represented in this study were placed in grades 9–11 depending on their age and school records, not ability levels. Redwood (pseudonym) was a large school with more than 1,600 students enrolled. The majority of the population was 43% Hispanic or Latino followed by approximately 21% Black, 17% White, 5% Asian or Pacific Islander, 1% Multiracial, and 3% other. MLLs made up 9% of the population, students with disabilities made up 15%, and 54% of the students were economically disadvantaged.

Participant Teachers

Mrs. Renj was part of a mathematics core professional development initiative within Redwood. As part of this team, teachers participated in the sheltered instruction observation protocol (SIOP) training and classroom coaching for a year with the first author, Carrie McDermott. This training was followed up by suggestions for co-teaching and collaboration for MLLs in the mathematics classroom. Students were struggling and teachers did not feel equipped to best meet their needs to help them succeed. The following year, the district invested in hiring several ESOL-certified teachers to meet the growing population of MLLs to support their needs in the content-area classes. The researchers were invited in the following year, 2019 to conduct visits and observe the first-year co-teaching team. No coaching took place during this time.

Mrs. Renj was a full-time, tenured teacher who was an educator for over 15 years and has taught MLLs, special education, and general education students in inclusive and integrated settings. Her courses included algebra one, two, and mathematical skills. Mrs. Renj was certified in mathematics from grades 7 to 12. Mrs. Renj was new to co-teaching.

Ms. Luna was a full-time, untenured, first year teacher. She was certified in ESOL from grades Pk to 12. She worked in five secondary co-teaching classrooms with concentrations in mathematics and ELA. Her partnerships included teachers that never co-taught and others that had for at least 3 years.

Data Collection and Sources

This study is part of a larger scale investigation of integrated collaborative practices to support MLLs in core content areas. Qualitative research methods were used to collect data through site visits, classroom observations, digitally recorded audio and video interviews with teachers, and text-based artifact collection that included lesson plans, teacher-created instructional materials, and student work samples. For the purposes of this chapter, we will only focus on one co-teaching team, Mrs. Renj and Ms. Luna. To fully capture the participating teachers' understanding of the CR-S framework (NYSED, 2019), the researchers developed an interview protocol. This tool incorporated the key features highlighted in the CR-S framework (NYSED, 2019), and expanded on it by asking teachers to reflect on specific examples of how they design their instruction and encourage MLLs' language and content attainment by "supporting multilingualism and multiculturalism" (Paris & Alim, 2014, p. 88) and how they ensure a continuing presence in students' collection of practices (Gutiérrez & Ragoff, 2003) by providing access to the academic language that constructs mathematical knowledge.

The researchers conducted four class visits throughout the 2018–2019 academic year and two interviews with Mrs. Renj and Ms. Luna, individually. In addition, each co-teacher individually completed the self-assessment tool, midway through the year with the pedagogical intent of deepening their own understanding of the CR-S framework (NYSED, 2019) through self-reflection. The researchers selected specific lesson segments from the class visits to illustrate how elements of CR-S support concept development and attainment through language-based instructional activities. Relevant excerpts from the interviews and the responses to the self-assessment tool were also woven into this case study to reveal the participating co-teaching team's metacognitive processes behind their instruction.

Data Analysis

Data were analyzed both preliminarily and at the culmination of the research. The different data sets were organized and coded in categories closely related to the research questions. Once complete, the individual data sets were merged. As Weber (1990) and Stemler (2001) suggested, revisions were made to the coding as necessary, and the major categories were refined to "maximize exclusivity" (Stemler, para 13). In addition, codes identified patterns of support in mastering core content, developing language proficiency, and acquiring disciplinary literacy skills in addition to the co-construction of the roles and responsibilities of collaboration in the integrated setting.

Major Findings

This case study ascertained how one co-teaching team supported MLLs in mastering mathematic content while developing language proficiency and disciplinary literacy skills in English. Three key themes emerged from this research which are directly aligned to the research objectives: (1) collaboration for a welcoming environment; (2) collaboration for rigorous instruction; and (3) collaboration for inclusive curriculum and assessment. A fourth, more subtle theme also emerged: (4) collaboration for ongoing professional learning.

Collaboration for Welcoming Environment

Students were exposed to a variety of learning opportunities where they intentionally participated in content focused lessons how they felt most comfortable. As Mrs. Renj mentioned, "students are given many different opportunities to participate in class and respond in their native language if they want." This was highlighted by Ms. Luna who stated, "We do a lot of group work. The MLLs talk to each other in their native language and build on it. They ask questions without being on the spot where everyone is going to turn and look at them." The co-teaching team also emphasized the importance of building relationships with the students and how they connect to get to know them better. Ms. Luna said, "I like to talk to the kids, I like to hear from them about their culture and know where they came from and why they came here." Mrs. Renj mentioned, "Some of them suggest what Netflix documentaries I should watch to learn about their country and things like that, so I get firsthand knowledge." The team found honoring students learning in a safe environment was pivotal to success.

Ms. Luna and Mrs. Renj also found they set a strong example of building relationships throughout the year as they "kind of fall into their roles" throughout the lesson. Mrs. Renj revealed, "My co-teacher will get them started and keep them on track and I will kind of deliver more of the math content of the lesson." Ms. Luna further elaborated by stating, "We've also established a relationship where we are able to bounce ideas off each other. We have no problem. If she interrupts to rephrase something or uses a teachable moment, we'll build off of it." They both explained the balance of co-teaching responsibilities and how "[they] hold each other accountable." Overall, the team emphasized how they work together and have an equal, 50/50 relationship in addition to their responsibilities in meeting the needs of MLLs going well beyond the classroom.

Collaboration for Rigorous Instruction

Embracing opportunities to challenge students through rigorous learning and encouraging students to take risks and grow was the second area of concentration for the co-teaching team. Mrs. Renj and Ms. Luna felt it was important to understand the students and build upon their assets throughout the instructional process. Mrs. Renj included, "I try to identify the gap...students who are more likely to solve the problem and be done or [others who] want to discuss it rather than one of us solving the problem." Ms. Luna stated,

> we have to modify and adapt to fit the needs of the group...I feel like it's always an evolution with us and our planning in our teaching and the rigor because the kids change often, sometimes from one week to the next.

Overall, Ms. Luna and Mrs. Renj expressed the need to challenge students and understand the process of learning both language and math simultaneously. They believed in creating building blocks to help students make meaning as they learn mathematics in a new language and then strengthening their understanding through application of these concepts.

Collaboration for Inclusive Curriculum and Assessment

Mathematics is not a universal language or content and Mrs. Renj found she needed to have a better understanding of what the students knew and how they accessed math in their prior experiences. In many cases, she felt students were not properly placed in the most suitable courses because students may have had different experiences and exposure to the concepts they were learning. She struggled with the density of the curriculum and how to teach through student assets instead of deficits. To work through this, Mrs. Renj mentioned, "we had all these issues with misplacing them." To remedy the situation, Mrs. Renj stated,

> I came up with my own entry exam that [the MLLs] take whether they are in middle school coming up to the high school or as a new entrant. At least we know where they are so that as soon as I get that test, I contact guidance and I let them know where they should be placed.

Ms. Luna chimed in about the importance of properly placing students to prevent them from "sitting and wasting a year." Once the teachers were comfortable with where the students were placed, they worked together to help them build on their mathematical knowledge and assets by "reinforcing and getting them stronger" in the areas they needed to know and building their knowledge in other areas. Mrs. Renj mentioned, "We create [our] own materials which makes it much easier to target the learning and hone in on the necessary elements the students need to understand." To elaborate this point, Ms. Luna stated "I have to teach them to look for the most important things...names are always going to look funny or weird and that's not the focus." The teachers concentrated on the process by telling students to "focus on the numbers, underline, highlight all the key words" to help them make sense of what they were learning while building connections to their prior knowledge.

Students were given opportunities to discuss how they solved a similar problem or what steps they learned to take previously, if they had already learned a similar concept in their earlier educational experiences. The teachers also gave ample opportunities for students to use their native language to make meaning. In the observations, students occasionally "translanguaged" throughout the lesson and focused on learning the concepts and bridging their knowledge. As we discussed earlier in this chapter, in the observed lesson, the students understood the words distribute and combine to be cognates in their own language (distribuir and combinar) and they used this to make meaning of the "Do Now" activity. They were able to engage in mathematical discourse which revealed that they understood the concepts as they explained it to their partner.

In addition to the learning, assessment was a key practice in the classrooms. The co-teachers utilized informal assessments to identify growth: "We try to informally assess as much as we can, especially because we have so many new students coming in at so many different times" (Mrs. Renj). In the observed class, Ms. Luna explained, "We do a lot of Kahoot! and online quizzes to make it more fun and engaging for the students." An inclusive curriculum and assessment process were important to the team. Throughout the planning process, Ms. Luna and Mrs. Renj created checklists and rubrics to ensure students were meeting the intended goals and worked cohesively to create an inclusive curriculum and assessment process in their class. The case study also highlighted individual student engagement with content and language development, student-to-student interaction, and student-centered learning environments.

Collaboration for Ongoing Professional Learning

A fourth and more subtle theme also emerged from this research. This theme addressed the opportunities for the co-teaching team to engage in professional learning. New York State teachers are required to maintain a certain amount of professional development hours and some of these hours are required to be dedicated toward MLL instruction. Teachers certified in ESOL and/or bilingual education are required to have 50% of their professional development hours targeted toward MLL instruction and those not certified in these areas are required to have 20%. Professional learning opportunities were offered through the district and outside entities. Although the teachers were permitted to select some of their professional workshops, they found it difficult to attend workshops at the same time unless required by the district. The teachers did find time outside the school day to share their learning and collaborate on new strategies and using more technology with their students. For successful teacher collaboration among math teachers or with their ESOL colleagues to take place, teachers need structured opportunities to engage in instructional and non-instructional professional activities.

Discussion

This case study provides evidence of how integrated collaborative instruction in mathematics supports integrated language and disciplinary literacy focused on equitable educational opportunities for MLLs. The research evidenced how mathematics co-teaching teams collaborate to better understand the needs of students and provide opportunities to develop conceptual understanding of core content through language.

Possibilities of Co-Teaching

We as researchers observed that Mrs. Renj and Ms. Luna co-constructed their roles as co-teachers of academic language and disciplinary literacy within a collaborative service delivery model. Prior to the lesson, Mrs. Renj and Ms. Luna co-planned and co-developed multileveled, differentiated instructional materials. During the lesson, Mrs. Renj focused on solving multistep equations using the distributive property to combine like terms in the lesson. Simultaneously, Ms. Luna helped students with academic language and breaking down the equations into more manageable parts. During the lesson, students were given ample opportunities to participate in class in English or their home language. This provided a welcoming and safe environment for the students. After the lesson, Ms. Luna and Mrs. Renj assessed students to identify learning outcomes to inform their instruction for the following day. Both teachers focused on maintaining rigor and challenging students to be their best.

The practices Ms. Luna and Mrs. Renj implemented throughout the observations are an important example of how collaboration in a co-taught math class offers possibilities to support MLLs in integrated language and disciplinary literacy. Professional learning opportunities further strengthened the team's collaborative efforts and supported their roles. This team focused on the five essential practices recommended for co-teaching: collaborative planning, co-developing instructional materials, co-teaching, collaborative assessment of student work, and joint professional learning (Honigsfeld & Dove, 2010, 2014, 2019) as shown in Table 8.1. To further explore the goals of these five practices and their applications in integrated math classes, an additional column has been added with considerations for collaborative teacher application.

Table 8.1 Collaborative Practices and Their Implications for Teacher Collaboration and Co-teaching in the Mathematics Classroom

Collaborative Practices Aligned to Instruction	Goals	Teacher Collaboration and Co-Teaching in the Mathematics Classroom
Collaborative planning	• To establish attainable yet rigorous learning targets • To share instructional routines and strategies • To align instructional content • To design appropriate formative and summative assessment measures	Teachers prepare daily lesson plans and unit plans reflective of the following: • language and content objectives • knowledge of diverse MLLs' needs • strategically selected instructional accommodations and accelerations • differentiated instruction according to students' academic and linguistic abilities
Co-developing instructional materials	• To scaffold instructional materials • To select essential materials that support accelerated learning	• Teachers develop differentiated, tiered, multilevel instructional resources as well as divide complex materials or tasks into manageable segments while also selecting essential learning tools.
Co-teaching	• To co-deliver instruction through differentiated instruction • To use various models of instruction to establish equity between co-teaching partners	• Teachers establish co-equal partnerships with other teachers and share ownership of teaching MLLs. • Teachers engage in the entire collaborative instructional cycle with colleagues.
Collaborative assessment of student work	• To jointly examine MLLs' language and academic performance • To analyze student data and identify areas that need improvement or targeted intervention	• Teachers develop, administer, and evaluate the outcomes of formative and summative assessment measures • Teachers set goals for MLLs and use assessment data collaboratively

| Joint professional learning | • To enhance pedagogical knowledge, skills, and dispositions about MLLs
• To established a shared understanding about MLLs' needs, best practices, and effective strategies
• To explore new and emerging directions in ELD/ESL education | Teachers utilize sustained opportunities and commitment to engage in
• Learning with colleagues
• Applying their new learning to teaching
• Reflecting on their new learning
• Showcasing their practices |

Source: Adapted from Honigsfeld and Dove (2019).

Challenges of Co-Teaching

The findings of this research suggest student exposure to mathematical concepts and technical language varied by individual experience. Additionally, the classroom population was often changing, sometimes from one week to the next. Throughout the observations, it was evidenced that Mrs. Renj struggled with differentiating the content to meet the various linguistic needs and educational backgrounds of the students. She further believed students needed to learn all aspects of algebra and was not necessarily comfortable with how to build prior skill sets and maintain the integrity and timing of the curriculum especially for the end of year Regents assessment (a state graduation requirement). She found it beneficial to collaborate with Ms. Luna to better understand how to make the content more accessible through language to help students feel individual successes along the way.

Although Mrs. Renj had worked with MLLs previously and had been trained how to meet their needs, having the collaboration on a daily basis brought about new challenges to the content she had been teaching for over 15 years. Ms. Luna was not certified in math and initially, both teachers had some reservations about their ability to make this collaboration work and more opportunities for joint professional learning may have helped alleviate any doubts. As first year co-teachers, the team needed to embrace collaboration and trust.

Throughout this case study, it was evidenced that teachers recognized multiple opportunities for their own ongoing professional learning; however, it was unclear how this professional development pertained to utilizing students' cultural and linguistic assets to maintain high levels of rigor and challenge for MLLs in integrated math courses. Many of the professional learning opportunities were not available to both teachers on the team due to budget and time constraints. Mrs. Renj and Ms. Luna wanted to direct their learning and were exposed to a variety of professional development opportunities throughout the year; however, they were often only permitted to attend one or two of them. They found it was better to attend a different professional development event and share the content with each other to maximize their time and learning.

Implications and Conclusion

As the population of students across the United States becomes more diversified, thinking about and acting on issues of equity for learning, considering both the conditions and outcomes, are our collective and individual responsibility (Gutstein et al., 2005). The dialogue and orientations of language in and around mathematics perpetuates positive and negative assumptions and labels of children and communities, the important knowledge, innovative practices, and culture students bring to mathematics should be recognized and embraced, not perpetuated by conforming to dominant practices, policies, and expectations (Aguirre et al., 2017). Cultural competence must expand content-based curriculum to embrace diversity multicultural knowledge and perspectives (McDermott, 2020) and could be further investigated to help researchers better understand how curriculum embraces this in co-taught high school math classes.

How do we ascertain equity for all students in mathematics education? This research evidenced one co-teaching team's effective collaborative practices to support MLL's core content attainment and language and disciplinary literacy development in a welcoming environment. Mrs. Renj and Ms. Luna used an asset-based approach for rigorous instruction, inclusive curriculum, and assessment. Additionally, the team utilized professional learning opportunities to further their collaborative practices to best meet the needs of their students. This case study offers a strong model for those seeking to co-teach in an integrated math classroom and offers opportunities for further research to investigate the implications of cultural competence on content instruction and the impacts on learning for MLLs. Additional research is also needed to help identify the types of professional learning opportunities available to help teachers utilize students' cultural and linguistic knowledge to maintain high levels of rigor and challenge for MLLs in content courses.

References

Aguirre, J., Herbel-Eisenmann, B., Celedón-Pattichis, S., Civil, M., Wilkerson, T., Stephan, M., Pape, S., & Clements, D. H. (2017). Equity within mathematics education research as a political act: Moving from choice to intentional collective professional responsibility. *Journal for Research in Mathematics Education*, 48(2), 124–147. https://doi.org/10.5951/jresematheduc.48.2.0124
Annamma, S. A., Jackson, D. D., & Morrison, D. (2016). Conceptualizing color-evasiveness: using dis/ability critical race theory to expand a color-blind racial

ideology in education and society. *Race, Ethnicity, and Education, 20*(2), 147–162. https://doi.org/10.1080/13613324.2016.1248837

Au, K., & Kawakami, A. (1994). Cultural congruence in instruction. In E. Hollins, J. King & W. Hayman (Eds.). *Teaching diverse populations: Formulating knowledge base* (pp. 5–23). Albany, NY: State University of New York Press.

Bailey, A. L. (Ed.). (2007). *The language demands of school: Putting academic English to the test.* New Haven, CT: Yale University Press.

Beninghof, A. M. (2020). *Co-teaching that works: Structures and strategies for maximizing student learning* (2nd ed.). San Francisco, CA: Jossey-Bass.

Calderón, M. E., & Slakk, S. (2018). *Teaching reading to English learners, grades 6–12: A framework for improving achievement in the content areas* (2nd ed.). Thousand Oaks, CA: Corwin.

Carr, J., Carroll, C., Cremer, S., Gale, M., Lagunoff, R., & Sexton, U. (2009). *Making mathematics accessible to English learners, Grades 6–12: A guidebook for teachers.* San Francisco, CA: Wested.

Celedón-Pattichis, S., & Ramirez, N. G. (Eds.). (2012). *Beyond good teaching: Advancing mathematics education for ELLs.* Reston, VA: National Council of Teachers of Mathematics.

Cohan, A., Honigsfeld, A., & Dove, M. G. (2019). *Team up, speak up, fire up! Teamwork to empower English learners.* Alexandria, VA: ASCD.

Davison, C. (2006). Collaboration between ESL and content area teachers: How do we know when we are doing it right? *The International Journal of Bilingual Education and Bilingualism, 9*(4), 454–475.

de Araujo, Z., Roberts, S. A., Wiley, C., & Zahner, W. (2018). English learners in K–12 mathematics education: A review of the literature. *Review of Educational Research, 88*(6), 879–919. https://doi.org/10.3102/0034654318798093

DelliCarpini, M. (2008). Teacher collaboration for ESL/EFL academic success. *The Internet TESL Journal, 14*(8). Retrieved from http://iteslj.org/Techniques/DelliCarpini-TeacherCollaboration.html

Erickson, F. (1987). Transformation and school success: The politics and culture of educational achievement. *Anthropology & Educational Quarterly, 18*, 335–356.

Ferlazzo, L., & Sypnieski, K. H. (2018). *The ELL teacher's toolbox: Hundreds of practical ideas to support your students.* San Francisco, CA: Jossey-Bass.

Fogle, L. W., & Moser, K. (2017). Language teacher identities in the Southern United States: Transforming rural schools. *Journal of Language, Identity & Education, 16*(2), 65–79. https://doi.org/10.1080/15348458.2016.1277147

Foldy, E., & Buckley, T. (2014). *The color bind: Talking (and not talking) about race at work.* Russell Sage Foundation. Retrieved from http://www.jstor.org/stable/10.7758/9781610448215.10

Friend, M., & Cook, L. (2012). *Interactions: Collaboration skills for school professionals* (7th ed.). Boston, MA: Allyn & Bacon.

Gay, G. (2000). *Culturally responsive teaching: Theory, research, and practice.* New York, NY: Teachers College Press.

Gay, G. (2002). Preparing for culturally responsive teaching. *Journal of Teacher Education, 53*, 106–116.

Gibbons, P. (2015). *Scaffolding language scaffolding learning: Teaching English language learners in the mainstream classroom* (2nd ed.). Portsmouth, NH: Heinemann.

Gottlieb, M., & Ernst-Slavit, G. (2014). *Academic language for diverse class-rooms: Definitions and contexts.* Thousand Oaks, CA: Corwin.

Gutiérrez, K., & Ragoff, B. (2003). Cultural ways of learning. *Education Researcher, 35*(5), 19–25.

Gutstein, E., Fey, J., Heid, M., DeLoach-Johnson, I., Middleton, J., Larson, M., Dougherty, B., & Tunis, H. (2005). Equity in School Mathematics Education: How Can Research Contribute? *Journal for Research in Mathematics Education, 36*(2), 92–100. Retrieved from http://www.jstor.org/stable/30034826

Honigsfeld, A., & Dove, M. G. (2010). *Collaboration and co-teaching: Strategies for English learners.* Thousand Oaks, CA: Corwin.

Honigsfeld, A., & Dove, M. G. (Eds.) (2012). *Co-teaching and other collaborative practices in the EFL/ESL classroom: Rationale, research, reflections, and recommendations.* Charlotte, NC: Information Age Publishing.

Honigsfeld, A., & Dove, M. G. (2014). *Collaboration and co-teaching for English learners: A leader's guide.* Thousand Oaks, CA: Corwin.

Honigsfeld, A., & Dove, M. G. (2019). *Collaborating for English learners: A foundational guide to integrated practices.* Thousand Oaks, CA: Corwin.

Hurst, D., & Davison, C. (2005). Collaboration on the curriculum: Focus on secondary ESL. In J. Crandall & D. Kaufman (Eds.), *Case studies in TESOL: Teacher education for language and content integration.* (pp. 41–66). Alexandria, VA: Teachers of English to Speakers of Other Languages.

Kaufman, D., & Crandall, J. A. (Eds.). (2005). *Content-based instruction in elementary and secondary school settings.* Alexandria, VA: TESOL.

Ladson-Billings, G. (1990). Culturally relevant teaching: Effective instruction for black students. *The College Board Review, 7*(15), 20–25.

Ladson-Billings, G. (1995). Toward a theory of culturally relevant pedagogy. *Journal of Educational Research, 32,* 465–491.

Ladson-Billings, G. (2006). "Yes, but how do we do it?" Practicing culturally responsive pedagogy. In J. Landsman & C. Lewis (Eds.), *White teachers/diverse classrooms: A guide to building inclusive schools, promoting high expectations, and eliminating racism* (pp. 33–46). Sterling, VA: Stylus.

Ladson-Billings, G. (2014). Culturally relevant pedagogy 2.0: a.k.a. the remix. *Harvard Educational Review, 84,* 74–84.

Leith, C., Rose, E., & King, T. (May 2016) Teaching mathematics and language to English learners. *The Mathematics Teacher, 109*(9), 670–678.

Martin-Beltrán, M., & Madigan Peercy, M. (2012). How can ESOL and mainstream teachers make the best of standards-based curriculum in order to collaborate? *TESOL Journal, 3,* 425–444. https://doi.org/10.1002/tesj.23

McDermott, C. (2020). Culturally responsive teaching in secondary, integrated mathematics class. *Impact on Instructional Improvement: Cultural responsiveness, 45*(1), 40–47.

Moschkovich, J. N. (2010). *Language and mathematics education: Multiple perspectives and directions for research.* Charlotte, NC: Information Age Publishing.

Murawski, W. W., & Lochner, W. W. (2017). *Beyond co-teaching basics: A data-driven, no-fail model for continuous improvement.* Alexandria, VA: ASCD.

NCTM (2013). *Teaching mathematics to English language learners: A position of the National Council of Teachers of Mathematics.* Retrieved from https://www.nctm.org/Standards-and-Positions/Position-Statements/Teaching-Mathematics-to-English-Language-Learners/

New York State School Report Card Data (2018–2019). Retrieved from https://data.nysed.gov/essa.php?year=2019&state=yes

NYSED. (2019). *Culturally Responsive-Sustaining Education Framework.* Retrieved from http://www.nysed.gov/crs/framework

Paris, D. (2012). Culturally sustaining pedagogy: A needed change in stance, terminology, and practice. *Educational Researcher, 41*(3), 93–97.

Paris, D., & Alim, H. S. (2014). What are we seeking to sustain through culturally sustaining pedagogy? A loving critique forward. *Harvard Educational Review, 84*(1), 85–100. https://doi.org/10.17763/haer.84.1.982l873k2ht16m77

Paris, D., & Alim, H. S. (2017). *Culturally sustaining pedagogies: Teaching and learning for justice in a changing world.* New York, NY: Teacher's College Press.

Parker Waller, P., & Flood, C. T. (2016). Mathematics as a universal language: Transcending cultural lines. *Journal for Multicultural Education, 10*(3), 294–306. https://doi.org/10.1108/JME-01-2016-0004

Peercy, M. M., & Martin-Beltrán, M. (2011). Envisioning collaboration: Including ESOL students and teachers in the mainstream classroom. *International Journal of Inclusive Education, 16*, 657–673. https://doi.org/10.1080/13603116.2010.495791

Peery, A. (2019). *The co-teacher's playbook: What it takes to make co-teaching work for everyone.* Thousand Oaks, CA: Corwin.

Schleppegrell, M. J. (2007). The linguistic challenges of mathematics teaching and learning: A research review. *Reading & Writing Quarterly, 23*, 139–159. https://doi.org/10.1080/10573560601158461

Sealey-Ruiz, Y. (2011). Learning to talk and write about race: Developing racial literacy in a college English classroom. *English Quarterly: The Canadian Council of Teachers of English Language Arts, 42*(1), 24–42.

Singer, T. W. (2018). *EL excellence every day: The flip-to guide for differentiating academic literacy.* Thousand Oaks, CA: Corwin.

Staehr Fenner, D., & Snyder, S. (2017). *Unlocking English learners' potential: Strategies for making content accessible.* Thousand Oaks, CA: Corwin.

Stemler, S. (2001). An overview of content analysis. *Practical Assessment, Research & Evaluation, 7*(17). Retrieved from http://PAREonline.net/getvn.asp?v=7&n=17

Villa, R., Thousand, J., & Nevin, A. (2013). *A guide to co-teaching: New lessons and strategies to facilitate student learning* (3rd ed.). Thousand Oaks, CA: Corwin.

Weber, R. P. (1990). *Basic content analysis* (2nd ed.). Newbury Park, CA: Sage.

WIDA. (2014). *WIDA standards: Framework and its theoretical foundations.* Retrieved from https://wida.wisc.edu/sites/default/files/resource/WIDA-Standards-Framework-and-its-Theoretical-Foundations.pdf

Zacarian, D. (2013). *Mastering academic language: A framework for supporting student achievement.* Thousand Oaks, CA: Corwin.

Zwiers, J. (2014). *Building academic language: Meeting Common Core Standards across disciplines, Grades 5–12* (2nd ed.). San Francisco: Jossey-Bass.

9 Collaboration for Culturally Relevant Pedagogy

An Extended Project Involving Content and ESL Teachers

Yvonne Pratt-Johnson

> Before this trip I didn't have any real training on how to begin or even think it necessary to relate culture to teaching science lessons. Through the experiences these 6 weeks I have [obtained] a completely different perspective. The workshop we had on culturally relevant teaching and also planning lessons together with [the ESL teacher] made me see that teaching ELLs is also my responsibility. Not only do I see the value in culturally relevant teaching, but I have ideas [on] how to include it in my lesson plans.
>
> – Teacher Participant

Knowledge of the backgrounds and experiences that English language learners (ELLs) bring to the classroom provides teachers and other school staff members with an advantage in their efforts to provide effective instruction to ELLs and to help them overcome the academic and linguistic challenges that they face. At its core, this assertion expresses a principle that is perhaps as old as pedagogy: that it is important for teachers to acquire and leverage *knowledge of the learner* (Powell & Kusuma-Powell, 2011; Rahman, Scaife, Yahya, & Jalil, 2010).

In today's multicultural world, however, this traditional best practice has taken on new meaning and new complexities. Some of the ELLs in our classrooms, for example, may be refugees or other new arrivals, and these students are particularly at risk from a variety of complex stressors that directly and indirectly impact their ability to thrive in school (Pratt-Johnson, 2015; Roxas, 2011; Suarez-Orozco, 2000). Indeed, even when their baseline physical and psychological needs are met, students with diverse heritage languages and cultures need to feel accepted and involved in the classroom and in the community in order to succeed in school and in life (Elizalde-Utnick, 2010; Roxas, 2011; Short & Boyson 2012; Sobel & Kugler, 2007). One way in which teachers can foster connectedness for diverse students is by practicing culturally relevant (or culturally responsive) pedagogy (CRP) (Ladson-Billings, 1994). In CRP, educators use the backgrounds, knowledge, and experiences of their students to inform their lesson content and methodology,

DOI: 10.4324/9781003058311-11

and this enables them to build bridges between students' home and school lives (Banks & McGee-Banks, 2016; Brown-Jeffry & Cooper, 2011; Catto, 2018; Edwards & Edick, 2013; Ladson-Billings, 2014; Rajagopal, 2011).

Practicing CRP does not detract from teachers' or schools' ability to meet district and state curricular benchmarks and performance standards. By contrast, failure to make our teaching culturally relevant shortchanges our students with respect to meaningful connections between a) the curricular content and the school experience and b) the students' daily lives and cultural backgrounds.

But how are teachers to acquire the knowledge and skills necessary to practice CRP effectively? One answer is to provide teachers with hands-on opportunities to explore and learn about their students' heritage cultures. In this chapter, in my role as researcher, I examine teacher collaboration that took place during an on-site learning excursion on which I served as project leader. Funded by a 2017 Fulbright grant, the program provided 12 New York City (NYC) public school teachers with a 6-week advanced introduction to the language and culture of West Bengal, India, a region from which an increasing number of US students originate (Asian American Federation, 2019).

The project offered teacher participants a unique opportunity to acquire firsthand knowledge of this particular region. Within this framework, one of our primary objectives was to explore the potential for collaboration, in particular, collaboration in planning for culturally relevant lessons among content area teachers and teachers of English as a second language (ESL).[1] Research questions were as follows:

1. How might pairs or groups of content and ESL teachers work collaboratively to develop culturally relevant lesson plans for ELLs?
2. What benefits might derive from such collaboration?

The present chapter provides provisional answers to these questions, based on participant feedback – that is, "teachers' voices" – collected during and after the program.

Literature Review

In this literature review, I first discuss scholarship on the benefits of CRP (both in general and in relation to ELLs) and then address research on the value of teacher collaboration (both in general and with ESL teachers). I begin, however, by noting some of the reasons why the organizers and funders of the project thought it important to target Bengali/Bangladeshi culture.

Why West Bengal?

Bengali, the predominant native language in West Bengal and in neighboring Bangladesh, is spoken by more than 260 million people worldwide. Immigration of Bengali speakers to the United States has increased considerably in recent years, and nearly one-half of these newcomers reside in NYC. From 2010 to 2015, for example, the population of NYC residents who self-identified as Bangladeshi (whether alone or in combination with other ethnicities) grew by 88% – from 35,275 to 66,197, a margin that far exceeds the city's overall 4% population growth and 13% growth rate for the total NYC Asian population during the same period (Asian American Federation, 2019). Yet despite the fact that over 6,500 Bangladeshi students – and over 10,000 Bengali-speaking students in total – are currently enrolled in NYC public schools (Luna, 2015), no program or institution, as far as I am aware, had previously undertaken the task of providing teachers with direct, on-site, experience-based learning about the language and heritage culture of these students. In other words, although Bengali is now the third largest home or heritage language group by representation in NYC public schools (Mayor's Office of Operations, 2016; New York City Department of Education, 2013), teachers and administrators throughout the city remain largely unfamiliar with the language, culture, and religions of their Bengali-speaking students. The project that formed the study context was intended to help address this knowledge gap.

Culturally Relevant Pedagogy

When teachers have knowledge of a culture, they are better prepared to empathize with the needs of their diverse students and to deliver culturally relevant pedagogy (Au, 2014; Delpit, 2006; Gay, 2010, 2013; Ladson-Billings, 1995, 2014). Taking their cue largely from Gloria Ladson-Billings' seminal work in the field, educators who practice CRP use the backgrounds, knowledge, and experiences of their students to inform their lesson content and methodology. This enables them to build bridges between students' home and school lives, as well as between curricular content and students' cultural backgrounds (Banks & McGee-Banks, 2016; Lee, 2010; Park, 2014).

It is often said that students are our best classroom resource (Banks & McGee-Banks, 2016), and this is particularly true with respect to CRP. ELLs, for example, stand to benefit strongly from instruction that is both culturally relevant and culturally affirming. Using the wealth of knowledge and diverse experiences that these students bring to the classroom is a good way for teachers to strengthen ELLs' interest and motivation to learn and participate (Lee, 2010; Park 2014). Nevertheless, as important as it is to leverage the knowledge and insights that students bring to the table, teachers themselves should have at least a basic understanding of the languages and cultures represented in their classrooms in order to proactively make connections between content and students' experiences and to build on students' strengths and backgrounds during instruction (Ladson-Billings, 2009).

Teacher Collaboration

Interest in collaborative learning in the classroom surged in the early 1990s among practitioners and scholars alike (Bruffee, 1993; Goodsell et al., 1992; Harding-Smith, 1993; Hargreaves, 1994; Johnson, Johnson, & Smith, 1991). Joint projects, small group assignments, and even group test-taking came into vogue, and such modalities remain a key feature of many classrooms today. Not long after, however, Schaible and Robinson (1995) and others began to examine the potential advantages of *teacher* collaboration. Since that time, a great deal of research has supported the notion that teacher collaboration can improve student achievement and school success (DelliCarprini, 2009; Dumay, et al., 2013; Friend & Cook, 2009; Goddard, et al., 2010; Honigsfeld & Dove, 2010; Mora-Ruano, et al., 2019; Ronfeldt, et al., 2015; van Garderen, et al., 2012).

Collaboration, in this context, is understood as "a style of interaction between at least two coequal parties voluntarily engaged in shared decision making as they work toward a common goal" (Cook & Friend, 1995 as cited in Dove & Honigsfeld, 2010, p. 4). When ESL and content area teachers work collaboratively, for example, they can address issues associated with academic reading and writing while delivering content instruction. Research has shown that such an approach can have advantages in meeting the curricular and instructional needs of ELLs (Sasson, 2010; York-Barr, Ghere, & Sommerness, 2007). As a result, many schools that formerly used the so-called "pull-out" format for ESL instruction, in which students are taken out of their content area courses (i.e., math, science, history, and so on) and taught English essentially in curricular isolation, have switched to more teacher-collaborative and/or content-integrating approaches (Dove & Honigsfeld, 2010; Dunne & Villani, 2007; Wertheimer & Honigsfeld, 2000).

Collaboration among ESL and content area teachers does not come without challenges, and often involves disagreements regarding the distribution of responsibilities. In particular, it is often found that content teachers view their role as someone who imparts or delivers knowledge and content-related skills only, and they may be reluctant to share responsibility for helping students to acquire the academic speaking, reading, and writing skills that they need in order to thrive in their classes. Several studies, for example, have found this attitude to be widespread among science and math teachers (Arkoudis, 2000, 2003; Tan, 2011). Similarly, research has shown that many content area teachers view ESL teachers as *aides* or *helpers* rather than full-fledged pedagogical colleagues or peers (DelliCarprini, 2009; Ernst-Slavit & Wenger, 2006; Turkan, 2018).

The aforementioned – and still widespread – practice of "pull out" ESL instruction has contributed to a sense of marginalization among ELLs, as in practice it has often led to instruction taking place in hallways, closets, storage rooms, and time-out rooms, with many distractions and few classroom resources (DelliCarprini, 2009; Liggett, 2010). Needless to say, such circumstances are not conducive to the emergence of collaborative work involving ESL and content teachers as "coequal partners." Rather, as Valdes (2001) claims and the present author's experience supports, collaboration can flourish only when ESL teachers *and* their ELLs feel valued and accepted as members of the school community.

A culture of trust and collaboration – in which teachers feel free to share their concerns and expose their weaknesses to their colleagues – is important for teachers' learning and for their ability to productively analyze students' progress. Once provided with such a context and with options and examples for change, however, teachers have to have the courage and willingness to alter their knowledge, beliefs, and perceptions. These shifts in perspective, in turn, challenge and encourage teachers to grow, learn, and transform their teaching (Colton, Langer, and Goff, 2016).

Engaging in ELLs' learning process in ways that go beyond or diverge from their typical modalities of content instruction is a challenge that some teachers either find daunting or may not have previously considered relevant to their practice. Yet research has shown that when content and ESL teachers collaborate and combine their knowledge and experience in an effort to provide CRP to ELLs, results can be extraordinarily positive and productive (Colbert, 2010; Colton et al., 2016; Ladson-Billings, 2014; Park, 2014). In such collaboration, ESL specialists can provide content teachers with the methods and strategies they need to help ELLs acquire content successfully. In this context, colleagues pool their knowledge, skills, and resourcefulness to find ways to use cultural elements to enrich the learning experience. With such a process and results in mind, the participants in the present study collaborated in planning lessons that engaged elements of Bengali/Bangladeshi culture, with the goal of enriching content and supporting learning for Bengali-speaking students in NYC public schools.

The Study Context

Participants

Twelve NYC public school teachers participated in the West Bengal project. Four participants were included from each K–12 teaching level – namely elementary, middle, and high school – and one participant at each level was an ESL teacher. At the middle and high school levels, the remaining three participants consisted of one teacher each from the content areas of math, science, and history. While all participants were from different schools in NYC, they all hailed from schools with large Bengali-speaking populations and had been recommended by their district supervisors and school principals. None of the teachers were Bengali speakers or had ever traveled to India. The average age was 37 years old, and the average amount of teaching experience was 12 years. Demographic data on teacher participants are provided in the Appendix. Both in the Appendix and throughout the chapter, pseudonyms are used to protect participants' privacy.

In addition to my role as researcher for the study presented in this chapter, I served as Project Director, in which capacity I monitored overall activities before, during, and after the trip. As a specialist in methods and strategies for teaching English to speakers of other languages (TESOL), as well as a knowledgeable and enthusiastic proponent of CRP, I observed and participated in conversations among ESL and content teachers on these topics throughout the program. During the lesson planning sessions, described below, I moved among the participants and observed their collaborative work.

Structure

The West Bengal project was organized into three main parts: language classes, lectures and fieldtrips, and collaborative lesson planning. Although this chapter focuses on the *collaborative lesson planning* component, all three parts are described here in order to explain the context in which teacher collaboration took place.

Appendix Teacher Participant Demographics

Participant*	Gender	Age	Teaching Level	Subject Taught**	Years of Teaching Experience
Ashley	F	32	Elementary	ESL	9
Rebecca	F	29	Elementary	AS	7
Brittany	F	45	Elementary	AS	15
Peter	M	34	Elementary	AS	9
Josephine	F	35	Middle	ESL	11
Mark	M	46	Middle	History	17
Rachel	F	48	Middle	Math	23
Li Wei	M	35	Middle	Science	8
Dorothy	F	38	High	ESL	13
Joyce	F	34	High	History	9
Jose	M	28	High	Math	5
Beth	F	39	High	Science	18

* All names are pseudonyms
** AS = All (elementary) subjects

Language Classes

The first objective of the project was to increase participants' knowledge of the language of West Bengal. This was accomplished through intensive study of the Bengali language at Jadavpur University in Kolkata, which hosted the teacher participants. The language study element consisted of 3 hours of daily classroom instruction for 4 days each week, followed by an additional hour of practical language exercise with tutors each afternoon. For most of the participants, this was the first time they had attempted to learn a non-European language. This is noteworthy because Bengali differs more substantially from English than other languages with which some participants were familiar. For example, as program participants soon discovered, certain sounds in Bengali do not exist in English, so not only their brains but also their tongues and mouths had to cope with new ways of doing things.

The 6-week program duration was not sufficient to support the goal that any of the participants would emerge as proficient in either spoken or written Bengali. Nonetheless, the organizers believed that the language component would be valuable not just for the background that it provided in the home language of many of the participants' students, but also because it provided them with firsthand insight into the challenges that others – particularly speakers of non-European languages – encounter when they learn English. Engaging in this experience as part of an immersion program, in which the environment provided constant reminders of the need to communicate in the host language, gave these teacher participants some idea of the pressure faced by ELLs in US schools, who typically need to master English quickly in order to succeed not only in school but in their new residential communities as well.

Lectures and Fieldtrips

The second component, lectures and guided field trips, was intended to provide participants with insight into the history, geography, and culture of West Bengal. Lectures were provided by faculty members from our partner university, including representatives of the departments of Economics, History, International Relations, Sociology (The Centre for the Study of Religion and Society), and Languages and Linguistics. Topics included Indian/West Bengali history; the economy, politics, and government of India; Hinduism, Islam, and other Indian religions; the school system in India; social customs and communication; and the ethnic minorities of India. Associated guided excursions took participants to a wide range of venues and institutions, including historical sites, museums, places of worship, and outdoor markets. On the weekends, participants traveled to places outside West Bengal. For example, teachers went to Agra to see the Taj Mahal and spent a weekend in Bangladesh, visiting

museums, markets, and historical sites. Also, participants visited a number of West Bengali schools, where they observed classes and spoke to the
teachers and administrators. This element was included in the program in
the belief that, of all cultural and social institutions, insight into the inner
workings of West Bengali schools could help teachers most to understand the expectations that Bengali-speaking students and their parents
struggle to transfer and modify as they seek to adapt to and flourish in
US school systems.

Collaborative Lesson Planning

The language and cultural components of the program related directly
to the framework of CRP and to the goal of improving this aspect of
teaching upon participants' return. The third component, in which ESL
specialists and other participants worked collaboratively to develop lesson plans in anticipation of this return, built upon this notion with the
further goal of spreading the benefits of such pedagogy across the curriculum and across the schooling experience. This is achieved by enriching
the curriculum through integrating insight into and reflections of West
Bengali culture and language into content classes as well as by increasing
synergy among these classes and the school's language instruction and
support components (viz., ESL instruction). To support this process, the
ESL teachers led six mini-workshops for their colleagues on such topics as culturally relevant teaching, stages of second language acquisition,
techniques for making instruction accessible to ELLs, and research-based
teaching strategies that help ELLs achieve language proficiency and academic grade-level standards. These workshops were conducted during
daytime hours, in between language classes, lectures, and field trips.

The collaborative lesson planning work, which is the focus of this study,
was carried out during evening sessions, Monday through Thursday,
throughout the 6-week stay. The focus of these sessions was on co-planning of lessons that would be delivered to students when the teachers
returned to NYC. Although variations can be found in the literature, the
co-planning process is aptly summarized in the following five-step model:

1. Review the standard and curriculum demands
2. Discuss learning needs of students
3. Decide on accommodations and who will implement them
4. Monitor, adjust, and provide feedback
5. Evaluate students.
        (Georgia Department of Education, Division for Special Education
        Services and Supports, n.d.)

As is typical in the literature on teacher collaboration, this scheme effectively presents co-planning as a precursor to co-teaching in that it assumes

that the co-planning partners will carry out steps 4 and 5 together. In the case of the present study, the teachers were planning lessons that they would deliver separately – that is, each at her or his own school, either alone or in collaboration with an onsite colleague. Another key difference was that in our case, we were operating with the dual goal of making lesson content and instruction accessible to all students *and* of practicing CRP using West Bengali/Bangladeshi themes, so the teachers worked collaboratively to choose and develop both the topics and the methods that would be used. Apart from these points, however, planning in the study context essentially followed the model presented above.

Co-planning groups were organized by content area, such that the middle and high school history teachers, math teachers, and science teachers were each joined, respectively, by one ESL teacher and one elementary teacher. Thus, each group had four members, two of whom specialized in the same content area. The groups began their collaborative work by identifying the target standards and curricular demands, and they proceeded to review the learning needs and particular characteristics of their students. In this regard, the content teachers typically presented most of the pertinent information to their ESL counterparts, such as the grade level of their students, the lesson objectives, key vocabulary and desired learning outcomes, and the English language proficiency level of the ELLs in the target classes.

Given this information, the ESL teacher would recommend research-based strategies intended not only to make the content more accessible to the ELLs in the class but also to reinforce important concepts from the lesson. Content-area and ESL teachers would then work together to further develop and refine the plan for delivery of the lesson, as well as for the assessment of the success of the approaches used and of the students' learning outcomes (that is, steps 4 and 5 in the above-quoted planning scheme). With respect both to assessment and to any homework that the content teacher might propose to assign, the ESL teachers would take the lead in proposing ways to differentiate assessment (assignments) for the ELLs in the class, depending on level of ability and learning needs.

Data Collection and Analysis

The findings reported and discussed in the following two sections are derived from two data sources: (1) my observations of the co-planning process, made during the collaborative work and reported here based on the notes I took at that time; and (2) the written reports, of 0.5 hour duration, that the participants completed during a "debriefing" session in which they participated upon their return to the United States. A group discussion also took place during that session, on which I also took notes. Subsequently, I coded and analyzed the data from these sources following the method for qualitative education research articulated in Saldaña (2013), which yielded four emergent themes regarding the benefits of teacher collaboration: (a) recognition of responsibility for teaching all students including ELLs, (b) recognition and value of ESL teachers' contribution, (c) recognition of growth and other new ways of enhancing lessons to make instruction accessible to ELLs, and (d) recognition that ESL teachers should learn curricula such that they are able to provide extra support to ELLs in their content area studies.

Findings

In this section, I first provide an account of the co-planning process, based on my observations but including teacher participants' voices wherever possible. This section provides the study's answer to Research Question 1: How might pairs or groups of content and ESL teachers work collaboratively to develop culturally relevant lesson plans? The response to Research Question 2 (What benefits might derive from such collaboration?) is twofold. First, continuing the focus on teacher voices, I present verbatim certain short selected excerpts from the written reports that I, as observer/researcher, felt to be particularly salient in representing the personal discoveries about ESL/content teacher collaboration that the teacher participants made in the course of the program (study) experience. The third subsection presents the aforementioned emergent themes relevant to Research Question 2: that is, the teacher participants' perceptions of the benefits of collaboration.

Observation: The Co-planning Process for Culturally Relevant Pedagogy

To fit in with a unit on *biographies* in the middle school curriculum, Mark, the participating middle school history teacher (see Appendix), asked his collaborative group to work with him on a lesson plan entitled *Investigating the Life and Achievements of Mahatma Gandhi*. Gandhi, as a person of paramount importance in Indian culture and history, was chosen as someone with whom ELLs from West Bengal would readily identify. The lesson was developed for a sixth-grade class of 26 students, half of whom were low-intermediate proficiency ELLs from Bangladesh and India. Together, the content teachers and the group's ESL teacher researched and developed material for this lesson, during and after which they carefully considered how each component could be taught meaningfully and purposefully with the particular class in mind. Throughout the course of this collaborative process, the ESL teacher offered a number of pointed questions and suggestions regarding the methods to be used in the lesson. Some of these are quoted here:

- *How are you going to introduce your key vocabulary?*
- *How will you ensure that your English learners understand the relevance of the quote from Gandhi, "Be the change you want to see in this world"?*

- *Have you thought about, after your initial presentation, using a PowerPoint presentation to further support and emphasize the highlights you present in the life of Gandhi?*
- *I don't see any opportunity in your lesson for students to speak. It is important for your English learners to speak because it gives them a chance to practice their new language [and] to use academic language, [particularly] the vocabulary you introduced in your lesson plan.*
- *Have you thought about group work to give them opportunities to interact with their American-born classmates?*

To the latter question, Mark responded by saying that he had not, but he also asked: "Will the English speakers in the class also benefit from this strategy?" As the discussion continued, it became clear that Mark had thought the strategies suggested by his ESL colleague were intended for use with ELLs only, and he was concerned that native speakers would find the lesson of little value. However, the ESL teacher convinced her colleague that the research-based strategies she suggested were good for *all* students; "Good strategies are good strategies!" she pointed out, and proceeded to explain how their implementation could be differentiated to accommodate various levels of proficiency.

The other collaborations between content area and ESL teachers, in general, followed a similar pattern. However, in addition to recommending instructional strategies to help ELLs (such as using graphic organizers, outlining, and engaging in vocabulary review before reading a text), and explaining how to use these strategies with all students, in many cases, the ESL teachers were instrumental in helping to make the lessons more culturally relevant for the target ELLs.

One such example had to do with a middle school science unit entitled *Examining an ecosystem/environment: The case of India.* For this lesson, the ESL teacher in the collaborative group recommended using photographs of the Indian environment taken during the study program. This would help engage both the ELLs – many of whom would be seeing recent photos of their heritage country – and the whole class, who would feel a sense of participation in their teacher's recent adventure. In another session, an ESL teacher asked Rachel, the middle school math teacher, who was working on a unit of lessons about measurement, "Why not use the Taj Mahal to teach your measurement lesson?" Rachel agreed that this was a good idea, as it would increase the level of cultural relevance for her ELLs from India. Hence, a new lesson was created: *Exploring the architecture of the Taj Mahal!*

In follow-up interactions, the content-area and ESL teachers collaboratively considered a range of aspects and issues relevant to the co-designed lessons: content, teaching and learning objectives, outcomes, formative and summative assessment, and practice of academic tasks and language skills (listening, speaking, reading, and writing) to increase learning success for ELLs in deliberate and purposeful ways. The teachers also co-developed instructional materials that would accompany their lessons, including multilevel, differentiated instructional resources designed to increase ELLs' understanding and acquisition of course content using Bengali and India-related themes.

Written Reflective Reports: Experiences and Impressions of Collaboration

For the retrospective reflections that the teacher participants wrote as part of their post-program debriefing process, they were asked to focus on their experiences collaborating with their colleagues. In keeping with the study's emphasis on teachers' voices, I begin by quoting a set of nine excerpts that I have selected for their saliency (concise, impactful wording) and because they collectively represent the range and tenor of participants' written comments regarding their collaboration experiences:

1   [Collaboration] was very meaningful to me. The way the ESL teacher helped me to see how I could improve my lessons to English language learners was great! (Jose, high school math teacher)
2   I can't express how much I learned working with my ESL colleague. She really explained to me the importance of being mindful of my English language learners when I teach. (Li Wei, middle school science teacher)
3   I did not realize the challenges in teaching history for ELLs. There are many, but my ESL partner helped me to see how I can make instruction more accessible to my ELLs with such tools as graphic maps. Because high school history is dense, Venn diagrams, for example, can be a good way to make my instruction (my words) visible and come to life for my ELLs. (Joyce, high school history teacher)
4   Before this trip I didn't have any real training on how to begin or even think it necessary to relate culture to teaching science lessons. Through the experiences these 6 weeks I have [obtained] a completely different perspective. The workshop we had on culturally relevant teaching and also planning lessons together with [the ESL teacher] made me see that teaching ELLs is also my responsibility. Not only do I see the value in culturally relevant teaching, but I have ideas [on] how to include it in my lesson plans. (Beth, high school science teacher)
5   The biggest take away for me was that I am not only in the classroom to teach math to my students, but I am also responsible to make sure that everyone is included, even my ELLs. The strategies I learned to assist in teaching them in the classroom are on my teaching speed dial. (Rachel, middle school math teacher)

6   Collaborating with my ESL colleague was not a chore that I supposed it would be. Rather, it was an opportunity to learn to do things
differently (for the sake of my ELLs), to give the students a chance
to succeed. Just by changing my way of doing things and incorporating a few new strategies into my teaching, I can make a difference
between the success or failure of an ELL. (Peter, elementary school
teacher)

7   As an ESL teacher, sharing my knowledge, skills, and resources
with my colleagues was an opportunity that I had never had before.
Offering workshops and engaging colleagues in discussions to plan
and strategize and create materials to reinforce content were experiences I cannot forget. And the nice thing about it was that there was a
real interest and genuine appreciation among my colleagues for what
I had to give. (Ashley, elementary school ESL teacher)

8   The expertise and classroom and instructional strategies that I brought
with me were tapped into and embraced by everyone. Whether I collaborated with my science, math or history colleague, I was armed
to help. There was a real collaboration and discussions that I think
should happen in our schools across the country. (Josephine, middle
school ESL teacher)

9   Working with my math, science, and history colleagues allowed me
to better understand the curricular goals of the content classes, and
so I was able to support these goals using appropriate instructional
strategies to better meet the needs of [my colleagues'] ELLs. (Dorothy,
high school ESL teacher)

In general, the written reports showed that all of the participants found
the experience of collaborating worthwhile. However, some of the specific points made in the above excerpts were echoed elsewhere in the
reports as well. Thus, for example, Ashley, who offered comment #7
above, was not the only participant who found herself sitting down with
an ESL specialist to co-plan lessons for the first time – and others, like
her, also reported having anticipated that it would be a "chore," but then
finding it to be fruitful. Overall, the mutual respect among the collaborating teachers was perhaps the most palpable and consistent element, both
in the reports and in my observations. The ESL teachers listened carefully
while content teachers shared their lesson plan ideas. Likewise, when the
ESL teachers shared ways in which their content-area colleagues might
enhance their lessons for their ELLs, the content teachers accepted and
embraced the new ideas.

Emergent Themes: Perceived Benefits of Teacher Collaboration

From the comments reported above, it is also clear that collaboration
helped the content teachers to understand the challenges involved in

teaching their specific content to ELLs. Some, like Joyce (excerpt #3), had never considered these challenges. However, collaborating with her ESL colleague allowed her to see lesson planning from a different and expanded perspective, and she eagerly embraced the new strategies that she learned.

Other specific collaboration-related themes that emerged from analysis of the observation data and written reports are as follows:

Recognition of Responsibility to Teach All Students, Including ELLs

Collaboration made the participating content teachers aware that they have a responsibility to all of the students they teach, even ELLs. All teachers are accountable for their students' progress, whereas previously most believed that the teaching of English was the sole responsibility of ESL teachers. Collaboration sessions helped them to see that they can provide and enhance lessons in ways that foster second language acquisition and increase academic learning for their ELLs. Participant comments #1 and #6, for example, clearly acknowledge that teaching all students in their classrooms has become a new reality for these teachers, one that they anticipate will guide their lesson planning in the future.

Recognition and Value of ESL Teachers' Contribution

The content area teachers were pleasantly surprised that their ESL colleagues were very capable of assisting them in learning ways to help their ELLs grow academically. In their reports, and in comments that I observed, content teacher participants in this study praised and recognized the value of their ESL colleagues for the knowledge they provided through both the mini-workshops and the one-on-one collaborative work (see comments 1–4, 6, and 8 above), which several participants stated had helped them grow and develop professionally (see the following theme).

Recognition of Growth, Including Acquiring New Ways of Enhancing Lessons to Make Instruction Accessible to ELLs

Another perceived benefit of collaboration was professional growth and development. Participants realized that there are other ways to share their content, including methods that they might not have used before but that can help ensure that ELLs make meaning of their instruction. In other words, they recognized that their previous training and experience did not provide them with all the pedagogical answers. Specifically, participants Brittany, Mark, Rachel, Jose, and Beth all stated in their reports that they had experienced professional growth and development as a result of the collaborations, and several of these comments connected this growth explicitly to increased teacher confidence and self-efficacy, particularly with respect to the ability to mobilize strategies that increase ELLs' acquisition of content and development of academic skills.

Recognition that ESL Teachers Should Learn Curricula Such That They Are Able to Provide Extra Support to ELLs in Their Content Area Studies

The ESL teachers in the study also felt that they had benefitted from collaboration, particularly to the extent that they had added to their knowledge of content and curriculum in various disciplines. This was indicated as beneficial in three ways:

a   increased understanding of what is expected of all students, including ELLs (e.g., Josephine:"I teach in isolation and don't really know what is going on in my ELLs' content courses. I only teach English. Having worked together with my content colleagues, though, I have a good idea of the kinds of things that happen in the content classes, like what my ELLs are expected to know…"),

b   more targeted understanding of what academic tasks and skills to focus on and emphasize for their ELLs (e.g., Dorothy: "As I worked with the math, science and history teachers, I learned the types of academic skills high school ELLs need to know to succeed in their classes—analyzing, synthesizing, describing, and so on. When I return home, I will begin to focus on ways I can better prepare my ELLs to meet the challenges in their content classes), and

c   increased self-efficacy as a result of feeling both better informed and more useful to their colleagues (e.g., Ashley: "It is a good feeling knowing that my colleagues see that I can be a bridge between what goes on in their classes and ways I can better reach out and assist young ELLs. Now that I know what my colleagues are doing, I am already thinking of ways to adapt my teaching").

Discussion

The project reported here provided a unique way in which to encourage collaboration among ESL and content area teachers. It extended well beyond the context of the US classroom to an overseas destination – which entailed various challenges but which also placed teachers temporarily outside the everyday business and distractions of school and district. The findings reported above, moreover, suggest that participants benefited from their guided 6-week excursion to West Bengal, India. The language and cultural components contributed to their ability to empathize with ELLs and to deliver CRP, and the context of the program allowed them to acquire a fresh perspective on content/ESL teacher collaboration.

Collaborative lesson planning and teaching are both widely held to better enable educators to meet the needs of all students in the classroom (Honigsfeld & Dove, 2008). This was certainly the opinion of the teacher participants in the present study, at least after completing the collaborative element of the program and based on the researcher's observations and the exit data (reports) that the participants provided. The participants found particular advantages – for both content and ESL teachers – to the specific practice of content/ESL teacher collaboration, despite challenges to this practice. In particular, as noted in the Literature Review, ESL teachers are often not seen as equal peers by and in relation to their content area counterparts, and thus they are often considered unqualified to co-plan with them (DelliCarprini, 2009; Ernst-Slavit & Wenger, 2006; Turkan, 2018). However, in this study, there was no evidence of such a prejudice or hierarchy, and no individual teacher dominated within any of the collaborative groups. Rather, each teacher brought her or his strengths to the collaboration table, and mutual appreciation was the norm across the groups.

Perhaps due to the heightened awareness of the language learner challenge and of the value of specialist input that the program fostered, the ESL teacher participants did not experience the sense of marginalization and slight regard that research and anecdotal evidence suggest is often the case in other contexts. Rather, as Ashley put it: "As an ESL teacher, sharing my knowledge, skills, and resources with my colleagues was an opportunity that I had never had before.... And the nice thing about it was that there was a real interest and genuine appreciation among my colleagues for what I had to give" (written response excerpt #7). Indeed, as Josephine, another ESL teacher, shared: "The expertise and classroom and instructional strategies that I brought with me were tapped into and embraced by everyone" (written response excerpt #8).

Content teachers in the program not only learned to better appreciate the challenges that their ELLs face, they also learned to better appreciate the positive impact that collaborating with ESL teachers can have on their ability to help students meet these challenges (e.g., Peter: "The strategies I learned to assist in teaching [ELLs] in the classroom are [now] on my teaching speed dial" (written response excerpt #6)). ESL teachers, too, benefitted from the collaborative work (e.g., Beth: "Working with my math, science, and history colleagues allowed me to better understand the curricular goals of the content classes" (written response excerpt #4)).

Overall, the project provided detailed evidence of what the content/ESL teacher collaboration process can look like, at least in one specific context. Furthermore, the lesson plans that emerged provide excellent examples of how this process can be used to achieve the substantial benefits – in terms of engagement and motivation – that can accrue from applying the principles of CRP to work with ELLs (Lee, 2010; Park 2014; Ladson-Billings, 2009). Moreover, although the present study did not look specifically at the impact of the program's language study component, it is notable that the project afforded participants the opportunity to experience language not only as an object of study, but also as it is embedded in a culture. Having learned first-hand something of the subtle cultural understandings that accompany language use, which we often take for granted when using our own heritage language, participating teachers emerged able to bring this experience to their schools and districts by foregrounding this cultural component in their teaching of ELLs at all levels and in all subject areas (Ladson-Billings, 2014).

This experience, together with the close collaboration with ESL teachers (which was new for some participants), helped the participating content teachers to achieve a new sense of responsibility to the ELLs in their classes, as well as a new sense of efficacy in their ability to contribute to these students' learning. Simply put, these teachers found that, as a result of the collaborative work, they had expanded their strategic toolkits (Honigsfeld & Dove, 2008) for working with ELLs (e.g., Joyce: "...my ESL partner helped me to see how I can make instruction more accessible to my ELLs with such tools as graphic maps" (written response excerpt #3)). This – in combination with the benefits of CRP – augurs well for the acquisition of content and for the overall academic success of language-diverse students in the schools in which these participants teach.

Implications and Limitations

The present study clearly leaves room for further research – for example, with larger samples or using methods that allow for greater quantification and/or screening for confounding variables. Nevertheless, the teachers' voices represented in the present study suggest that there are broad and deep benefits to participation in onsite guided language and culture studies, such as the program examined in this chapter. Indeed, the author recommends – and has participated in – the establishment of further such programs, enabling more teachers to visit and learn about other major "donor cultures" for diverse students in their schools.

It must be noted, however, that this approach alone cannot be expected to ensure that all students receive the benefits of empathetic teaching, specialized methods, collaborative teaching, and CRP. It would be logistically and financially impossible for all or even most of the teachers whose schools include linguistically and culturally diverse students to participate in programs abroad, particularly in a large country like the United States, where many of the most diverse school districts are also the most financially challenged. Here, however, it may be that precisely the element of *collaboration*, on which this chapter has focused, is key to expanding the benefits of programs of this kind. In other words, it is of immense value for teachers to extend the professional collaboration begun on such projects upon their return to their own schools, and to include in this process "homebound" teachers, new education graduates, and administrators. In my experience, teachers who return from study projects abroad are almost always fountainheads of both relevant knowledge and enthusiasm for CRP, and letting their voices be heard – and their example be followed – can set off chain reactions that spread the benefits of a few teachers' experiences to large numbers of colleagues and students.

Conclusion

Effective teachers are those who are committed to being active learners and who value and practice collaboration with their colleagues. Collaboration is not easy, nor is it without issues or problems, especially considering the historical legacy of marginalizing the ESL profession. The program examined in this chapter, however, transformed this challenge into an opportunity. It helped participating content teachers to realize that, irrespective of what they teach, they also have a responsibility to support ELLs' learning; it helped them to obtain both insight and skills that will better enable them to do so; and it created a context in which ESL and content teachers worked together as coequal partners to develop culturally relevant lesson plans.

In the study reported here, the teachers' own voices demonstrate that, as language learners in a cultural immersion program, they developed greater empathy for the challenges faced by their ELL students, as well as a heightened sense of responsibility for their role in making content accessible to these students and in promoting academic reading and writing skills for all. The research-based strategies provided by the ESL teachers promoted this goal by giving content teachers new and improved ways in which to provide ELLs with language support as they learn in content areas such as math, science, and history. Content teachers expressed appreciation for the value of the input of the ESL teachers and of the collaborative process, and ESL teachers appreciated the fact that they were treated as equal partners in their collaborative efforts with their content area counterparts. Further research into the impact of cultural immersion study abroad for teachers is certainly warranted.

Nonetheless, these findings suggest that participants who return from programs of this kind do so as advocates not only of CRP but of teacher collaboration as well, and that their efforts and enthusiasm will help engender further collaborative efforts, including much-needed exercises in bridging the already narrowing gulf between ESL and content instruction.

Note

1 Note that this more traditional term is used throughout the present chapter, although some scholars now prefer *English as a new language* (ENL), in light of the fact that many ELLs are already multilingual learners.

References

Arkoudis, S. (2000). '*I have linguistic aims and linguistic content*': ESL and science teachers planning together. *Prospect, 15*(2), 61–71.

Arkoudis, S. (2003) Teaching English as a second language in science classes: Incommensurate epistemologies? *Language and Education, 17*(3), 161–173. doi:10.1080/09500780308666846

Asian American Federation. (2019). *Profile of New York City's Bangladeshi Americans*. New York, NY: Author. Retrieved from http://www.aafederation.org/cic/briefs/2019bn.pdf

Au, W. (2014). *Rethinking multicultural education: Teaching for racial and cultural justice* (2nd ed.). Milwaukee, WI: A Rethinking Schools Publication.

Banks, J. A., & McGee-Banks, C. A. (2016). *Multicultural education: Issues and perspectives* (9th ed.). New York, NY: Wiley/Jossey Bass.

Brown-Jeffry, S., & Cooper, J. E. (2011). Toward a conceptual framework of culturally relevant pedagogy: An overview of the conceptual and theoretical literature. *Teacher Education Quarterly, 38*(1), 65–84. Retrieved from https://www.jstor.org/stable/23479642

Bruffee, K. (1993). *Collaborative learning: Higher education, interdependence, and the authority of knowledge*. Baltimore, MA: Johns Hopkins University Press.

Catto, S. (2018). More than one voice: Utilizing students' home languages and cultural experiences in reading recovery. In E. Ortlieb & E. H. Cheek, Jr. (Eds.), *Literacy research, practice and evaluation: Addressing diversity in literacy instruction* (Vol. 8, pp. 17–36). Bingley, UK: Emerald Publishing Limited. Chicago: The Danielson Group.

Colbert, P. (2010). Developing a culturally responsive classroom collaborative of faculty, students, and institution. *Contemporary Issues in Education Research, 3*, 17–26. doi:10.19030/cier.v3i9.231

Colton, A., Langer, G., & Goff, L. (2016). *The collaborative analysis of student learning: Professional learning that promotes success for all*. Thousand Oaks, CA: Corwin.

Cook, L., & Friend, M. (1995). Co-teaching: Guidelines for creating effective practices. *Focus on Exceptional Children, 28*(3), 1–16. Retrieved from https://core.ac.uk/download/pdf/162644006.pdf

DelliCarprini, M. (2009). Dialogues across disciplines: Preparing ESL teachers for interdisciplinary collaboration. *Current Issues in Education, 11*(2). Retrieved 20 May 2021 from file:///C:/Users/The%20Johnson/Downloads/1573-Article%20Text-6816-1-10-20150515%20(15).pdf

Delpit, L. D. (2006; originally published 1995). *Other people's children: Cultural conflict in the classroom*. New York, NY: New Press.

Dove, M., & Honigsfeld, A. (2010). ESL coteaching and collaboration: Opportunities to develop teacher leadership and enhance student learning. *TESOL Journal, 1*, 3–22. doi:10.5054/tj.2010.214879

Dumay, X., Boonen, T., & Van Damme, J. (2013). Principal leadership: Long-term indirect effects on learning growth in mathematics. *Elementary School Journal*, 114i225–251. doi:10.1086/673198

Dunne, K., & Villani, S. (2007). *Mentoring new teachers through collaborative coaching: Linking teacher and student learning.* San Francisco, CA: WestEd.

Edwards, S., & Edick, N. (2013). Culturally relevant teaching for significant relationships. *Journal of Praxis in Multicultural Education*, 7(1), 1–18. doi:10.9741/2161-2978.1058.

Elizalde-Utnick, G. (2010). Immigrant families: Strategies for school support, *Principal Leadership*, 10(5), 12–16.

Ernst-Slavit, G., & Wenger, K. (2006). Teaching in the margins: The multifaceted work and struggles of bilingual paraeducators. *Anthology and Education Quarterly*, 37(1), 62–82. Retrieved from https://www.jstor.org/stable/3651375

Friend, M., & Cook, L. (2009). *Interactions: Collaboration skills for school professionals.* (5th ed.). Boston, MA: Pearson Education Inc.

Gay, G. (2010). *Culturally relevant teaching: Theory, research, and practice* (2nd ed.). New York, NY: Teachers College Press.

Gay, G. (2013). Teaching to and through cultural diversity. *Curriculum Inquiry*, 43(1), 48–70. doi:10.1111/curi.12002.

Georgia Department of Education, Division for Special Education Services and Supports. (2019). Co-planning for student success: Module 2. Retrieved from https://www.gadoe.org/Curriculum-Instruction-and-Assessment/Special-Education-Services/Documents/Co-Teaching%20Models/Module%202/ONE%20PAGER%20for%20Module%202%20-%20Co-planning%20for%20student%20success.pdf

Goddard, Y., Miller, R., Larsen, R., Goddard, G., Jacob, R., Madsen, J., & Schroeder, P. (2010). *Connecting principal leadership, teacher collaboration, and student achievement. Paper presented at the American Educational Research Association Annual Meeting*, Denver, CO. Retrieved from https://files.eric.ed.gov/fulltext/ED528704.pdf

Goodsell, A., Maher, M., Tinto, V., Smith, B. L., & MacGregor, J. (Eds.). (1992). *Collaborative learning: A sourcebook for higher education.* University Park, PA: National Center on Postsecondary Teaching, Learning, and Assessment.

Harding-Smith, T. (1993). *Learning together: An introduction to collaborative learning.* New York, NY: Harper Collins.

Hargreaves, A. (1994). *Changing teachers, changing times: Teachers' work and culture in the postmodern age.* New York, NY: Teachers College Press.

Honigsfeld, A., & Dove, M. G. (2008). Co-teaching in the ESL classroom. *Delta Kappa Gamma Bulletin*, 74(2), 8–14. Retrieved from http://questgarden.com/17/33/5/100410231246/files/coteaching%20article.pdf

Honigsfeld, A., & Dove, M. G. (2010). *Collaboration and co-teaching: Strategies for English learners.* Newbury Park, CA: Corwin Press.

Johnson, D. W., Johnson, R. T., & Smith, K. A. (1991). *Active learning: Cooperation in the college classroom.* Edina, MN: Interaction Book Company.

Ladson-Billings, G. (1994). *The dreamkeepers: Successful teachers of African American children.* San Francisco, CA: Jossey-Bass Publishing Co.

Ladson-Billings, G. (1995). Toward a theory of culturally relevant pedagogy. *American Educational Research Journal*, 32(3), 465–491. doi:10.3102/00028312032003465

Ladson-Billings, G. (2009). *The dreamkeepers: Successful teachers of African American children* (2ndrev. ed.). San Francisco, CA: Jossey-Bass Publishers.

Ladson-Billings,G.(2014).Culturallyrelevantpedagogy2.0:Akatheremix.*Harvard Educational Review, 84*, 74–84. doi:10.17763/haer.84.1.p2rj131485484751

Lee, J. S. (2010). Culturally relevant pedagogy for immigrant children and English language learners. Yearbook of the National Society for the Study of Education. *Teachers College Record, 112*(14), 453–473.

Liggett, T. (2010). "A little bit marginalized": The structural marginalization of English language teachers in urban and rural public schools. *Teaching Education, 21*, 217–232. doi:10.1080/10476211003695514

Luna, J. (2015, October 2). *Bengali students need teachers who speak their language.* New York, NY: WNYC Public Radio. Retrieved on April 30, 2020 https://www.wnyc.org/story/wanted-teachers-who-speak-bengali/.

Mayor's Office of Operations. (2016). *Social Indicators Report.* The City of New York. New York: Author.

Mora-Ruano, J. G., Heine, J. H., & Gebhardt, M. (2019). Does teacher collaboration improve student achievement? Analysis of the German PISA 2012 sample. *Frontiers in Education, 4*, 85.

New York City Department of Education. (2013). *Demographic Report New York City Department of Education's Division of Students with Disabilities and English Language Learners.* New York, NY: Author.

Park, M. (2014). Increasing English language leaners' engagement in instruction. *Multi-cultural Education, 22*(1), 20–29. Retrieved from https://files.eric.ed.gov/fulltext/EJ1065395.pdf

Powell, W. and Kusuma-Powell, O. (2011). *How to teach now: Five keys to personalized learning in the global classroom.* Alexandra, VA: ASCD.

Pratt-Johnson, Y. (2015). Stressors experienced by immigrant and other non-native English-speaking students in U.S. schools and their families. *Journal of Social Distress and the Homeless, 24*(3). doi:10.1179/1053078915Z.00000000018

Rahman, F. A., Scaife, J., Yahya, N. A., & Ab Jalil, H. (2010). Knowledge of diverse learners: Implications for the practice of teaching. *International Journal of Instruction, 3*(2), 83–96. Retrieved from https://files.eric.ed.gov/fulltext/ED522935.pdf

Rajagopal, K. (2011). Create Success! ASCD. Retrieved from http://www.ascd.org/publications/books/111022/chapters/Culturally-ResponsiveInstruction.

Ronfeldt, M., Farmer, S., McQueen, K., & Grissom, J. (2015). Teacher collaboration in instructional teams and student achievement. *American Educational Research Journal, 52*(3), 475–514. doi:10.3102/0002831215585562

Roxas, K. (2011). Creating communities: Working with refugee students in classrooms. *Democracy and Education, 19*(2). Retrieved from https://democracyeducationjournal.org/home/vol19/iss2/5

Saldaña, J. (2013). *The coding manual for qualitative researchers.* Thousand Oaks, CA: Sage.

Sasson, D. (2010). *Benefits of general education and ESL teacher collaboration.* Retrieved on May 15, 2020. http://EzineArticles.com/3510148.

Schaible, R., & Robinson, B. (1995). Collaborating teachers as models for students. *Journal on Excellence in College Teaching, 6*(1), 9–16.

Short, D. J., & Boyson, B. A. (2012). *Helping newcomer students succeed in secondary schools and beyond.* Washington, DC: Center for Applied Linguistics.

Sobel, A., & Kugler, E. G. (2007). Building partnerships with immigrant parents. *Educational Leadership*, 64(6), 62–66.

Suarez-Orozco, C. (2000). Identities under siege: Immigration stress and social mirroring among the children of immigrants. In A. Robben & M. Suarez-Orozco (Eds.), *Cultures under siege: Collective violence and trauma* (pp. 194–226). New York, NY: Cambridge University Press.

Tan, M. (2011). Mathematics and science teachers' beliefs and practices regarding the teaching of language in content learning. *Language Teaching Research*, 15, 325–342. doi:10.1177/1362168811401153

Turkan, S. (2018). *The role of the ESL teacher in relation to science teachers*. Washington, DC: National Academies of Sciences. Retrieved 20 May 2021 from file:///C:/Users/The%20Johnson/Downloads/1573-Article%20Text-6816-1-10-20150515%20(15).pdf.

Valdes, G. (2001). *Learning and not learning English: Latino students in American schools*. New York, NY: Teachers College Press.

van Garderen, D., Stormont, M., & Goel, N. (2012). Collaboration between general and special educators and student outcomes: A need for more research. *Psychology in the Schools*, 49(5), 483–497. doi:10.1002/pits.21610

Wertheimer, C., & Honigsfeld, A. (2000). Preparing ESL students to meet the new standards. *TESOL Journal*, 9(1), 23–28. doi:10.1002/j.1949-3533.2000.tb00223.x

York-Barr, J., Ghere, G., & Sommerness, J. (2007). Collaborative teaching to increase ELL student learning: A three-year urban elementary case study. *Journal of Education for Students Placed at Risk*, 12(3), 301–335. doi:10.1080/10824660701601290.

Part III

Implications and Suggestions for Future Research and Practice on Teacher Collaboration

10 What Can a Principal Do to Support Teacher Collaboration for ELLs?

Implications for Building Leadership Practice

Suzanne E. McLeod

I had the privilege of reading all of the chapters in this edited book. The experiences and insights of these researchers reminded me of what I, as an educational leader, can do to support teacher collaboration for our English language learners (ELLs). As someone who spent 43 years working in schools in the United States, specifically in Missouri, Michigan, Massachusetts, and New York, and 29 of those years as a school and school district administrator, the role of a principal in supporting and enhancing student achievement cannot be underestimated. From Hattie (2009) to Marzano (2005) to Dufour (2004), with legions of educational researchers preceding them, it is the principal that stands out as the person who has the power to support change in the instructional setting, if they also have the capacity. Indeed, during my time as a principal – in a building that literally sat at the crossroads of a suburban sideroad and an arterial highway leading to New York City – my husband would occasionally stop in when traveling to or from a meeting. (This was well before the days of American school buildings being locked up tight to the outside world.) After a short visit, my husband would always comment, "You're the mayor of a very small town. Everything from the health and well-being of everyone here, to schedules, to lunch getting served on time, is your responsibility."

This collection of studies, and the best practices that have the potential to truly help our ELLs succeed in schools, highlights the potential impact a principal could have on this often underserved population. With consideration to the fact that this population is growing in some states exponentially, it best serves us as educators and, more specifically, as educational leaders, to mindfully implement the best practices noted in this edited book. Specifically, the percentage of public school students in the United States who were ELLs was higher in fall 2017 (e.g., 10.1%, or 5.0 million students) than in fall 2000 (e.g., 8.1%, or 3.8 million students). In the fall of 2017, the percentage of public school students who were ELLs ranged from 0.8% in West Virginia to 19.2% in California (National Center for Education Statistics, 2020).

DOI: 10.4324/9781003058311-13

Drawn from the studies in this collection, I highlight six areas of both effective educational leadership and school management, some within a principal's direct control and some requiring outside professional support. Listening to these researchers' voices from the field and working toward implementing as many of these areas as possible could go a long way in improving educational opportunities and, ultimately, the academic achievement of our ELLs. I provide specific suggestions for school principals who seek new ideas to support effective teacher collaboration for ELLs.

Suggestions for School Principals to Support Collaborations to Benefit ELLs

Suggestion 1: Create and Lead with Building Goals for Enhancing ELLs' Student Achievement

I first suggest school leaders take the lead to establish building goals for ELLs' successful learning. In 2001, No Child Left Behind (NCLB) ushered in a sea change in American education in taking us literally into the 21st century with accountability as part of the public education equation. Suddenly, the full access to education promised with Brown v Board of Education of Topeka, KS (1954) ran headlong into the lofty dreams of the nation's governors, Congress, and the President with the passage of The Goals 2000: Educate America Act (1994), to shift American educational practice to focus on standards-based academic achievement for all American children, regardless of their backgrounds. And, even though we are 20 years past the passage of NCLB, the promise of ensuring academic achievement for our ELLs is as critical as it was when the standards movement commenced. Indeed, the current federal requirements of the Every Student Succeeds Act (ESSA), which replaced NCLB in 2015, maintain specific requirements for growth in ELLs' academic achievement.

Suddenly, principals were not just responsible for ensuring that students in their schools got in the door and where they were supposed to be for the next 6.5–7 hours, but that they actually learned, with the focus turning to outcomes and research-based educational practices. With NCLB, and its successor ESSA, principals needed to broaden their skills beyond being managers into true educational leaders. As noted in virtually all of the studies included in this book, this meant that the principal needed to create, implement, and facilitate systems for true, equitable, and student-focused collaboration among teachers. Indeed, in "Both Teachers' Names on the Door: Elementary ESL and Classroom Teacher Collaboration" (Chapter 3), the principal is called upon to ensure that content area teachers increase their personal level of responsibility for the successful academic outcomes of the ELLs. As noted by Uliassi, the chapter author, too often our English as a Second Language (ESL) teachers, especially when integrated into a classroom setting, become nothing more than highly paid classroom aides serving often as translators or note takers during the class period itself, but solely carrying the heavy responsibility for the ELLs actually learning the subject matter. If the ELLs do not do well on their assessments, that was considered the fault of their ESL teacher. Thus, ESL teachers faced the daunting task of reteaching when the students failed to learn the material during the content area class period.

However, with NCLB and ESSA, and the shift to subgroup accountability, schools no longer could waste the time spent in co-taught content-area classes. The ESL teacher needed to be fully integrated into the full building curriculum and supported, especially if the school was serious about achieving their accountability goals for all of their subgroups, of which ELLs were one.

Schools with principals that successfully implemented Richard Dufour's (2004) Professional Learning Communities (PLCs) structures for professional collaboration between teachers met with greater success in breaking down the established structures and power dynamic between classroom teachers and teachers of ELLs (DuFour, 2004). With successful implementation of PLCs, as highlighted here in "Co-Taught Integrated Language and Mathematics Content Instruction for Multilingual Learners" (Chapter 8), the teacher of the ELLs can help the classroom teacher implement instructional practices that work better for the ELLs (and, I would argue for all students in the classroom) and the classroom teacher can help the ELL teacher better understand the content area curriculum to better support the ELLs.

Suggestion 2: Develop Building Schedules That Maximize ELLs' Success

My second suggestion is grounded in the current scheduling reality and complexity for ELLs in our schools. For example, in the United States, city schools host many more ELLs than suburban and rural schools. These students made up 14% of total public school enrollees in city school districts in fall 2015, compared with just 4% in rural areas. Districts in suburban areas (9%) and towns (6%) fell in the middle. Districts located in an urban city with a population of 250,000 or more had the highest share of ELLs (16%) (Pew Research, 2018).

However, in a state such as NY, with half the children attending public schools being part of the New York City School system, and with 62.1% of the total New York State ELLs in the NYC school district (New York State Education Department, 2019), principals of schools throughout the rest of the state often see a much smaller percentage of ELLs. Even some of the larger suburban school districts, with student populations greater than 10,000, potentially see fewer than 100 ELLs spread throughout the grade levels and having a wide variety of first languages.

Thus, the question which arose in several of the included studies, "How are these students scheduled?," might speak more to trying to make mandated ELL services fit the existing structure of the school schedule in the most cost-effective manner, and still honor state regulations, rather than answering the higher question of developing and implementing systems that address the learning needs of all students. I would ask principals to seriously reflect on the findings here, notably "Reimagining Collaboration: Exploring how ESL Teachers and Technology Coach Perceive Collaboration to Improve ELLs' Language Skills" (Chapter 5), and ask themselves whose voice is in your ear as you begin the development of your master schedule for the following year? Are you, as we encourage our PLC's to do, beginning with data and developing a schedule that places the learning needs of our most challenged learners – the very subgroups that NCLB called on us to help – at the center? Or, are you implementing a schedule more centered on the needs of adults, for example building a schedule around who gets last period "free" to attend to their own (adult) priorities?

Essentially, these studies in this book call for principals to broaden their scope to include themselves as part of the team who "own" the ELLs. Too often, we see that role falling solely on the shoulders of the teacher of the ELLs. With effective teacher collaboration, that ownership broadens to include all of the classroom teachers who work with ELLs, too. The principal needs to be able to innovatively see beyond ELLs as a place (the ESL teacher's room) or a role (the ESL teacher). Instead, the principal needs to both envision and enact an instructional program designed and facilitated by both a leadership and instructional team to meet the needs of the ELLs within the total school environment. If accomplished, scheduling the ELLs becomes something more than an afterthought.

Suggestion 3: Facilitate Collaboration between Content Area and ESL Teachers

I also suggest that principals actively work to ensure systems to support collaboration between classroom and ESL teachers. As noted in several of the research studies included in this book, notably "Reflections on Co-Teaching and Collaboration: Communication, Flexibility and Congruence" (Chapter 4) and "I See Myself as Another Teacher": Co-Teaching Practice for ELLs in a Science Class" (Chapter 7), the school culture must foster a climate of both empathy and mutual respect. On November 24, 2020, the American Education Research Association (AERA) and the Organisation for Economic Co-operation and Development (OECD) hosted an interactive policy forum to discuss new results from the Teaching and Learning International Survey (TALIS) Video study. TALIS Video Study gathered evidence from about 700 teachers with over 17,000 students and observed, via video, the instruction of a unit on quadratic equations. Utilizing both the videos and test data of students' learning gains, the forum noted that the factors positively impacting student learning fell, first, to effective classroom management skills; second, to providing students' social and emotions (SEL) support; and then, third, to effective instructional techniques (OECD, 2020).

SEL strategies are the current hot topic in schools, and it would appear that the OECD work bolsters the importance and positive impact that SEL can have on student learning. However, principals should pay heed to Kathleen Porter-Magee's (2020) work examining school culture as a crucial predecessor to social and emotional learning. In my experience, many successful collaborations between content or grade level teachers and ESL teachers helped the ELLs feel emotionally supported in the general education classroom. Successful collaborations embody both a focus on strong instruction and a classroom environment where students feel safe. For many ELLs, the ESL teacher is the first teacher to understand their unique needs, both academically and emotionally. Within a successful collaboration, the ESL teacher can help guide the content area/grade level teacher to a better understanding of the ELLs' social–emotional needs, just as the content area teacher can help the ESL teacher to better understand the content the students need to learn to be academically successful.

Too often, this collaboration is left to chance. The teachers are assigned to work together and everyone hopes for magic to happen. Again, too often, that does not occur. I argue that the building principal needs to nurture a school culture that actively facilitates collaboration. The Association of Supervision and Curriculum Development (ASCD) is the national professional organization that American school administrators look to for guidance and support in the development of their professional learning and leadership skills. ASCD hosts an entire section of their website on the topic of School Culture and Climate, with links to articles, books and publications, webinars, digital learning, and experts and events all focusing on the goal of building educational leaders' skills in creating, enhancing, and maintaining positive school culture (e.g., how the adults in a building treat each other) and school climate (e.g., how this positive culture results in success for the students in that school).

Specific to the needs of the ELLs, it is essential that principals continuously work to build a culture of trust within their school. This need to have a school based upon mutual respect means that the principal must navigate political, socio-economic, and cultural biases that may be baked into the culture of the building. Areas a principal needs to be both cognizant of and to address if necessary include:

- Are some classes/courses the destination for students of high social capital? Or, do all students have access to the teachers/courses most necessary for academic success?

- Are ELLs mainstreamed only into classes with either the most willing classroom teachers (or the low status/seniority teachers) because high status/seniority teachers do not want them (and potentially their Special Education peers also)?
- Does the school as a whole make an effort to learn about the backgrounds and cultures of their ELLs in order to both personalize the educational experience and create a climate of understanding and hospitality for all students who attend that school?

Suggestion 4: Supervise Well

In addition, I recommend that building principals need to reflect deeply on the current reality of their legal responsibility to supervise the teachers in their buildings. This, in essence, is what all of the authors of this collection of studies are asking to have happen in schools in order to best respond to the needs of the ELLs. Notably, "Collaboration for Culturally Relevant Pedagogy: An Extended Project Involving Content and ESL Teachers" (Chapter 9) calls out the too-common practice of content area teachers only viewing themselves as the subject area specialists in the classroom, with this particularly evident in mathematics and science classrooms.

Supervision and evaluation of teachers has undergone much change with the advent of the American Recovery and Reinvestment Act's (2009) competitive grant Race to the Top hitting American schools at the depths of the great recession. Participating states were required to implement evidence-based accountability systems in their public schools for both teachers and principals. In some states, notably New York, this led to a huge backlash from teachers' unions and is believed to be one of the inspirations for the Opt Out movement of parents who refuse to allow their children to participate in mandated grades 3–8 testing.

Thus, we embarked on a decade of "supervising well." We established systems that were indeed evidence-based, hearkening back to the work of Larry Lezotte (1997) and ensuring that principals carefully scripted everything they saw and heard in their mandatory classroom observations in order to hold evidence up to the light of a rubric, some with almost 100 indicators, to judge a teacher's skill as ineffective, developing, effective, or highly effective.

To be sure, there were some successes in this radical departure from the (perhaps) annual soft assessment. It got principals out of their offices and into classrooms to actually see what was going on. The rubrics were selected on the basis of research (Danielson, 2009) and professional development was provided to principals to help build their instructional leadership skills. And, for teachers operating at the top of their game, it gave them a well-deserved acknowledgement of the specific areas of excellence of their skills.

In the decade since, while evidence-based accountability systems are still in place, schools have moved much more toward a coaching model of instructional supervision, with principals being encouraged to build their coaching skills. As noted by Frontier and Mielke (2016), teacher supervision must be part of a balanced system, one that encourages a school that is a learning environment where supervision is one part of system supporting professional growth. Too often, traditional supervision looks to capture just one moment in time of a teacher's work, not this shift of thinking to one of continuous professional growth and improvement.

One of the key factors in a principal's ability to effectively coach their teachers is the nature of the relationships between the principal and the teachers. In *The Coach Approach to School Leadership*, Johnson, Leibowitz, and Perret (2017) lay out specifics of how principals can and should coach, rather than just supervise, their teachers to support their growth. With a focus on building positive trusting relationships and providing direct feedback to teachers in a collaborative manner, rather than judgmental, the principal can encourage the teamwork necessary to achieve student achievement goals. Principals embedding coaching within their supervision practices can suggest specific practices (e.g., collaborative lesson planning with ESL teachers or specific instructional and/or technological tools) in order to improve collaboration and instruction, with the desired outcome of improved student achievement for the ELLs.

Suggestion 5: Seek Professional Supports, within and outside the Schools

Drawn from the studies in this edited book, I also suggest that principals constantly seek professional levels of support as it is crucial to enhancing ELLs' academic achievement. The forms that support takes, however, can be diverse – from within the school, from within the school district, and from outside agencies. School principals need to educate themselves as to what support they and their school district can directly provide to the teachers and students, but also to what may be offered from local and statewide organizations, too.

Several studies included in this book, in particular "Collaboration for Culturally Relevant Pedagogy: An Extended Project Involving Content and ESL Teachers" (Chapter 9), referred to the need for quality professional development for both ESL and content area teachers who support ELLs. Even in larger school districts, where professional development might be overseen by district-level administrators, efforts need to be made by both building and district level administrators to be aware of teachers' professional development needs. And, sometimes, it may be in areas that may not occur to them. As principals set the tone for their building, they also set a tone of continuous improvement for all. Through a culture of professional development, and a keen eye as to how things are going in classrooms and data related to student achievement, targeted professional development can enhance teacher collaboration for the benefit of the ELLs.

In "Reflections on Co-Teaching and Collaboration Communication, Flexibility, and Congruence" (Chapter 4), Jeong and Eggleston accurately describe the goal of teachers with strong "profession capital," specifically their strong knowledge of how to co-teach. This can only be developed through consistent administrative (both building and district level) support for all teachers, differentiated to meet their needs much like we ask our teachers to differentiate their teaching to meet their students' needs.

Resources outside of a school district that offer benefits to ELLs often rest in institutions of higher learning. These supports can include formal partnerships where university students are placed in K–12 ENL classrooms as a resource. The students on both sides of the equation can benefit from practicing English skills to having extra sets of hands for activities (e.g., science experiments) in the classroom. Further, many universities also can offer school districts access to resources to help them implement needs-based services, such as under the community schools model.

Suggestion 6: Actively Seek Out ELLs' Voice

Finally, I suggest that principals actively seek out ELLs' concerns and attend to them. There are many voices chirping in principals' ears. Many principals utilize the "open door" policy in an attempt to provide open lines of communication between themselves and stakeholders. While it may be a deterrent to administrative productivity, it does provide the opportunity for faculty, staff, and community to share their needs and points of view with the principal, with the hope that their needs are then acted upon. With this rotation of teachers and staff sharing their concerns throughout the day, and parent and supervisor calls and emails (and now texts) sharing theirs, where is room for the student voice? And, specifically, where is room for our ELLs' voice? Ironically, if you ask virtually any school or school district administrator how they make decisions, they often respond that they always make decisions that are in the best interest of the children. But, are they actually listening to what the children want or need? And, are they actively seeking out the voices of their ELLs?

The importance of the ELLs' voice is evident in the chapter entitled "Leadership Roles at Different Points": Collaborating to Plan for and Teach ESL Students in a Secondary Social Studies Classroom" (Chapter 6). Often, these students, limited by their ability to communicate in our language, as well as by cultural norms that emphasize respect for adults and educational institutions, make no real attempt to share their needs. Further, in schools that do try hear the student voice, they often do so through elected student officials who disproportionately represent the dominant social class of the community. If principals sincerely want to hear all voices, and make informed decisions regarding the effective running of their schools, they need to ensure that they reach out to all subgroups of students to hear their voices, too.

Conclusion

Even with my extensive experience as a public school administrator, I learned a lot from reading all of the chapters in this edited book. The key ideas of the chapters on teacher collaboration for ELLs helped me construct specific suggestions for school principals who seek ideas on supporting teachers. This book stands to make a significant impact on the culture and practice of public schools in the United States and in other countries, and changes necessary to make education more fully accessible to all students, notably our ELLs.

While I spent my career in K–12 public schools with small subgroups of ELLs, my responsibility to them as an educational leader was as great, if not greater, as that to all of the children we educated. The recommendations for enhanced collaboration between content-area and ESL teachers outlined in this book should be taken to heart. As Jeong and Eggleston stated, our ELLs deserve excellence in co-teaching "so smoothly flowing like a hawk flying in the sky." It is my hope to embed the deep learning I gained from this book into my role in training the next generation of school principals.

References

Danielson, C. (2009). *Implementing the framework for teaching in enhancing professional practice.* Alexandria, VA: ASCD.

DuFour, R. (2004). *Whatever it takes: How professional learning communities respond when kids don't learn.* Bloomington, IN: National Educational Service.

Frontier, T., & Mielke, P. (2016). *Making teachers better not bitter.* Alexandria, VA: ASCD.

Hattie, J. A. C. (2009). *Visible learning: A synthesis of over 800 meta-analyses relating to achievement.* New York, NY: Routledge.

Johnson, J., Leibowitz, S., & Perret, K. (2017). *The coach approach to school leadership: leading teachers to higher levels of effectiveness.* Alexandria, VA: ASCD.

Lezotte, L. (1997). *Learning for all.* Okemos, MI: Effective Schools Products.

Marzano, R. J., Waters, T., & McNulty, B. A. (2005). *School leadership that works: From research to results.* Alexandria, VA: ASCD.

National Center for Education Statistics (2020, May). *The condition of education, English language learners in public schools.* https://nces.ed.gov/programs/coe/indicator_cgf.asp

New York State Education Department (2018–2019). *Percentage of MLLs/ELLs as a share of total student population by county and district 2016-17 (PowerPoint*

Slides). Retrieved from https://www.google.com/search?rlz=1C1GCEU&ei=pl_
jX-y0J-GO5wKY5L7ICA&q=NYSED+nyseslat+2018+ELL+demographic+sli
des&oq=NYSED+nyseslat+2018+ELL+demographic+slides&gs_lcp=CgZwc3
ktYWIQAzoECAAQRzoFCAAQzQJKBQgHEgExSgUICRIBMUoGCAoSAjY-
zUJyMAVjPqAFgxa8BaABwAngAgAGQAYgBtgiSAQMxLjiYAQCgAQGqA-
Qdnd3Mtd2l6yAEIwAEB&sclient=psy-ab&ved=0ahUKEwjsn5KSs-TtAhVhx
1kKHRiyD4kQ4dUDCA0&uact=5

Organisation for Economic Co-operation and Development. (2020). *Global
teaching insights: A video study of teaching*. Paris, France: OECD Publishing.
doi:10.1787/20d6f36b-en.

Pew Research (2018, October 25). *6 Facts about English language learners in
US public schools*. https://www.pewresearch.org/fact-tank/2018/10/25/6-facts-
about-english-language-learners-in-u-s-public-schools/

Porter-Magee, K. (2020, May 18). *Why school culture is a key underpinning to
social and emotional learning*. American Enterprise Institute. https://www.
aei.org/research-products/report/why-school-culture-is-crucial-to-social-
and-emotional-learning/

11 Implications and Suggestions for Effective Teacher Collaboration for ELLs

Bogum Yoon

What do the findings of the case studies in this book imply to us as educators and researchers? What are the common elements that the studies offered for effective teacher collaboration for the needs of ELLs? This chapter attempts to address these questions. As shared in the previous chapters, the case examples in diverse settings and across the curriculum provide educators with important theoretical and practical insights. Educators who seek ideas of effective collaborative practices may find the case study examples helpful.

In the following section, I first discuss the implications by focusing on what possibilities and challenges the studies in various settings and across the curriculum shared in the chapters. Next, as conclusion, I offer suggestions and directions for future research and practice for effective teacher collaboration to meet the needs of ELLs.

Cross-Case Analysis

My cross-case analysis shows that there are several common elements across the studies on effective collaborative practices between ESL/bilingual and content area teachers. As shown in Chapters 3–9, the authors conducted their studies in the different content area classrooms (e.g., ELA, math, science, and social studies) and in different contexts (e.g., elementary, middle, and high schools). Yet, I found that the common elements that the studies show are consistent. The findings of the studies in this book confirm the four key elements that are required for effective teacher collaboration, which I shared in Chapter 2 (e.g., co-planning time for shared goals, teacher agency for voluntary collaboration, mutual trust, and equal positioning between two parties). However, I found that there were unique elements that the studies showed in this book: the ESL and classroom/content teachers' views of their roles and approaches to challenges in the process of collaboration. This analysis will be supported by the case examples below.

DOI: 10.4324/9781003058311-14

ESL Teachers' Leading and Co-Equal Roles

The presented case studies show that an important element for effective collaboration is related to the ESL teachers' positioning of themselves as leaders and co-equal partners in the process of collaborative practices. In the context in which the ESL teachers were recognized as professional experts who have a wide range of content knowledge and experiences, there were more possibilities for both groups of teachers to engage in collaborative practices. For instance, as shown in the interview data of the classroom/content teachers in Chapters 3 (e.g., ELA for 4th–5th graders), 4 (e.g., ELA and math for K–2nd graders), 6 (e.g., social studies for 8th graders), 7 (e.g., science for 7th graders), and 9 (e.g., multiple content areas for K–12th graders), all of them (e.g., both experienced and less experienced teachers) viewed the ESL teachers as professional experts and co-equal partners. The findings show that when the ESL teachers were in the context that allowed them to take a leadership role in planning and teaching lessons, more active collaborative practices were possible in the co-taught content classrooms.

This finding in the chapters extends the findings of the previous studies (e.g., Arkoudis, 2006; Burgess, 2011; Yoon, 2015). The previous studies suggest that effective collaborative practices did not occur under the tension between ESL and content area teachers because ESL teachers were often positioned as "supporting" members in the general education classroom. The ESL teachers who were perceived as having a supporting role did not actively seek out collaborative relationships with content area teachers. Yet, the insights from the current studies in this book illustrate that the ESL teachers' leading and co-equal roles (e.g., "I am at the center of the class" in Chapter 7; "an equal, 50/50 relationship" in Chapter 8), not as assisting roles, influenced the positive process of collaboration with the content teachers. This finding is ground-breaking in our understanding on teacher collaboration. It provides evidence on what would happen when ESL teachers are viewed as professional capital and co-equal partners. Yet, the question remains on what element contributed to the ESL teachers' positioning of themselves as leaders and co-equal partners. This question leads to the following element that I found through the case studies.

ESL and Content Teachers' Professional Capital

My analysis shows that the major factor that influenced the ESL teachers' active roles in collaborative practices might be connected to their thorough knowledge beyond their TESOL background. For instance, as shown in the observation data from the studies in primary (e.g., Chapters 3 and 4), secondary (e.g., Chapters 6 and 7), and both primary and secondary levels (Chapters 5 and 9), the ESL teachers were positioned as "mentors," or "resources" by the classroom/content area teachers during the collaborative process (e.g., managing class, teaching content curriculum, and integrating technology). The classroom/content area teachers' voices from the studies demonstrate their trust and respect for their partner teachers' professional knowledge and experiences. The ESL teachers were welcomed and appreciated in the content area teachers' classrooms where the co-teaching instructions were implemented for the needs of ELLs.

Given that collaboration is dynamic and not unilateral, the professional capital from the ESL teachers' side only is not all that is needed for successful collaboration. The content area teachers' professional knowledge beyond their subject matter including TESOL knowledge and experiences (e.g., Chapters 3 and 8) is also a contributing factor. For example, as particularly shown in the study in Chapter 3, the classroom teacher who had a solid knowledge base in ESL (e.g., TESOL certification) had more meaningful and deeper discussions with the ESL teacher (e.g., attending conferences together), compared to the teacher who was beginning to establish a relationship with the ESL teacher. It shows that effective teacher collaboration might need both groups of teachers' professional capital (e.g., ESL teachers' content knowledge and content teachers' TESOL knowledge) beyond their certification areas.

As Arkoudis (2006) pointed out, there is a sense of curriculum hierarchy and power issues between content and ESL teachers that hinder establishing equal partnership. Although the previous studies show that equal partnership is essential for teacher collaboration, they did not show how it can be established. The findings of the case studies provide a possible answer. The ESL teachers' professional capital including content knowledge beyond TESOL knowledge (e.g., ELA, reading, experiences as classroom or special education teacher) helped their positioning as leaders, not as supporting roles. Likewise, the content area teachers who have a better understanding of the needs of ELLs were successful in establishing collaborative partnerships with the ESL teachers. Under the current imbalanced power structure between ESL and content area teachers, these findings provide important insights for the importance of both groups' professional capital.

No Dichotomized Role as Content or Language Specialists

Another common theme that I found in the case studies is that both groups of the teachers showed their perceived roles broadly beyond subject (e.g., content area teachers) or language specialists (e.g., ESL teachers). Most of the studies' interview and observation data showed that the teachers viewed themselves as teachers for all students (e.g., "we both are viewed as being teachers" in Chapter 4; "we're both everyone's teacher" in Chapter 7) and served all of the students together through a flexible instructional approach. Rather than viewing their roles from their certi-fied qualifications (e.g., content teachers focus on content and ESL teach-ers focus on language), they viewed their roles from the students' needs. That is, the teachers' roles were more holistic. In the context that the ELLs' needs were prioritized, the teachers' roles were different based on the students' academic needs. They alternated their leading roles based on individual students' specific needs (e.g., math concepts such as "dis-tribute" and "variable"; vocabulary such as "peel"; science concepts such as the human reproductive system).

These findings also extend to those of the existing studies that I pre-sented in Chapter 2. The previous studies show that both groups of teachers have challenges in establishing collaborative partnership due to their uncertainty of their own roles and responsibilities for ELLs (e.g., Burgess, 2011; Yoon, 2015). Dichotomized roles were evident in the pre-vious studies (e.g., I am an ESL teacher for ELLs; I am a content teacher for general education students). The findings from the case studies pro-vide evidence that both groups of the teachers took responsibilities for all students, both ELLs and non-ELLs. In the co-teaching context, flexibility was a common element (e.g., changing leading roles) and there was no clear-cut, fixed form of "co-teaching" (e.g., one teaches/one observes). Both groups of teachers "chimed in" and "chimed out" in their instruc-tions to promote ELLs' understanding on language, literacy, and content, as demonstrated in the studies (e.g., Chapters 3, 7, and 8).

Shifting Challenges to Successful Collaboration

The way that the teachers handled challenges, such as the lack of time, was unique. As shared in Chapter 2, each study on teacher collaboration reported numerous challenges including time constraints. There was no exception in the case studies in this volume of the book. Most of the teachers in the case studies shared that the lack of common planning and co-instructional time was an obstacle to further sustain collaborative relationships. The scheduling structure in their schools seemed to affect their quality of collaborative practices. This finding is aligned with the literature review that I presented in Chapter 2 (e.g., Collinson & Cook, 2001; Yoon, 2004; Yoon & Haag, 2012).

Yet, the way that the teachers handled the limited time was different from the previous studies. The teachers attempted to overcome this chal-lenge rather than giving up collaborative partnerships. Instead of using the limited time as an excuse not to pursue collaboration, both groups of teachers negotiated the lack of time by prioritizing the ELLs' needs. As notably shown in the studies (e.g., Chapters 3 and 4), both groups of teachers continued to engage in "frequent open communications" by uti-lizing their informal time (e.g., discussing over lunch, communicating in the hallway, short classroom visits between classes). In short, the findings of the studies in this book illustrate that the teachers face challenges in the process of collaboration. Yet, they handled the challenge of the time constraints by focusing on the ELLs' areas to grow and by utilizing informal time (e.g., lunch, hallway).

Additionally, the challenges that teachers felt in the beginning stage of collaboration were used as learning opportunities through conversations and reflections as notably shown in Chapters 4, 6, and 9. Specifically, in Chapter 6, the ESL teacher and the social studies teacher learned that the ELLs' learning outcomes on the content were not positive during the initial stage of collaboration. They discussed the involved issues, reflected on them, and improved their collaborative practices, which resulted in positive results of ELLs' learning. The teachers' continuous dialogues, communications, and reflections on their co-planning and co-teaching made their collaboration effective and successful.

In sum, these examples show how the teachers used challenges to create opportunities for their learning on collaboration. Successful collaboration between ESL and content teachers takes time. Yet, the studies provide evidence that it can happen when both groups of teachers can use the challenges as their professional learning opportunities for ELLs' success in learning.

Implications and Suggestions for Future Research and Practice

The cross-case analysis shows both possibilities and challenges in teachers' collaborative practices, but possibilities prevail. One of the most intriguing findings is that uneven power dynamics between the ESL teachers and content teachers were not visible in the studies. Although the studies in this volume of the book might not provide a full picture of teacher collaboration, they do provide a certain pattern and a current trend on teacher collaboration. Based on these findings, I provide implications and suggestions for future research and practice.

First, the findings of the case studies provide implications for teacher education programs. I suggest that teacher education programs have a course on teacher collaboration, as well as more cross-listed courses between the TESOL program and the subject-area program. This approach will provide further opportunities for pre-service and in-service teachers in both programs to interact and to build professional relationship with one another.

As the study in Chapter 9 showed, when the professional opportunities were offered to both groups of the teachers in designing lessons by integrating ELLs' cultural references into the content curriculum, it brought benefits to both groups of teachers. As the author of the chapter reported, the professional opportunity brought "an increased sense of responsibility and self-efficacy for content teachers in teaching ELLs and an improved sense of equality among peers for ESL teachers." The teachers' reflections on their co-designing lessons and interviews demonstrate that both groups of teachers need to have more professional opportunities to work together before going out into the teaching field. The teacher education program can offer more collaborative opportunities for the teachers both in the TESOL program and the subject-area program.

Second, I suggest that teacher education programs include more content courses to help pre-service and in-service teachers in TESOL programs to build professional capital. Likewise, teacher education programs continue to include more courses that focus on the academic, cultural, and social needs of ELLs for pre-service and in-service teachers in content area programs. I also suggest that teacher education programs adjust the course objectives of existing courses to include the focus on the diverse needs of ELLs.

Professional knowledge on the needs of ELLs is equally important to both groups of teachers. As particularly shared in Chapter 8, the teachers who engaged in collaboration initially "had some reservations about their ability to make this collaboration work." If ESL teachers know that content area teachers have a deep knowledge of the process of ELLs' learning while content teachers know that ESL teachers have a solid knowledge of the content, then they have a better chance to build mutual trust and to engage in effective collaborative practices. As with the teachers in the studies illustrated, it took much time to establish a successful relationship. If the teacher education programs prepare pre-service and in-service teachers before they go out into the teaching field, it will help the teachers to engage in more meaningful collaborative practices, rather than spending time to learn the basic ideas of collaboration.

Third, I also recommend that the studies on teacher collaboration include more voices of students as a way to triangulate the data of the teachers' interviews and observations in the classroom. Although the majority of the researchers in the case studies included ELLs in their observation, the interview data that could show their learning through their voices were limited. Effective teacher collaboration can take various forms, and the teachers' choice of the forms could be decided based on what ELLs share about their learning process through their voices and experiences. Given that multiple data sources are critical in any qualitative study, the student's data will provide more evidence on the findings of the effective teacher collaboration.

Fourth, more studies on teacher collaboration could be conducted by the researchers from the field of the content area to have more balanced and diverse perspectives. After the call of chapters for this book were sent out, I learned that almost all of the researchers on this topic of teacher collaboration were from the field of TESOL education, and it was rare to find the researchers from the field of the content area. Given that researchers play a significant role in selecting research questions and focus based on their experiences, more studies from the researchers in the field of the content area would provide a clearer picture of co-equal partnerships between ESL teachers and content area teachers.

Finally, it is important for teachers to continue to engage in professional development in teacher collaboration through school and district supports. As shown in the examples, particularly in Chapters 5 and 8, both groups of teachers who received school and district supports were able to learn "systematic" collaborative practices from teacher educators. Additionally, the teachers who received school supports in terms of scheduling (e.g., regular meeting time daily) helped them to establish and sustain positive relationships. As suggested in Chapter 10, it is important that school leaders consider adjusting curriculum schedules to promote collaboration between both groups of teachers.

Conclusion

In conclusion, my position in this edited book is that collaboration between ESL/bilingual and content area teachers is essential to meet the diverse needs of ELLs. It creates a school culture in which learning from each group of teachers is promoted (Cochran-Smith & Lytle, 2009). As shared in my position earlier, we cannot approach teacher collaboration from a romanticized view in that this dynamic is possible in any setting. Collaboration between ESL/bilingual teachers and content area teachers is complex because it involves many external, internal, and political factors, including school culture, teachers' beliefs of their roles, and power issues between them.

All of the case studies in this book demonstrate these complexities through the teachers' collaborative dynamics. Despite the difficult situations and time constraints, neither group of teachers stopped pursuing collaboration because they understood that it positively influenced students' learning. The teachers continued to engage in collaborative practices because they knew it broadened their teaching realm and deepened their understanding of the needs of ELLs who learn English in a new context. I hope more researchers conduct research on the complexities of teacher collaboration to refine and extend the findings of the current studies in this book. I also hope that teacher educators across the curriculum bring this important topic of teacher collaboration into discussion when they work with pre-service and in-service teachers on a regular basis. The possibilities of the teachers' learning will be endless.

References

Arkoudis, S. (2006). Negotiating the rough ground between ESL and mainstream teachers. *The International Journal of Bilingual Education and Bilingualism*, 9(4), 415–433.
Burgess, M. (2011). *Best practices for collaboration between ESL and general education teachers*. Theses, Dissertations, and Other Capstone Projects. Minnesota State University at Mankato.

Cochran-Smith, M., & Lytle, S. L. (2009). *Inquiry as stance: Practitioner research for the next generation.* New York, NY: Teachers College Press.

Collinson, V., & Cook, T. F. (2001). I don't have enough time: Teachers' interpretations of time as a key to learning and school change. *Journal of Educational Administration, 39*(3), 266–281.

Yoon, B. (2004). Uninvited guests: The impact of English and ESL teachers' beliefs, roles, and pedagogies on the identities of English language learners (Doctoral dissertation, University at Buffalo, 2004). *Dissertation Abstracts International, 65*, 885.

Yoon, B. (2015). A case study: One novice middle level teacher's beliefs, challenges, and practices for young adolescent English language learners. In K. F. Malu & M. B. Schaefer (Eds.), *Research on teaching and learning with the literacies of young adolescents* (pp. 3–19). Charlotte, NC: Information Age Publishing.

Yoon, B., & Haag, C. (2012). The epistemological and institutional challenges of teacher collaboration for English language learners' literacy learning. In M. T. Cowart and G. Anderson (Eds.), *English language learners in 21st century classrooms: Challenges and expectations* (pp. 244–257). Denton, TX: Canh Nam Publishers.

Index